W9-DIL-939

OCR

Jane Pepper's Garden

*Getting the Most Pleasure and
Growing Results from Your Garden
Every Month of the Year*

Jane G. Pepper

President,
The Pennsylvania Horticultural Society

Camino Books, Inc.
Philadelphia

Manufactured in the United States of America

The chapters of this book were adapted from material originally published in The Philadelphia Inquirer. This book is published by arrangement with The Philadelphia Inquirer.

1 2 3 4 5   99 98 97

Library of Congress Cataloging-in-Publication Data

Pepper, Jane G.
    Jane Pepper's garden: getting the most pleasure and growing results from your garden every month of the year / by Jane G. Pepper

            p.   cm.
    Includes index.
    ISBN 0-940159-39-2 (alk. paper)
    1. Gardening   I. Title.
    SB455.P46   1997
    635—dc20   96-44183

Photos copyright © 1997 by Derek Fell, The Pennsylvania Horticultural Society, Laura Lewis, and Vicki Valerio (The Philadelphia Inquirer).

Line drawings by Mary Thompson.

Book design by Robert LeBrun.

This book is available at a special discount on bulk purchases for promotional, business, and educational use. For information write to:

Publisher
Camino Books, Inc.
P.O. Box 59026
Philadelphia, PA 19102

*To The Gardening Partner,
my favorite lima bean.*

Contents

Introduction

Gardening is the perfect pleasure for people like me. My idea of a great Saturday is to dress in my oldest clothes, put on my boots, and head out for a day of digging and planting. By sundown, I'm filthy and my back aches, but it's the relaxation I was looking for at the end of the week.

And then there's the produce. As I write this, it's nearly the end of the summer and the kitchen is filled with tomatoes and beets, eggplants, lima beans, and peppers. Above all in our garden, I get the greatest satisfaction from the edibles—the vegetables, herbs, and fruits. It's fun to dream up a storm in winter and order seeds from a catalog, then watch the seedlings struggle to life on a windowsill in early spring. Planting days are a bustle of activity, followed by months of nurturing before it's time to harvest. Every step of the way is a new experience each summer, and even if I mess it all up this year, I know I always have another chance next year.

Let me introduce you first to The Gardening Partner, then to the piece of ground that we call our garden, which is southwest of Philadelphia.

The Gardening Partner is the anonymous character in my newspaper columns and in the rest of these pages, but he's hardly anonymous in real life. He's my husband, Wing, or G. Willing Pepper when a nickname won't do. As for the garden that he and I have worked in for nearly 30 years, this suburban plot is no showplace— the lawn is more crabgrass than turf, our landscaping mistakes are evident front and back, and the dogs' scratchings are there for all to see. But it's a place where we have had lots of fun over almost three decades, and in the years I have written gardening columns for The Philadelphia Inquirer, readers have become familiar with my gripes about The Gardening Partner, the deer, and, sometimes, the neighbors who have a hard time understanding my desire to grow vegetables all over what had looked to them like perfectly good lawns.

Gardening may be in my genes. I grew up in a large family in Scotland with parents who loved to garden. The allocation of duties was traditional—my mother took care of the flowers and, at our first house, the geese, chickens, and ducks, while my father tended the vegetable patch, the fruits, and the Highland cattle. Together, they tackled the lawns and major pruning jobs. From early spring through late autumn, we rarely bought a vegetable.

My father was a trial lawyer, later a judge, and in his gardening costume he was a strange apparition. Instead of jeans and T-shirts, he gardened in clothes too worn for court appearances—black-striped pants on the bottom, with a frayed black coat, green at the edges, on top. His shirts were pin-striped but devoid of the starched, winged white collars he wore in court. Wet soil is common in Scottish gardens, so he topped off the outfit with a pair of gumboots. Mother's gardening costume was less bizarre, but she rarely went out without an old brown felt hat. In what she would call her "debutante days," in the late 1930s, this was the headgear she had worn to many a chic horse-race meeting.

My father was way ahead of the recycling movement. He reused envelopes and saved little pieces of string. But for me, his best recycling effort was the container in which he stored his vegetable seeds. For court appearances as a judge he wore a wig, which was stored in a tall, elegant black tin with gold edging. When he retired, the wig tin retired with him to protect his seeds from rodent damage. My four brothers and I were regularly roped into gardening projects, but my mother firmly believed that none of us would ever embrace gardening as a desirable occupation until we had "places of our own."

In 1967, I came to the United States planning to spend a few months before returning to a secretarial job in London. Romance interfered with my plans, and within nine months of leaving home, I reappeared in Scotland to tell my family that I planned to marry the man they had met for the first time that day. They wasted no time in putting Wing Pepper to work. In fact, one of the photographs in my mother's album from that visit shows him digging in the compost heap.

That same year, we bought the house in which we still live, surrounded by a lawn, some trees, and some shrubs described by the real-estate agent as "foundation plantings," a term that was new to my Scottish vocabulary. In the early years of our marriage, Wing was constantly traveling overseas as head of the Scott Paper Company's international division. I went with him to Asia, to South America, and back to Europe, but after a few years, I became restless living out of a suitcase and was lucky enough to find a secretarial job at Haverford College. There, thanks to the friendship of Steve Fletcher, the college's landscape architect, I learned that you could actually study "gardening."

Six years after leaving Haverford, I received a master's degree from the College of Agriculture at the University of Delaware and returned to Haverford College to work for the arboretum association. Many of my idols in the horticulture world worked for the

Pennsylvania Horticultural Society in Philadelphia, so in my spare time I volunteered for any jobs that came along there. I was thrilled in 1979 when its president, Ernesta D. Ballard, invited me to join those idols and become the society's public information coordinator. When she retired 15 months later, I was surprised to find myself sliding into her shoes.

A friend once said to me that I have the best job in Philadelphia, and I have to agree. Every day, I am surrounded by a subject I love and by people I enjoy and admire. Across the United States and around the world, the society is best known as the producer of the Philadelphia Flower Show, attended in 1996 by more than 300,000 visitors. The Philadelphia Flower Show is the world's largest indoor flower show, held annually for eight days in late February or early March. Each show is planned four to five years ahead, starting with the development of a theme and an overall design. Fifty major exhibitors are invited to stage landscapes that include massive waterfalls, elegant perennial gardens, and elaborate floral arrangements. More than 300 exhibitors—home gardeners and professionals from many backgrounds—also compete in classes that range from small gardens to single pots of begonias and ferns. Some 120 vendors sell all kinds of horticultural products, from bulbs to topiary. A highlight of my year is the 10-day setup period when we witness the fruits of the society's and our exhibitors' planning, which come together to produce 10 acres of early spring—a magical, colorful, fragrant landscape that provides a stark contrast to the dreary days of winter outside.

Another endlessly satisfying aspect of my job is the opportunity to work with our team of 80 staff members and 3,000 volunteers, who are involved in all aspects of our activities at the Pennsylvania Horticultural Society. Many help with the Flower Show. Others help orchestrate our Harvest and Junior Shows, attend to the interests and enthusiasms of our 8,000-plus members, answer our Horticultural Hotline, and judge our annual City Gardens Contest.

With proceeds from the Flower Show, city contracts, and generous donations from many sources, the society also operates Philadelphia Green—the nation's most ambitious community greening and public landscapes program. Staff members in this program have worked with more than 700 community groups on about 2,000 planting projects throughout Philadelphia. Lots in inner-city neighborhoods that were once vacant and trash-filled are now covered with beautiful, productive gardens, and we have planted hundreds of street trees and helped neighbors establish and maintain community parks. These neighborhood gardeners contend with the usual pests and predators as well as the vicissitudes of life in a big city.

Among them are some of the best gardeners I know, and their advice appears often in my newspaper columns.

We in the Philadelphia area are fortunate to have an unusually large number of botanic gardens, arboretums, excellent garden centers, small nurseries, garden clubs, and gardening enthusiasts. When gardeners from other parts of the country ask why this is so, I am hard-pressed to come up with a good answer, but here are a couple of possibilities. First, the horticultural traditions in and around Philadelphia are deep and old; John Bartram, one of the founding fathers of horticulture in the United States, made his home in Philadelphia. And despite our complaints about it, the climate allows us to grow a wide range of plants, a feature that keeps the curious gardener moving forward in the quest to grow new and different things.

The Pennsylvania Horticultural Society was founded in 1827. Since then, like a butterfly, it has been through many metamorphoses. Today, it is a vibrant organization in which everyone shares an interest in and a love for plants and gardens. To me, just as important as the plants are, for want of a better phrase, the social aspects of gardening and the opportunities that this activity offers for people to work together. The project may be an exhibit in the Philadelphia Flower Show, a community garden in North Philadelphia, or a plant sale at an arboretum. When I look back at the first few years of my life in the United States, everything was new and exciting, but it was lonely. Once I discovered the joys of the garden and the community of people connected to gardening and horticulture, I never looked back.

In the following chapters, beginning with March, the start of the gardening year, I have tried to distill what I have learned from puttering in our garden. In addition, you will find advice from some of the hundreds of gardeners I have interviewed over the years for my columns. Only a few of these gardeners are mentioned by name, but their willingness to trade tips and plants has enriched my writing and gardening.

In their busiest months, gardeners have little time to read, so each chapter starts with timely tips, followed by seasonal suggestions applicable to different sections of the garden. Each chapter proceeds with more detailed information on specific gardening topics for that month.

Just as I am based in the Philadelphia area, so is the material in this book. References to "my region" or "this area" are meant to apply to the Greater Philadelphia region and to other locales where the weather conditions are similar. To help gardeners determine whether different plants will survive outdoors, the Arnold Arboretum of Harvard University has produced a map dividing the United States and Canada into 10 hardiness zones. Information for this map is based on average annual minimum temperatures and is meant only as a guide. Philadelphia-area gardens straddle zones 6 and 7. Even within one metropolitan area, climates can differ widely and are often dotted with warm and cold pockets. If you live with a different climate, whether within the Philadelphia area or in another region of the country, be prepared to adjust my advice.

New gardeners often shy away from the Latin botanical names for plants. In the text that follows, I have tried to include both the botanical names and the common names for all plants except vegetables, which are identified only by their common names. If you want to check out a particular plant in a reference, the easiest way to find it is by using its botanical name. Similarly, if you want to buy the plant you read about or your friend recommended, the only way to be absolutely sure that you get what you want is to go shopping armed with the botanical name. A frustration for gardeners is that botanists are continually updating plant nomenclature. In this text, plant names follow the New Royal Horticultural Society Dictionary of Gardening (The Stockton Press, 1992).

The Appendix lists resources, including catalogs, books, magazines, and plant and horticultural societies, that I believe gardeners will find especially useful.

Acknowledgments

It has been more than 20 years since I first took the plunge into horticulture, and many people have helped me carve out a wonderful life in this field.

First and foremost and the most important of my helpers has been my husband, G. Willing Pepper—known in these pages as The Gardening Partner, and to me and his friends as Wing—who has not only dug, weeded, and harvested beside me but has also been the inspiration for so many of the things I've done in the almost three decades since we met. Fortunately for me, he has a well-developed, tolerant sense of humor, because not every husband would cheerfully take the abuse The Gardening Partner has to take in my twice-weekly gardening columns for The Philadelphia Inquirer.

To Dick Lighty, I extend grateful thanks for his encouragement when I was a student at the Longwood Graduate Program in Public Horticulture Administration at the University of Delaware. Ernesta Ballard gave me my first job at the Pennsylvania Horticultural Society and has supported me ever since. Jean Byrne, the society's director of publications, took a chance and published my first article in Green Scene, the society's magazine.

Four volunteer chairs of the society, Hank Reichner, Bob Ryan, Don Felley, and Morris Cheston, have shaped my career as the society's executive director, then president, and all of the society's achievements while I have been its chief executive officer would not have been possible without our staff and volunteers. Many thanks to present and former staff members with whom I have worked the closest over the longest period of time: Blaine Bonham, Carol Lindemann, Ed Lindemann, Cheryl Monroe, Lisa Stephano, and Ellen Wheeler. Special thanks to one special volunteer, guiding light, and good friend to us all, Liddon Pennock.

The Pennsylvania Horticultural Society has a wonderful library, made accessible to me in doing research for my columns and in the preparation of the appendix for this book by librarian Janet Evans, assistant librarian Jane Alling, and former librarian Mary Lou Wolfe.

My thanks go to all the gardeners who have let me pester them on weekends or evenings about their gardens and gardening practices, and especially to five good friends who provided expert help during the preparation of the manuscript: Steve Mostardi, Alan and Charlotte Slack, and John and Ann Swan.

Thanks also to the editors I have worked with over the years at The Inquirer and finally to Ken Bookman, editor of this book. He's the one who has sifted, condensed, and organized all the material in the pages to follow. Friends have often suggested that I should "make a book out of all those columns." Without Ken, it would never have happened.

MARCH

The Start of the Gardening Year

To me, March is the most exciting month in the gardening year. It might start with snow, ice, and gale-force winds, but it will end with a few early shrubs and bulbs in bloom. And with any luck, you will have sown your peas, onions, lettuce, spinach, arugula, and mustard greens. With all that to look forward to, I welcome March with open arms.

Some tips for early March ...

❧ Longing to start work in the vegetable garden? Then this may be the most important tip of the year: Pick up a handful of soil and squeeze it in your hand. If it stays in a ball, don't get out the spade yet. But if it crumbles, it's dry enough to start digging. If you're able to work the soil in the vegetable garden, scratch slow-release fertilizer into the soil around asparagus and rhubarb plants. Clean off any debris you left in the garden last fall. The longer you leave this, the more opportunities pests have to get a good start right where you plan to plant this year's crops.

❧ Have your soil tested—before the laboratories get too busy. Buy a soil sample bag from your local agricultural extension office or some nurseries. The results will guide you in applying lime and fertilizer; in fact, they'll help you avoid wasting fertilizer while ensuring the best possible yields.

ê❧ Early fall is the best time to completely re-do a lawn, but spring is a good time to reseed certain spots. By doing those spots as early as possible, the seedlings will have time to develop roots before the dry, hot weather sets in. The longer you let it go, the more the grass seedlings will have to compete with weeds.

ê❧ If the ground is dry enough, this is an excellent time to plant shrubs and trees as well as move them around your garden. If spring-blooming shrubs such as azaleas are on your list, move them just after they bloom, then give them adequate moisture through the growing season.

ê❧ **In the vegetable garden:** For planting outside in mid-April, sow broccoli and cabbage seeds inside in a sterilized seed-starting mixture. In my garden, I have found that cauliflower rarely makes good heads before the hot weather, but it makes a good fall crop. ... Rhubarb is one of the most rewarding plants for the home gardener, so if you like the tart taste of a rhubarb pie or crumble, pick up a few plants this spring. Within several years, you'll have enough to feed the family. Once the plants are established, you can harvest stalks from April through June. Always pull, never cut, rhubarb stalks. Unlike many perennials, rhubarb seems to produce well for years without division, but if you need to slice off a piece for a friend to start a rhubarb patch, now is the time to carve out a section from the mother plant.

ê❧ **For the flowers, shrubs, and trees:** If you mulched perennial flowers or strawberries last fall, don't be in too much of a hurry to remove the cover. The purpose of a winter mulch is to keep the plants from heaving out of the ground when it alternately thaws and freezes.

Some tips for late March ...

ê❧ If you order plants by mail, open the boxes when they arrive to check the plants. Most of the plants will be in a dormant state, so don't worry if the foliage is brown and dead or if the roots look limp; in some cases, you'll see dormant buds in the center of the plant. If you intend to plant within a few days, rewrap the plants in moist (not soggy) packing material and leave them in a cool, dimly lighted place. But if the weather or soil conditions will not allow planting for a longer period, place the plants into a shallow trench and cover the roots with a mixture of equal parts sand and peat moss.

≀♨ One of the luxuries of a garden is having lots of fresh parsley available from spring through fall. It's one of the cook's most useful herbs, and it's a snap to grow it in the garden or even in a pot on a terrace. The more dedicated herb lover probably sowed seeds inside in late February, but parsley germinates slowly and I prefer getting half a dozen plants to set out in my garden in late March. They grow beautifully in full sun, but, unlike many herbs, parsley can also do adequately with less than full sun. Keep it well watered and fertilized, and pick the oldest leaves from the outside first.

≀♨ Fertilize bulbs with bulb fertilizer or bonemeal as they emerge from the soil, scratching the fertilizer into the surface of the soil before rainfall. Hardy bulbs that were forced into bloom inside can be planted outside after the last frost in May. Tender bulbs, such as paperwhites, will not bloom again, so discard them.

≀♨ Don't let the lawn get ahead of you, but don't cut it too short either. Let it go to three inches before cutting. Leave the grass clippings on the lawn to provide nutrients.

≀♨ Become a garden scavenger. Start saving gallon plastic jugs and other clear plastic containers to protect seedlings when you transplant them into your garden.

≀♨ **In the vegetable garden:** My ideal would be to have pea seeds in the ground by St. Patrick's Day, but this rarely happens because the soil usually isn't dry enough to plant until later in the month. The goal is to allow as much time as possible for a crop to mature before the weather turns warm. Plant the first rows as soon as you can, and continue planting at two-week intervals through mid-April. Lettuce, arugula, and spinach, too, should go in now if the soil is dry enough. ... The impatient gardener will already have tomato seedlings decorating every windowsill, stretching for light. For the patient ones who want stocky seedlings to plant outside in mid-May, this is the time to plant seeds inside. Sow in sterilized soil, and place flats or pots where the soil will remain at 70° to 75° F. ... Like many other vegetable and flower seeds, pepper, tomato, and eggplant will germinate best if you can provide bottom heat and maintain a soil temperature of 70° to 75° F. You may have the ideal radiator handy, or you can buy a propagating box or heating cable.

≀♨ **For the flowers, shrubs, and trees:** Woodchips make wonderful mulch for shrub beds. Find a local tree company to make a delivery for you. If the chippings are fresh, let them sit for several months before you spread them on your planting beds. If you use them too soon, you might rob your shrubs of nutrients. ... In preparation for spring repotting and seed sowing, disinfect seed trays and pots by soaking them overnight in a solution of one part bleach to ten parts water. ... Check daylilies, hostas, Siberian iris, and other such perennials to see whether the new growth is above ground yet. If you wish to transplant or divide them, the time to do it is as soon as the growth shows. Divide and move early-spring bloomers later, after flowering. ... If your forsythia needs pruning, do it as soon as the bloom is over. Remove stems from their base to encourage the development of new shoots, rather than trimming from the top. ... Resist the temptation to give each plant a neat haircut from above. Rather, reach into the plants and remove one-third of the older canes at soil level. ... Late March through early April is a good time to fertilize evergreens. You can spread fertilizer around the base of the plants and let the spring rains soak it down to the roots. ... Acid-loving plants such as rhododendrons, azaleas, junipers, and hollies require an acid-forming fertilizer. For junipers and deciduous plants such as spirea and viburnum, use a slow-release standard fertilizer. ... As new growth starts to show on roses, give them a spring lift by scratching a handful of slow-release fertilizer specified for roses into the soil around the base of each shrub. ... Remove strangling vines, such as Japanese honeysuckle, Virginia creeper, bittersweet, and wild grape from trees.

MARCH: PENCILS, PAPER, PLANNING, PATIENCE

A monthly overview

March is a month in which to make long-delayed decisions. Try to establish a plan of attack so that you make the most of your precious gardening hours. Arm yourself with a pad and pencil and stroll around the garden listing the jobs in order of importance. Bear in mind the planting schedule for the vegetable garden, leaving time on appropriate weekends to turn over the soil and get the seeds in place at the right time. And set aside some time to work on the lawn, including adding lime if the pH is low.

Map out your coming year's vegetable garden on a piece of graph paper or with a scale ruler, leaving plenty of room on the plan to make notes on planting dates and crop successes or failures. Then, list all the vegetables that are popular with your family and figure out how many plants or row-feet you need for each crop. I'm half of a two-person family with large vegetable appetites, and we like to freeze some of our harvest for the winter. Ten tomato plants, for example, planted in full sun provide ample yield for salads, plus some soup and tomato sauce to freeze. With vegetables that don't freeze well, such as snap beans, we plant only enough seeds to produce a crop to eat at harvest time, then sow additional rows at two-week intervals. In addition to the family's requests, slip in something new each year to surprise them.

And tack up the plan in a convenient place so you can make notes as the season progresses.

Dig! Dig! But when?

Your seed list may include lettuce, snap beans, and tomatoes—favorites in our home and plants that have to be sown at different times and in different ways. Both vegetables and flowers fall into one of two categories—those you can sow from seed directly into the ground and those you will grow from transplants that started either from seedlings that you have grown yourself or have purchased at a garden center. The purpose in using transplants is to get a jump on the season. With tomatoes for instance, there would be no point in sowing seeds directly into the ground until it had warmed up, say in mid-May. By starting the seeds inside, you can gain six to eight weeks.

In early spring, the seeds of some crops germinate well in cold soil. Lettuce falls into this category, as do peas and leafy vegetables such as mustard greens, arugula, and spinach. These plants could also be started indoors a couple of weeks ahead of time, but, with the exception of lettuce, they don't transplant well, so it's not worth the effort. Cole crops (cauliflower, cabbage, and broccoli) are almost as cold-tolerant as lettuce and peas, but you will benefit greatly by starting seedlings or buying them at the garden center to plant in mid-April.

By early May, the soil is warm enough to plant seeds of snap beans into the garden and by mid-May, with the last chance of frost in most of my area supposedly past, you should be able to put out those tomato seedlings in the ground. The last plants to go in are crops such as eggplants, peppers, and lima beans, which all like really warm weather.

The seed packets themselves have lots of information to help you determine which vegetable and flower seeds to start when. Many catalogs have that information, too.

Start by dividing your seeds into those to be sown outdoors and those that should be started inside in a small container. With the ones that start in containers, start with the appropriate planting date and work backwards to figure out when to sow the seeds indoors. Resist the temptation to add just a couple of weeks "to be sure." Invariably, the seedlings will develop faster than you had thought and you will end up with a windowsill full of flats of leggy plants. The transition from flat to garden will be less traumatic for plants that are small and sturdy.

Remember, the most common cause of failure with most seed-germinating projects is that the gardener buries the seeds too deeply. Never cover a seed with soil more than three to four times the depth of the seed. Some flower seeds require light to germinate, so these should just be scattered on top of the soil.

Another important concept for spring gardeners is that of "hardening off" your plants. In a greenhouse or on a windowsill, your transplants live the best of lives—sheltered from the hottest sun, the harshest winds, and the danger of frost. Outside, conditions are very different, and if you make the transition gradual for the delicate seedlings, they will reward you handsomely with better growth than if you jerk them from the comforts of the windowsill straight into the garden. Harden off plants by putting them in a coldframe for a week or so, or on a sheltered porch where they'll get plenty of sun during the day. Then cover them at night. Alternatively, put them outside during the day and return them to a cool room at night.

Just when to begin digging in the garden is a point over which The Gardening Partner and I haggle each year. He is at the ready with his spade on the first warm day in March, while I am overly cautious. Remember that digging the garden when the soil is too wet will harm the soil structure, so have a little patience and use the squeeze test I mentioned in the March tips to determine when you can dig.

If you garden in raised beds, early spring planting is a treat because you can work without treading on the garden and compacting the soil. In a traditional, row-type garden, you have no alternative but to wade in and turn it over. If you have a wooden plank handy, lay it alongside the row to distribute your weight as you plant.

Planning the vegetables

I space the summer crops such as tomatoes, eggplants, and peppers four feet apart, then plant a row of early vegetables in between. If planted early enough, peas, lettuce, spinach, beets, radishes, mustard greens, and several other cold-hardy crops will mature by the Fourth of July, by which time the summer crops will need the additional space.

I lay aside another section of the garden for vegetables that mature in late June or during July, vegetables such as cabbage, broccoli, string beans, and onions. When they are finished, I turn this area over to the hardy varieties of fall, such as lettuce, spinach, and other leafy vegetables.

To get the earliest harvest from your garden, check the catalogs or seed racks in garden centers for varieties with the shortest date to maturity. With lettuce, for example, go for the looseleaf varieties such as Salad Bowl or Red Sails that mature in less than 50 days. The butterhead varieties—Burpee Bibb and Buttercrunch—will need 75 days from the planting date.

Other leafy vegetables grow rapidly in cool weather and add interest to your salads. Mustard greens, spinach, and arugula are well-known suggestions, and you will find an increasingly wide selection of other possibilities in seed catalogs. Many of them are Asian in origin and include Japanese Greens and Edible Chrysanthemum.

With peas, grow a combination of peas to shell and the snap edible-podded varieties. Among the former, choose something that matures early, such as Maestro, as well as midseason varieties such as Lincoln and Green Arrow. Sugar Bon is the earliest snap pea to mature.

Despite what the catalogs say, I find that all varieties of peas are more productive if they are grown on supports, so I use three-foot-tall chicken wire anchored with four-foot metal stakes. I use four stakes per 25-foot row. If you can work it out, install the wire first, then sow one row of peas on each side, two to three inches from the wire.

Sow lettuce both indoors and in the garden in March. At the beginning of the month, sow seeds in a flat for transplanting outside at the end of the month. When the soil is dry enough, plant additional seeds outdoors.

Supermarket potatoes have been chemically treated to retard sprouting, so buy certified seed potatoes from a nursery or garden center and plant in late March or April. Certified potatoes should sprout easily and are guaranteed disease-free. One friend mulches her potato patch with leaves in the fall and then just slips the seed potatoes under the mulch, thus avoiding tramping around in the soil to dig holes.

Carrots are a crop I used to sow directly into the garden in late March. Come harvest time in midsummer, the roots were half-eaten by the carrot rust fly, a pest that works underground, which means that you may not realize there is a problem until you start harvesting.

To avoid the carrot rust fly, plant seeds in midsummer. By that time, the pest has laid its eggs elsewhere. If you get the carrot seeds into the ground by July 15 and keep them well watered and mulched through early fall, you ought to have an excellent yield.

Choose a variety to suit your soil. In heavy or stony soils and in containers, shorter varieties such as Short 'n Sweet or Thumbelina will work best. Carrot seeds are slow to germinate, so mix them with seeds of lettuce or radish that will germinate first and will help not only to mark the rows but also to break up the crust on top of the soil. Harvest lettuce and radishes first and you will have less thinning to do on the carrots.

Carrot seeds are tiny and therefore hard to handle. You may find it worth the extra expense to buy pelleted seeds that make these fine seeds easier to handle.

Excessive nitrogen will give you hairy, fibrous roots, so stay away from nitrogen-rich animal manures or commercial fertilizers such as 10-10-10 with a high percentage of nitrogen for carrots; 5-10-5 will serve you better.

What's a coldframe?

Throughout this book, you'll find many references to a coldframe. So what's that? you might ask. In Victorian gardens, you would find row upon row of wooden frames that gardeners would fill with manure, then cover with glass sashes. As the early spring sun would beat down from above, the manure would heat up from below and seeds and seedlings would flourish in these structures. In fall, the gardeners would return to plant late crops of lettuce and to dig in the bulbs to be forced into bloom.

Early in my gardening days, I built a coldframe out of concrete blocks and covered it with a plastic cover. It worked well for hardening off seedlings from the house and I also used it for forcing bulbs, finding it much more pleasant to dig the bulbs out of the coldframe than out of the frozen soil in the garden.

Hindsight is great, and if you start thinking about a coldframe, I suggest buying a lightweight, readymade one that you can move around the garden, depending on the exposure you wish. In my garden, the trees have expanded near our concrete structure and I don't

Coldframes are handy for starting seedlings and hardening off transplants in spring and for providing cold storage for bulbs and cuttings over winter.

get as much sun as I once did in that spot, so that now limits its use. Coldframes are offered in catalogs, and I suggest you invest in one that's equipped with an automatic opening system, governed by the temperature. If you want to increase the temperature for starting seeds in the spring, use a heating cable—today's answer to manure.

Skinnier eggplants

The Gardening Partner has a voracious appetite for eggplant and is very disappointed if we don't have it on the menu every night for supper from early July until frost. And he doesn't like just any old eggplant. To him, there's nothing as good as the long, skinny varieties that we grow in pots on our deck.

Equally important, he would like you to know, is how we cook them. We skin the fruits, then cut them into half-inch-thick slices, lay them on pieces of paper towel, sprinkle them lightly with salt, and leave them to "sweat" for about half an hour. We then lay them on a lightly greased baking pan, coat each slice with garlic butter, and put them under the broiler until the tops brown. We turn them over to brown the other sides.

I like to experiment with different varieties of eggplant. But once The Gardening Partner has found something he likes, he never wants to change, and although he rarely remembers its name, he never wants a summer without Ichiban eggplant. After some experiments that I'll discuss in a moment, I've decided that I agree with him: Ichiban is the best. The plants produce early and they keep on producing for at least eight weeks—assuming, that is, that The

Gardening Partner has remembered to water the pots during the middle of the day on hot days and that I have remembered to fertilize them. The fruits never seem to get bitter, even if we let them get a little beyond the stage when the skin is deep, shiny purple.

The closest I can get to Ichiban is Pintung Long. The taste isn't quite as delicious, but the redeeming feature of this variety is the glorious, pale lavender color of the fruits. In addition, the plants are slightly smaller and are less likely to drop their leaves and become as ratty as Ichiban by early September. One year, we tried Osterei, which was not a success. Its white fruits seem bitter at all times, which is too bad because the leaves and fruits are very decorative and the plants hold up well.

Growing blueberries

If you want to grow blueberries, plant the bushes any time from early spring until mid-May. But first, prepare the soil properly.

The ideal medium is well-drained, organic soil with a pH of 4.0 to 4.5. With a higher pH, the plants will grow poorly and show signs of iron deficiency, with leaves yellowing at the tips and margins and between veins. Organic supplements such as peat moss and leaf mold will help lower the pH, but for substantial changes you must rely on ferrous sulfate or aluminum sulfate. A soil test kit, available at county agricultural extension offices, will guide your applications.

Blueberries will grow in part shade, but you will find them much more productive if you plant them in full sun. Start with a half-dozen plants and space them on six-foot centers. Select early-, mid-, and late-season varieties to ensure not only a long harvest season but also good pollination.

For the first couple of years following planting, your chores will be light, mainly consisting of keeping the weeds under control. Mulch to deter the weeds and help the soil retain moisture. Use whatever you can lay your hands on—salt hay, rotting leaves, or wood chips all are good. Immediately after planting, fertilize each plant with a slow-release, acid-forming fertilizer. In subsequent years, fertilize in early spring and again in late May.

Pruning should be light for several years after planting. Let the bushes develop by removing only dead or crossing branches. Once the bushes are established, your goal will be to rejuvenate each bush by pruning the oldest canes at the base. Prune any time from October through mid-March.

For The Gardening Partner, the greatest challenge in the blueberry department is the flock of birds that seeks to deprive him of his breakfast bounty. His ideal bird-proofing system would be to surround each plant with a wire-mesh cage fitted with a security alarm that would sound when a bird settled. Fat chance. We make do with a black plastic net draped over posts and fastened with clothespins, a barrier that the birds frequently penetrate. If we were to start again, I think we would build a fruit cage such as you see in British gardens, with more substantial posts as a framework to hold a covering of wire whose mesh is small enough to deter small birds. If you plan such a structure, bear in mind that some blueberry bushes may eventually grow six to eight feet tall.

Magnolias and peonies, spring stars

Among the magnolias, you can find plants suitable for landscaping anything from a grand estate to a tiny garden. The bigleaf magnolia, *Magnolia macrophylla*, for example, has leaves up to 32 inches long, with giant-sized white, fragrant flowers. I enjoy this tree in the park near my home, but it's not a plant I would like in my backyard because the leaves are just too big.

For home gardeners, the smaller varieties, such as the star and saucer magnolias, are more practical. The star magnolia, *M. stellata*, is a small, shrubby tree, growing to about 15 feet high with a slightly smaller width. It's the first magnolia to bloom, so your recollection of this tree may be of its frosted, blackened blossoms. If you plant it, avoid locating it on a southern exposure because the buds tend to open more quickly in such situations and are therefore more likely to get damaged by late frosts.

The saucer magnolia, *M.* x *soulangiana*, will grow taller, to an ultimate height of 20 to 30 feet with as wide a spread. Within this hybrid, you will find cultivars with flowers ranging from white to dark red and purple. Also, the National Arboretum in Washington has introduced a whole series of smaller-growing cultivars with flowers as large as the original hybrid. Known as "little girls," these plants have names such as Ann, Betty, Judy, and Jane. Shop according to your color preference and look for mid-April bloom.

In late April or early May, magnolia aficionados enjoy a splash of yellow flowers, resulting from breeders crossing *M. acuminata* with *M. denudata*. *M.* Elizabeth was one of the first introductions from a breeding program at the Brooklyn Botanic Garden. Its flowers are large and fragrant, but be prepared for it to grow quickly into a large tree.

Apparently, one of the problems with yellow-flowered magnolias is that their flowers fade in warmer-than-usual spring temperatures.

A cultivar called Butterflies is popular because its flowers are darker than others and are less likely to fade.

There's another flower that shines this time of year. The colors of the flowers, the lush petals, and the good smells all make me think there's little more luxurious in spring than a huge vase of herbaceous peonies. Peony plants will bring you years of good dividends so long as you invest in their initial planting. In spring, you will find container-grown peonies available in many colors in garden centers. In fall, you can order bareroot plants from specialty catalogs or buy them at some nurseries. Choose a site with full sun and well-drained soil, and be sure you don't plant the crowns too deeply. Place the bud only one to two inches below the soil line. For the first couple of years after planting, pick only a few blooms per plant to allow the roots to develop. When you pick, cut the flowers when the tight balls start to show color. Unlike some flowers that don't come out unless you pick them after they've started to open, peonies will go from tight bud to full bloom in a vase.

Shopping for trees and planting them

When you shop for trees, it's best to buy a small to medium-sized tree, with a good-sized rootball in relation to the size of the canopy. Trees with large canopies and small rootballs do not establish well. If you are buying a balled and burlapped tree, make sure the ball is intact and that there are no scars on the trunk. Overly tight rope and burlap will scar or wound the bark.

Until a few years ago, tree specialists were advising us to dig large holes, settle in the trees, then backfill with a rich, well-drained soil mixture and stake each plant. These days, the story is different. If you buy a tree in a container, the advice is to remove the loose soil that surrounds the roots, plant the tree, then backfill with the soil you dig from the planting hole. The theory is that if you place the roots in a rich, well-drained mixture, they will grow round and round each other rather than venturing out into the surrounding soil. If you're planting a balled and burlapped tree, dig a hole slightly wider than the ball, lower the ball into the hole, cut the string that binds the burlap, loosen but do not remove the burlap, and backfill the hole with the soil you removed.

In either case, plant the crown slightly higher than it was in the container to allow room for settling, then water generously. Remove all grass surrounding the tree and replace with a two- to three-inch layer of mulch. Keep mulch several inches away from the trunk of the tree.

When planting trees and shrubs, either from containers or balled and burlapped, place the top of the rootball slightly higher than before to allow for settling of soil.

Most trees, research now shows, can be planted without staking. If the tree is unable to stand on its own, stake low on the trunk and remove stakes as soon as possible. Unstaked trees have freedom of movement and will develop stronger root systems. If you stake them, once they grow beyond the stakes, the tops whip around in the wind and often break off.

And while we're on the topic of trees, let's talk about siting trees in the landscape. Every tree has an ultimate height and width, and before you plant it's your responsibility—both to the tree and to your landscape—to find out those parameters. You may have moved into a house and rued the decisions of the prior owners who planted a blue spruce or an oak by the front door, where a small shrub would have been much more appropriate. Further away, large trees would have been fine, but as they are now, you know that you will have to remove them before many more years go by.

We've all done it. The Gardening Partner reminds me each season about the stewartia I planted too close to the back of our house. So far, I've been able to prune it myself, but I know that time is running out.

Also consider the utility lines that run through your property. Keep towering ashes and spreading sycamores away from these lines, or future generations will have to mutilate the trees to keep them from interfering with the wires.

Another compulsion gardeners have is to plant under a tree. Anything you plant under a tree ultimately robs the tree of water and nutrients. Add a simple layer of mulch and don't make it a huge layer. I hate to see those mounds of mulch that people put under their trees. Two to three inches will do, but any more will suffocate the tree roots. And remember, pull the mulch away from the trunk to avoid creating the perfect site for fungal diseases to settle in.

Pruning needs tools and timing

For large trees, most gardeners need the services of an arborist (November, p. 147). Shrub pruning, however, can be done by the gardener. It's just a matter of sharp tools and correct timing.

The tools first. For starters, you will need a pair of hand pruners. Buy a well-built pair that will last several years and test the grip for comfort. For larger branches, you will need a pair of loppers; those with ratchet-cut movement are easiest to use. I also love my small pruning saw, which folds neatly into my back pocket. If you plan to do your own small-tree work, a pruning pole saw will come in handy.

Establish a pruning schedule. Summer-flowering shrubs such as buddleia can be pruned now. Take all stems back to within a few inches of the soil line. Spring-flowering plants such as forsythia and azaleas should be pruned immediately after they flower. Evergreens can be pruned in early spring, but you can also wait until late June after the heavy spring growth. Plan to take a rest from early July through mid-October to avoid stimulating late-summer growth that may not harden before winter.

Houseplants want spring cleaning, too

In the house, you will find your plants picking up and starting active growth as they respond to the longer days and brighter light. That makes now an excellent time to get them shipshape for the spring and summer. Some of my plants are in pots crusted with salts. Others, with roots poking out the drainage hole, are in obvious need of a new pot. If you're not sure, tip the pot over, turn the plant out, and inspect the roots. If they are starting to circle inside the pot, it's time to repot.

How you repot a houseplant depends on whether you want the plant to grow much larger. If you do, select a pot a couple of inch-

To stimulate root growth after repotting houseplants, pull roots apart before replanting.

es larger in diameter. If you think the plant already is big enough for your space, remove it, scrub away the salts, and return it to the pot.

In either case, you'll want to stimulate root growth, and this will never happen if you just stuff the rootball back with a little new soil. If the ball is a mass of fibrous roots, cut away the outside with an old knife and tease the roots apart to stimulate growth. If the roots are thicker and more distinct, you can unwind them and prune selectively.

As a general rule, prune as much from the top as you do from the roots when repotting. Sometimes it's not possible to take an equal amount from the top without ruining the shape of the plant. In these cases, you should be particularly careful about reacclimating the plant, allowing time for new roots to develop under optimal conditions.

Fertilizer basics

Once the gardening year starts in your area, you will be bombarded with advertisements promoting *the* best fertilizer for your flowers, vegetables, or lawn. To help you figure out what to buy, here are a few basic points about fertilizers and comments about those that The Gardening Partner and I have used over the years.

Fertilizer comes in spikes, tablets, liquid, 50-pound bags, and two-ounce bottles. As a gardener, your challenge is to determine the most appropriate formula for your needs and to figure out how to use it wisely with little waste.

Most fertilizer packages carry a series of numbers, such as 5-10-5, indicating the analysis of that particular product. The three numbers represent the percentage of three major elements: nitrogen, phosphorus, and potassium. Nitrogen is the chief source of vegetative growth. Phosphorus develops early root growth and is responsible for bud set, color development, and the general maturation of the plant. Potassium acts as a binder or catalyst and promotes sturdy growth.

Many fertilizer packages also list the minor elements, such as calcium, magnesium, and sulfur, present in smaller quantities along with trace elements such as boron, manganese, and zinc. Each element plays a vital role in plant growth and development and if one is short, this will be the limiting factor in determining the crop production.

At several points in the gardening year, I've recommended that you invest a few dollars in a soil-testing kit from your local agricultural extension office, so you can make the best use of your fertilizer. Within a few weeks, you will receive a computer printout indicating the current fertility of your soil and recommendations for improving its potential. These recommendations are based on the type of crop or ornamental planting you plan for a particular site. For example, if you plan to grow blueberries on one site and vegetables on another, buy more than one soil test kit.

Important information on the printout will be the pH level indicating the alkalinity or acidity of your soil. Each plant has a specific pH range within which it can absorb nutrients. Before you even consider adding fertilizer, amend the pH level as outlined in the recommendation from the lab. Expensive fertilizer will be wasted unless you adjust the pH before you add fertilizer.

Many soils in my area have low pH, in the 4.5 to 5.5 range, providing ideal conditions for acid-loving plants such as rhododendrons, azaleas, some hollies, and blueberries. Vegetables, most annuals, perennials, and lawn grasses flourish in the 6.0 to 6.5 range.

Applications of ground limestone will raise the soil pH. Peat or ground sulfur can be used to lower pH. Use the quantities recommended by the extension office on your soil test report. Soil structure is another important factor that will determine whether you get maximum benefit from your fertilizer. Soils high in organic matter will hold both fertilizer and moisture, whereas these quickly leach out from sandy soils. To improve soil structure, add compost, rotted leaves, sawdust, or other organic materials such as mulch during the growing season and dig this into the soil in fall.

Careful timing of your fertilizer applications will help conserve vital nutrients. For woody plants, the most efficient use of fertilizer results from late winter applications. Roots can absorb nutrients in winter whenever soil temperatures exceed 35° F. For flower and vegetable beds, hold your fertilizer until spring. Nitrogen, the essential element, leaches from the soil during the winter when the ground is empty.

In the days of cheaper fertilizer, vegetable gardeners would broadcast their applications before spring planting, covering the whole garden. Fertilizer can be conserved if you sprinkle a little in the trench below the seed before planting. Cover the fertilizer before adding seed to avoid the possibility of burning new roots. Later, as plants develop, additional fertilizer can be added as a side-dressing, that is, the granules can be scattered alongside a row of vegetables. Either scratch the fertilizer in, or water heavily. Beware of using too much fertilizer. Excess fertilizer can produce more disastrous results than a shortage of the elements mentioned above.

As gardeners continue to debate the merits of organic as opposed to inorganic fertilizers, it is important to understand the differences between them. Organic fertilizers such as manure (both dried and fresh), bonemeal, and dried blood are less caustic, so there is less danger of burning plants. Organic fertilizers become available to the plants slowly because they must be broken down in the soil into inorganic forms before the plants can use the nutrients. However, this type of fertilizer remains in the soil longer than an inorganic material.

Inorganic fertilizers have higher concentrations of the required elements, are more speedily available to plants, and come in several forms. First is the water-soluble form, which provides the quickest action. An example of this is 20-20-20 fertilizer recommended for houseplants and container plants. Recently, products with high phosphorus content that provide benefits to flowering houseplants have come on the market with names such as Blossom Booster.

Granulated fertilizers are also quick-acting. A typical example of this kind of product is 5-10-5, recommended for vegetables. For leafy crops, you may want to use a product with a higher nitrogen content, such as 10-10-10.

For shrubs and trees that don't need such a quick-acting fertilizer as vegetables, there are slow-release products in which the nutrients are coated, which makes them available to plants over a longer period of time. Their release is governed by temperature and moisture. For shrub plantings such as azaleas and rhododendrons that require acidic soil, look for acid-forming, slow-release fertilizers.

Then there's an even slower form of release, made possible by encapsulated products, such as Osmocote, which become available to plants over three to four months. I use this for orchids and also for all the container plants on my deck. At planting time, I add Osmocote to the soil mixture, then also fertilize during the peak of the growing season with a water-soluble fertilizer.

No matter what fertilizer product you decide to use, your first step should be to get that soil test kit from your local agricultural extension office—or from some nurseries. Test results will show not only soil fertility, but also the pH.

APRIL

Something New
Every Day

This is the month that gardening starts to be fun. If I had my way, April would have 60 days instead of 30, each marked by a new blossom, a new blade of grass, or a different tree coming into bloom. The parade starts with magnolias, continues with shadblow, daffodils, early tulips, fragrant viburnum, and azaleas, then ends with the dogwoods turning creamy white. For the gardener, April's 30 days are filled with feverish activity.

Some tips for early April ...

❧ Plant seeds of tender annuals indoors.

❧ Dill and basil are wonderful herbs for kitchen use. Dill grows best in cool periods, so sow it outside now, then again in late summer. Sow basil seeds inside in mid-April for transplanting outdoors after the last frost in mid-May.

❧ Hydrangeas make good temporary houseplants—provided you give them plenty of light and moisture.

❧ When planting container-grown plants, pull apart the roots before you put them into the planting hole. This rough treatment will encourage new root growth, and your plants will become established more easily.

❧ Old pantyhose has lots of garden uses. Cut into strips for tying staked peppers, tomatoes, and eggplants, or use the strips instead of broken pieces of terra cotta in the bottom of clay and plastic pots.

ᘓᕀ Spring makes gardeners want to get out and plant, but don't plant everything all at once. May 15 is the last date on which frost can be anticipated in my area, so in your zeal to plant, make sure that you don't set out tomatoes, eggplant, peppers, and tender flowers such as marigolds and zinnias too early. Find out whether your frost date is different; if you live in a city, where the soil will warm up more quickly, you can plant 10 to 15 days earlier than those who live in less protected locations, and if you're in a frost pocket, you may need to wait until around Memorial Day.

ᘓᕀ Also, be sure you harden off (March, p. 6) the plants before setting them out. A coldframe is ideal for hardening off, but you can also set the containers in a protected area and cover them with light plastic at night.

ᘓᕀ **In the vegetable garden:** Keep plantings of strawberries weeded. Heavy weeds encourage moisture and subsequent fruit rot. Use a porous mulch, such as salt hay, that will keep the weeds down and will also provide a quick-drying layer on which the maturing strawberries can rest. Remove blossoms from newly planted strawberry plants to prevent fruit set. Harvest fruit the second year after planting. ... Continue planting potatoes, onion sets, and onion plants outdoors. ... Sow seeds of tomatoes, peppers, and eggplants in small seed pans, place in an area where soil will remain between 70° and 75° F., and cover containers with polyethylene to retain moisture to encourage germination. If your seedlings already have germinated, move them to cooler temperatures for sturdy growth. ... Get the peas into the ground, continue to plant lettuce and spinach, and put transplants of cabbage and broccoli into the garden for early yield before the weather gets warm. ... Soil maggots can reduce a gardener to tears by ruining the roots just as crops start to produce. Protect your plants by surrounding each with a maggot mat to discourage flies from laying eggs at the base of the plant. Small squares of carpet underlay seem to do the job. Slit them from edge to center, and carve out a hole for the stem to allow room for expansion.

ᘓᕀ **For the flowers, shrubs, and trees:** Take advantage of any mild days to prune overgrown and leggy blooming shrubs. Concentrate first on such late summer bloomers as buddleia and caryopteris. In subsequent weeks, after they've bloomed, work on those that produce flowers in early spring. ... Caladiums make wonderful plants for cool, shady spots. Buy a few now and enjoy them inside the house. Put them outside on a terrace in pots or plant in the ground after the last frost date. ... Complete pruning your roses.

Some tips for late April ...

⁊ Late spring is a good time to check on the houseplants. Toss out those that have succumbed to diseases and pests and see if the rest need repotting. Turn each one over and knock out the rootball. If the roots are winding round and round, making a white mass, it is time to repot. Always untangle the roots before you repot to encourage them to reach out into new soil. If you remove a lot of root growth, also remove foliage. If you expect the plant to bloom this spring, save your surgery on roots and tops until later in the year, right after bloom.

⁊ Excess seeds will germinate better in future years if you store them in a cool area with low moisture. Place two tablespoons of powdered milk (from a freshly opened packet) in four facial tissues and secure the package with a rubber band. Put this in a wide-mouthed canning jar with the seeds, and seal the jar tightly. Place the container in the refrigerator, as far away as possible from the freezer. Replace the powdered milk, which absorbs damaging moisture, once or twice a year.

⁊ Hold fertilizer for strawberries until plants have fruited. If you fertilize now you will encourage leaf rather than blossom development.

⁊ Wait until mid-May to plant out ageratum, cockscomb, vinca, begonias, impatiens, salvia, and other tender annuals. Alyssum and lobelia are two half-hardy annuals that can be planted outside in late April. Petunias also seem able to take colder weather, although not frost. In mid-April, sow seeds of marigolds and zinnias inside to have good-sized transplants for your garden by mid-May.

⁊ **In the vegetable garden:** It's getting late to sow peas, but if you had trouble getting them in because of a cold, early spring, sow a couple more rows, using a more heat-tolerant variety, such as Wando. ... Collect milk jugs and cartons to use as mini-hothouses to protect the early seedlings as you move them from house or coldframe to open garden. ... Plant out seedlings of cole crops (broccoli and cabbage) no later than the end of the month to allow them time to mature before the hot weather. After planting, surround each seedling with a small collar (one to two inches deep) to deter cutworms from severing the stem. Look around for discarded objects to reuse for this purpose, such as drinking cups from which you can remove the bottom. … Continue to plant lettuce. Hold the string beans until early May. … If flower stalks appear on your rhubarb plants, remove them promptly; if you leave them in place, they will sap strength from the edible shoots.

🍂 **For the flowers, shrubs, and trees:** Fertilize each rose plant with one-third cup of slow-release fertilizer. Work lightly into the soil, then cover the ground with two inches of organic mulch. If planting roses, look for a sunny, well-drained area with good air movement. … Bulbs forced into bloom in the house cannot be made to bloom again inside, but if they're hardy, there's another life waiting for them outdoors. Keep them growing, in good light and with adequate moisture, until early May, then plant them outside. As with all bulbs, allow the foliage to mature and yellow naturally. (Nonhardy bulbs, such as paperwhites, will not make it outside, so you should put these on the compost heap.) … Now's the time to plant shrubs and trees, both bareroot and from containers. Never set the plants lower in the new hole than they were planted previously, whether it was in the field or in a pot. … Check climbing shrubs and vines, retying where necessary in preparation for heavy growth in the months ahead. … When the daffodil blooms fade, do me a favor and neither remove the leaves nor tie up the foliage with string or rubber bands. It may satisfy your desire for a neat garden, but either move restricts the amount of nutrients the bulbs can store for additional blooms next spring. Let the foliage mature naturally, then remove it once the leaves are brown. … Perennials, except for spring bloomers, can still be divided in the next couple of weeks. If you receive perennials by mail, wrapped in dry packing material, soak the roots in water for several hours before planting. … If your forsythia has finished blooming, it's time to prune. If you want to remain in my good graces, do not give the whole plant a haircut, slicing it across the top and down the sides. Rather, remove old canes from the base to encourage new growth. … Plant roses by the end of the month so they have a chance to get roots established before the hot weather arrives.

APRIL: LAUNCHING GARDENS

A monthly overview

April is when buds break, seedlings germinate, and bright yellows and fresh greens overtake the dreary grays and browns of winter.

If you didn't do it last winter, clean off last year's debris before you dig over the vegetable garden, disposing of plants that may harbor insects and diseases. Building the structure of your soil is an ongoing task, so add whatever compost, leaf mold, or other organic matter you have available before you start to dig or till. You may also want to dig in fertilizer granules in specific areas.

Although the April sun may feel warm, the soil is still relatively cold, so restrict your planting to crops that will germinate at low temperatures. Seeds of peas, lettuce, and other salad greens, such as mustard, arugula, radishes, and spinach, should all be sown before the third week of April to allow sufficient time to mature before a flash of hot weather.

Hardy herbs (sage, mint, tarragon, and chives) should also be planted into the garden in April. If you need only a couple of plants, you probably will find it more practical to buy plants of these herbs, rather than sowing them from seed. Indeed, French tarragon, which has the tasty leaves, does not come true from seed and must be propagated by cuttings. Be sure to pinch tarragon leaves before buying. If there's no smell, it's probably Russian tarragon. Leave it on the bench and check another garden center. Mint is invasive, so take care to plant it where it cannot spread over less vigorous plants. Once you have it in the garden, it's hard to get rid of it.

In the ornamental gardens, remove all the leaves that have settled on shrubs and ground covers since last fall. Rake them out of the way into a pile. Later, when they have decomposed into leaf mold, spread them on the vegetable garden to retain moisture and reduce weeds. If you can reduce their size in a shredder, so much the better.

As you work in the flower garden, tread carefully among emerging shoots of peonies, daylilies, and other perennials. When most plants have put up several shoots, scratch fertilizer around the base of each plant. Where you plan to plant annuals, spread fertilizer and dig it into the soil.

When buying perennials, look for strong, vigorous plants, rather than those with the most flowers per container. Buy early for the best selections and the freshest plants. In general, the less time a plant spends in the garden center sales area, the healthier it will be.

When planting shrubs and trees, be prepared to water them in dry weather until late fall to ease the shock of transplanting. When you plant balled and burlapped specimens, the burlap can remain on the balls, provided it is a natural fiber and provided you cut the strings around the stems after lowering the plants into the hole. "Plastic burlap" must be removed at planting time.

Of all the goofy things I've done in the garden; the one with the "plastic burlap" keeps coming back to haunt me.

Shortly after I took up horticulture with a vengeance, I became enamored with the elegant Hinoki false cypress, *Chamaecyparis obtusa* Nana. This evergreen caught my eye on a garden tour, so the next spring I bought four Hinoki cypress and planted them below a low stone wall.

First mistake: I didn't know enough to check the labels to make sure the plants I was buying were the dwarf (Nana) variety. The plants loved the location, and much to my surprise, within a couple of years they were shooting way above the stone wall. If only I had thought to check, I would have found out that the species, *Chamaecyparis obtusa*, which I had bought, matures at around 50 to 75 feet with a spread of 10 to 20 feet. Clearly, these plants had to be moved and that's when I discovered my other mistake. They were too big for me to handle, so I asked a landscaper to move them and was horrified when he asked whether I knew I had left the "plastic burlap" on the rootballs.

Of course not. At the time of the first planting, I had no idea that you should treat "plastic burlap" with great suspicion—certainly removing it before planting.

So here we are, at least 10 years after the second planting of the cypress to create a background for a perennial garden. Over this past winter, deer removed the foliage from every lower branch, leaving four ugly sticks at the bottom with leaves above. The time had come to move the chamaecyparis again—to the dump.

When my current landscaper called after he'd finished the job, he casually said, "And guess what we found below the soil line?" Apparently, the first landscape crew had only pulled the burlap back, which had allowed the trees to develop side roots, but there was little root activity below the ball, which was still totally enclosed in "plastic burlap."

I'm told that there's a move afoot among nursery companies to banish "plastic burlap" from the trade, but in the meantime, may this serve as a warning to all gardeners: Don't forget to remove the plastic-type burlap!

The first vegetable garden

"Flowers and shrubs are okay," says The Gardening Partner, but if I'm looking for togetherness with him in garden activities, the end product has to be edible. Over the years, we've had a lot of fun in our vegetable patch, so here's some advice for the family that is planting its first.

First, consider the size of your garden. A large garden looks great on paper, and you can quickly label sections with cucumbers, eggplants, tomatoes, and squash—maybe even pumpkins. But later in the season, when it's hot and dry and every vegetable has some disease, it may become a weedy nightmare. For the first year, start small in a location where you can expand in future years in proportion to your enthusiasm.

Ample sun is essential, but to get maximum light throughout the growing season, keep in mind, as you study potential sites, that the sun's path will change throughout the summer. Look for a piece of ground with full sun for a minimum of six hours a day. Keep away from trees, not only because of the shade their canopies will cast, but also because their roots will rob your vegetables of valuable nutrients. If you have a black walnut on your property, be aware that many vegetables, especially tomatoes and eggplants, will not grow in association with this tree's roots.

Good drainage is as important as good light. Avoid low areas where you see water standing after a storm. Gardening on a hillside can provide excellent drainage that can often allow a gardener to work the soil several weeks ahead of neighbors who cultivate flat spots. Drainage and light are hard to modify, and without reasonably good conditions, your garden may be a struggle. The soil, however, is something you can modify and improve over the years.

The results of the soil test I have urged you to conduct will tell you the pH (acidity and alkalinity) of your soil and the amount of fertilizer required for best growth. The pH measurement must be correctly adjusted because availability of nutrients depends on an appropriate pH. On the scale of 1 to 14, most vegetables grow best between 5.5 and 6.5.

Lime to adjust pH and fertilizer are immediate applications. Your long-term goal for the soil should be to build in as much organic matter as possible by adding compost and mulch and by sowing a cover crop such as winter rye in the fall to turn under the following spring.

In most areas, it takes a few years before the soil "cuts like butter" under your spade. Become a neighborhood scavenger and search for leaves, grass clippings, and other organic materials to incorporate into your soil. I mulch heavily with leaves each June, after the soil has warmed up, and then I dig these into the garden in the fall.

The beauty of a vegetable garden, as compared to permanent plantings, is that every year it's a fresh experiment, and that allows you to try new techniques and varieties. As you start on your first garden, get into the habit of making notes and keeping records so you can follow up on your experiments and adjust the following year.

In basic terms, vegetable crops divide into those that thrive in cool weather and those that should not be planted until after the last frost. Early crops include greens such as lettuce, spinach, Swiss chard, and mustard, as well as peas, onions, beets, and cole crops (broccoli and cabbage). Some you sow by seed, such as the leafy greens (tiny seeds) and beets (slightly larger). When you open a packet of beet seeds, you'll find small, knobby objects, each one a small natural package containing several beet seeds in a group.

Onions grow slowly from seed; in future years, you may want to start seeds in late January. But for this first year, buy small plants, or buy bulbs, or sets, through the mail or at a local nursery. Peas come easily from large, wrinkled seeds; cole crops are best started from transplants, readily available in April in garden centers. Life for the above crops—except onions and beets—is short because they have to mature before hot weather comes, usually about the end of June.

For peas, you will need supports to provide a firm hold for the vines. We use three-foot-high chicken wire supported by metal stakes. You may prefer a net trellis or brush cut in the woods.

Green beans require warmer soil than those other crops. You can usually plant the seeds for your beans during the first week of May and have a crop by the Fourth of July. Snap beans are high producers; we sow only one 20-foot row at a time, then plant another several weeks later for a succession of harvests. If you have the space, keep planting until mid-July.

Those staples of high summer—tomatoes, peppers, eggplants, and lima beans—should not be planted until after the last frost, about May 15. Tomatoes seem slightly more cold-tolerant than the other crops.

The selection of varieties in seed catalogs and on the seed racks at garden centers is dizzying, but it's just a question of figuring out family favorites and how you will use the fruits of your labors. Take tomatoes: The Gardening Partner longs all winter for big red tomatoes, so there's no point in our growing "interesting" yellow varieties or cherry tomatoes.

The pepper selection is also wide. One year, I got carried away by the catalog photographs of beautiful purple peppers. My main goal with peppers is to gather enough to make jelly. Red-pepper and green-pepper jellies are gorgeous; purple-pepper jelly is plain ugly.

Once you decide to grow tomato and pepper plants, you must

also decide whether and how to support them. If you have plenty of land, you can afford to let them sprawl, figuring you'll lose some to ground pests and rot. With a smaller planting area, every one counts, so stake or support plants in cages.

If you have the time and are able to prune suckers and tie shoots on a regular basis when the plants are growing rapidly, staked tomatoes probably provide the highest yields with the best fruit, but, lazy gardener that I am, I find caging easier. Use five-foot lengths of five-foot-tall turkey or reinforcing wire to make cages about 18 inches in diameter. (Chicken wire isn't strong enough and the small holes make it very hard to harvest large tomatoes.) You can also grow pepper plants in cages.

Peppers need attention

With a name like Pepper, you would have thought The Gardening Partner would have been a pepper grower from his early days. But no, his mother brought him up on okra, tomatoes, and eggplant, and he just could not see the point of wasting garden space on peppers. It has taken a few years, but I've converted him. Now we grow peppers not only in the vegetable garden, but also in containers on our deck. Peppers like it warm, so I suggest that you wait until after May 15 to plant.

If you get itchy feet and just *have* to get the pepper transplants out early, protect them for a couple weeks—perhaps with large plastic milk jugs with their bottoms removed—to give them a good start.

Some summers, despite your best efforts, pepper plants will grow lush and full with abundant foliage and little fruit. The cause is climatic; first it's too cold, then too hot or too dry for the plants to set fruit. For good fruit, the air temperature should be 70° to 80° F. and the soil should be moist.

Plant peppers closely, 24 inches between plants in a row and 24 inches between rows, so when the plants mature, you have a good leaf canopy to cover the soil. Mulch heavily with a material that will hold moisture in the soil. Grass clippings are good for pepper mulch, as long as your grass has not been treated with herbicides. Leaf mold or salt hay are alternatives. Be generous with the mulch, placing a two- to three-inch layer around the plants. When the late summer drought hits, be sure to water the plants thoroughly a couple of times a week.

Wire cages, similar to those that many gardeners use to support tomatoes, are a great way to contain and support pepper plants. For each cage, cut a 12-inch-wide strip of black roofing paper or plastic, and wrap this around the base of the cage. The black paper captures the heat and protects the transplants from drying and damaging winds. Leave the tar paper in place for three to four weeks, until the transplants are well established.

If you plan to grow hot peppers, be sure to label them in such a way that the labels will stay throughout the summer. One year, I got our hot peppers mixed up with the sweet peppers and an unsuspecting friend received a basket of hot Hungarian Wax instead of a sweet variety. My friends John and Ann, who are avid pepper growers, also recommend separating hot from sweet peppers in the garden. In years when they have planted them side by side, they have found hot, bell-shaped peppers on a sweet pepper plant. Jalapeño and Serrano Chili are varieties for those who like their peppers real hot. You'll even find varieties bred especially for making salsa.

A good time for shrubs

April is the time to plant all manner of shrubs and trees, whose root systems will take advantage of the cool temperatures of early spring to become established before the cruel heat of summer.

When setting out bareroot plants, be sure to spread out the roots and force soil between them to ensure maximum contact between roots and soil. With containerized plants, a tendency among gardeners is to disturb the root systems as little as possible on the theory that what's good for the plant in the pot must be good for it in the garden. This is not the case. The roots of a containerized plant continue to grow round and round in circles, eventually girdling the stem, unless they are forced to break out into the surrounding soil.

You do that by removing the plant from its container and making a slit through the middle of the rootball, starting at the bottom and going up about one-third through the ball. Then slash the sides of the rootball to encourage the roots to break out on all sides. When you plant, spread the ball out at the bottom and fill the hole left by the slit with soil.

Perennials, American-style

For centuries, British gardeners have been famous for their large, colorful perennial borders filled with a wide variety of plants. Until the mid-1980s, American gardeners, on the other hand, planted mostly shrubs and annuals, and the selection of perennials available in nurseries was dismal. How times have changed. Large nurseries throughout the United States now carry a broad range of perennials.

Books on the subject abound, and a host of small nurseries have sprung up, concentrating on everything from daylilies to geraniums. There's even a Perennial Plant Association and a Hardy Plant Society with study groups for several types of perennials.

Herbaceous perennials, commonly referred to as perennials, are plants that grow and flower for more than three years. The stems and foliage of a perennial plant die to the ground each winter and regrow in the spring.

There's a perennial for almost every site, from hot, sunny banks to moist, shaded areas in woodland gardens. By definition, a perennial continues to flower and seed year after year. Some plants will die down soon after flowering; others will become unattractive after hard frosts and should be cut back; still others, such as ornamental grasses, will provide interest throughout the winter in foliage and seed heads and should not be cut down until early spring.

Most plants will benefit from well-drained soil. When you establish a perennial bed, put extra time and effort into preparing the soil. In future years, your only chance to build up the soil will be through fall or spring applications of manure or compost, or by replacing soil when you divide the perennials.

During the growing season, be prepared to stake the plants if you expect them to grow tall; many a potentially beautiful sight in our garden has been ruined because I was too slow in getting the stakes and twine in place. In the spring following planting, fertilize perennials, scattering a handful of slow-release fertilizer around the base of each plant, and then scratch it into the soil. In later years, be prepared to divide the plants when they start to bloom with less abandon. Most perennials, except for a few such as peonies, should be divided once every three to four years.

There are several times in the year when you can divide perennials. For spring-blooming plants, one of the best times would be just after flowering. Summer-blooming perennials can be divided in early spring, or most perennials can be divided in the fall. Just try to do it sooner rather than later, so the plants can put out some new roots before hard frost.

Dig up the whole plant and place it on a piece of burlap or tarp to avoid spoiling your lawn. You'll be able to pull apart some plants with your hands. Tougher plants, such as daylilies and ornamental grasses, are much harder to separate. If you have two large forks available, place these back to back in the center of the plant and force the roots apart. Alternatively, slice the plant into pieces with a spade. With some ornamental grasses, I have had to resort to an ax.

Here's a smattering of easy-to-grow perennials for new gardeners to try. First, for sunny sites:

Catmint. Some gardeners complain about the scent of its foliage, but it's hard to beat catmint for planting in a sunny, dry location. *Nepeta mussinii* has lavender blue flowers. Look for cultivars such as Blue Wonder and Six Hills Giant. Cut back all catmints in late summer to rebloom in fall.

Columbine. In spring, I love to see these plants come into bloom with their red, pink, and blue flowers that include little birdlike spurs. Many columbines are easy to grow, especially the native *Aquilegia canadensis,* which has red and yellow flowers and some of the hybrids of *A. vulgaris,* such as the McKana Hybrids, with pastel flowers. The smaller *A. flabellata* Nana Alba, with sturdy white flowers, has seeded itself into several locations in our garden and does not seem to be attractive to deer. Columbines will grow in full sun or partial shade.

Daylilies. Gone are the days when you had only a few cultivars of Hemerocallis from which to make your choice. Breeders now produce a dazzling array of sizes and flower colors, from deep mahogany to pale peach, and have placed considerable emphasis on repeat bloom. The cultivar Stella d'Oro was one of the first in this group. Happy Returns blooms just as well, is also of medium height, and has prettier, pale-yellow flowers.

Geranium. Not to be confused with the tender geraniums we grow on terraces and in window boxes, whose scientific name is *Pelargonium,* these hardy geraniums are gaining popularity as nurseries offer more varieties. Flower colors range from white to pink and mauve, through deep blues and purples. Some varieties will tolerate shady sites.

Heuchera. Here's another plant that has attracted the attention of breeders because of its ability to survive severe climates and also because of the wide range of leaf variations that have evolved through hybridization. *Heuchera micrantha* Palace Purple is a popular hybrid, but there are many others with leaves from deep purple to those with silvery veins. Plant in well-drained soil. Heuchera will survive in full sun or partial shade.

Japanese anemones. These are stunning plants with dark green leaves and late-summer flowers in white and pink, single and double. They will flower in some shade.

Lady's mantle. On a May morning after a rain shower or heavy dew, the leaves of this plant glisten. Its delightful foliage is yellow-green and, because it stays low, this is a good plant for the front of your flower border. When the blooms fade, remove these and some of the older, coarser leaves of *Alchemilla mollis.*

Lamb's ears. For a soft, fuzzy mat at the front of the garden, there's little to beat these plants. *Stachys byzantina* has oval, gray-silver leaves. *S. byzantina* Helene von Stein has broader, gray-green leaves and does not produce flowers, which I prefer because the pink flowers of the species are not an asset in some color combinations. The leaves on *S.* Primrose Heron are a tasteful lemon yellow-green. Lamb's ears resists deer browsing.

Purple coneflowers. Gardeners who enjoy having butterflies in their gardens should plant these coneflowers in tough, dry sites. *Echinacea purpurea* is sturdy and coarse, but the flowers are so broad, they make wonderful landing platforms for butterflies and will also last well if picked and brought into the house. There are cultivars with purple or white flowers, and if you keep removing the deadheads you should have flowers from early through late summer.

Russian sage. With filigreed leaves, tall stems, and blue flowers, Russian sage, or Perovskia, makes an airy presence toward the back of a border and can handle difficult, very dry sites. *Perovskia atriplicifolia* Filgrin has good habit and flowers.

Sedum. For the hottest, sunniest spots in your garden, there are tall-growing sedums as well as those of more modest proportions. These plants are tough and durable. *Hylotelephium* Autumn Joy grows one to two feet tall and produces rounded heads of flowers in late summer that open pink and later fade to deep rust. *Sedum kamtschaticum* will sprawl over a rocky ledge or alongside a path and will produce yellow flowers in midsummer.

Threadleaf coreopsis. Sometimes known as tickseed, this plant has many excellent cultivars that grow well in hot, sunny areas. The foliage is bright green and threadlike, the flowers yellow and abundant over several weeks. *Coreopsis verticillata* Moonbeam is popular for its pale yellow flowers that combine well with blue-flowered perennials. Zagreb is a tougher, taller cultivar, but its flowers are a brassy yellow.

Veronica. Some of the most spectacular hybrids, such as Sunny Border Blue, have bright blue flowers. *Veronica incana*, with gray leaves and pink summer flowers, has proved resistant to deer browsing in our garden.

Yarrow. For a sunny border, yarrow is an excellent addition because it can survive in the hottest and driest of summers and you can use the flowers for dried arrangements. Flower colors range from white to deep yellow and tangerine. My favorite is *Achillea* x Moonshine for its pale yellow flowers; I find the white cultivars look messy.

31

And now some perennials suited to shady sites:

Astilbe. These plants are easy to grow in shady sites with good soil and can even grow in boggy soil. Their leaves are fine, and most varieties flower in May and June. Among the hybrid cultivars, you will find flowers in red, pink, lavender, and white and heights ranging from 18 inches to three feet.

Aruncus. Similar to astilbe in form and preference for growing conditions, these plants are also useful for shady sites. *Aruncus aethusifolius* resembles a small, low-growing astilbe with creamy white flowers and can be used as a ground cover to the front of a planting.

Bleeding heart. *Dicentra spectabilis* is the best known in this genus for its pink May flowers. The leaves are gray-green and will die down in midsummer. Plants will grow two feet tall with a spread of 18 inches. *D. eximia* has blue-gray leaves that remain in good condition through much of the summer. Flowers will be white, pink, or red, depending on the cultivar.

Epimedium or **barrenwort.** A tough, low-spreading perennial with wiry stems that seems to resist deer browsing. Flowers will be white, pink, or yellow, depending on species and cultivar.

Hellebores. These plants are an early joy in the garden for their waxy flowers that look like roses and, in some species, for their shiny, evergreen foliage. The Lenten rose, *Helleborus orientalis*, is one of the easiest to grow. Flowers are mostly mauve pink; some are spotted. Bearsfoot, or stinking hellebore (*H. foetidus*), is poorly named because although it has a slight odor, it's not offensive. The charm of this plant is its dissected foliage.

Hostas. The hosta could be called the daylily of the shade and as such enjoys a well-deserved popularity. There are huge hostas with gigantic green, crinkled leaves; hostas with variegated leaves that brighten up shady corners with their yellow or white markings; tiny hostas that grow in the shaded section of a rock garden; and fast-growing types such as *H. sieboldii* Kabitan that spread to form large mats. If you are seeking to expand hosta plantings, divide them in early spring, just as shoots start to appear above ground.

Siberian bugloss. This bugloss produces clumps with fuzzy leaves and forget-me-not-type flowers in May. *Brunnera macrophylla* has blue flowers and dark green foliage; some cultivars have variegated leaves. Again, this plant has resisted deer browsing in our garden.

Disbudding and pinching

Disbudding and pinching are two methods by which you disrupt a plant's normal growth habit to produce either larger flowers or bushier plants. Disbudding is often used on plants such as roses and chrysanthemums where you remove some flower buds while they are still small, so those remaining will develop into larger flowers. You can do this as soon as the buds are large enough to handle, such as the size of a small pea. The sooner you do it, the better to allow the remaining flowers to develop.

Pinching creates a stockier plant. In the spring, when you plant annuals such as impatiens, petunias, coleus, and salvia, for example, pinch out the terminal shoots to encourage branching. One pinch may do the trick. Chrysanthemums should be pinched three or four times until late July.

Plant now, have roses later

Just imagine a bouquet of roses, freshly picked around dawn on a June morning. Sound tempting? Then get to work now to prepare a rose bed and get your plants established by the end of April.

To produce larger flowers on plants such as roses and chrysanthemums, remove side buds to force growth into terminal buds. This practice is known as "disbudding."

My rose-growing expertise is limited, but Judy McKeon, chief horticulturist at the Morris Arboretum of the University of Pennsylvania, has lots of good advice for rose growers.

Roses require at least six hours of direct sun daily, good air circulation, well-drained soil, and adequate water and fertilizer. To prepare a rose bed, dig the soil over to a depth of 18 inches, mixing organic matter such as peat moss, chopped leaves, manure, or compost into the soil. If your soil is heavy, add sand or perlite to improve the drainage.

You can buy roses bareroot, in a package, or with soil in a container. Try to get those sold bareroot or in a package in the ground as soon as possible. When bareroot roses arrive, they will be dormant, but the canes should look smooth, with a green or reddish color. If you can't plant them right away, make sure the material in which they are wrapped is moist, then store them in a cool place or in the refrigerator for up to 10 days. When you are ready to plant, McKeon suggests soaking the roots for several hours or overnight in water.

Before planting, prune off broken canes or roots and cut back the canes by about one-half to one-third, leaving two or three buds. Dig a hole 18 inches deep by 24 inches wide, replacing some of the soil in cone formation. Spread the roots and set them over the cone so

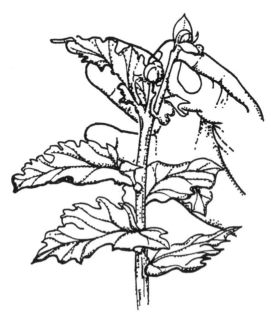

When you plant annuals, pinch terminal shoots to encourage branching, which will give you stockier plants later in the year.

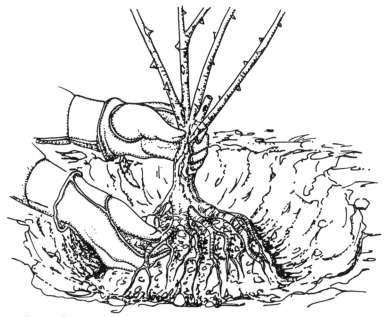

When planting bareroot roses, create a mound on which to spread out roots, then cover with soil.

the bud union is level with the soil. Replace the soil, packing it tightly, then water well to eliminate air pockets. The planting procedure is similar for packaged roses, but McKeon warns gardeners to be sure to remove the package before planting.

If the rose is in a pot, you can plant it later in the spring, but the sooner you get it into the ground, the easier it will be for the plant to become established. Remove the plant gently from the container, first tapping the container on a hard surface to loosen the soil. If it does not fall out easily, cut the container rather than yanking the plant out by its roots. Roses can be planted in spring or late summer, and no later than mid-September.

After planting, mulch roses with a three-inch layer of chopped leaves or woodchips. Newly planted roses do not require fertilizer, but established roses should be fertilized with a slow-release fertilizer in early spring. If you have several roses, buy a product formulated for roses. McKeon suggests fertilizing everblooming and reblooming roses again in June to encourage later blooms. In all cases, she suggests not fertilizing roses later than early July because the fertilizer will stay in the soil and could push late-season growth that will be damaged by an early frost.

Roses are a challenge to the gardener because pests and diseases favor these plants. Rose growers in my area have experimented with a variety of alternatives to toxic chemicals. For aphids and mites, Pat Los, a member of the grounds crew at Pennsylvania's Swarthmore College and the person in charge of the school's rose plantings, has had success with beneficial insects, specifically lacewings and predatory mites, which she has ordered by mail. Japanese beetles have long been a problem for rose growers and now another insect, the rose midge, has growers baffled. An extract from the neem tree, sold by a variety of trade names, is a product with which growers have had some success in controlling both insects.

Among the diseases that favor roses, black spot and powdery mildew can defoliate a rose garden in wet summers. According to McKeon, one of the most effective controls for black spot is to regularly clean up dead foliage, especially at the end of the season, to remove spores from the site. In addition, prune canes hard in early spring to remove those with spores on them and, as soon as the leaves come out, treat the bushes with a preventive organic spray. McKeon recommends mixing garden sulfur with a fungicidal soap, combined with an antitranspirant. Throughout the season, be rigorous in promptly removing dead flowers and repeat the spray twice later in the summer, at monthly intervals.

Some roses are more resistant to fungal problems than others, so consider planting cultivars recommended as disease-resistant. Pat Los suggests some of the David Austin cultivars, introduced in the last few years from England, such as Graham Thomas, Mary Rose, English Garden, and Pertita. McKeon recommends Alba Semi-Plena, Stanwell Perpetual, and Madame Plantier.

Also investigate the full range of landscape roses, which have been bred for maximum disease resistance. Lowest to the ground are the Meidiland series, with red, pink, and white flowers. All are designed to cover large areas and grow vigorously, so plant these only in an area where they can spread. Shrub roses are taller and can be used in borders and for hedges. Bonica was the first introduction, followed by Carefree Beauty and Carefree Wonder. Carefree Wonder is superior to Carefree Beauty in flower production and disease resistance, but it does not produce hips. The Fairy, a polyantha rose, is smaller in stature but is a dependable bloomer and is also disease-resistant.

Dogwood distress

The end of April and beginning of May used to be a time I looked forward to each year, simply for the pleasure of waiting for the buds on the dogwood trees to open. In the initial stages, the show is cream-colored, then white, and the countryside seems to dance with the layers of blossoms.

In recent years, the number of native or flowering dogwood (*Cornus florida*) in gardens and natural areas has declined because of a fungus called anthracnose. In our garden, we lost several trees in the late '80s; those left seem to be holding their own. If you decide to plant a flowering dogwood, place it in a partially shaded area, perhaps on the edge of woods, and try to surround the base with a layer of mulch to help avoid nicks to the trunk when mowing.

Two alternatives to the native dogwood in the same genus are the Korean dogwood (*C. kousa*) from Asia, and hybrids between the American and Asian species, developed by Dr. Elwyn Orton at Rutgers University in New Jersey. Dr. Orton released six hybrid cultivars, which bloom between the American and Asian species and appear to be resistant not only to anthracnose, but also to the dogwood borer, a troublesome pest of the American flowering dogwood. Unlike the native dogwood, which produces its flowers before the leaves, the Korean dogwood comes into flower in the middle of June, with creamy white bracts. The tree itself is beautiful, with branches more upright than the native dogwood, but age gives it a graceful, spreading habit. The bright red fruits are attractive starting in September, and the peeling, colorful bark is an asset in winter. Be sure to plant in full sun. My trees look great, but they would bloom much better if I hadn't planted them too close to a red maple.

Two of the hybrids developed by Dr. Orton and especially recommended for growing in this area are Aurora, with an upright growth habit and white flowers, and Ruth Ellen, which has a spreading habit more similar to that of the native flowering dogwood.

If you're looking for other alternatives, outside the dogwood family, there are a number of trees of similar size from which to choose.

Japanese snowbell or **styrax** (*Styrax japonicum*). This is a small tree with white flowers. Styrax produces small bells in early June, and some years, you may even notice the delicate fragrance of these blooms, particularly in early evening. This plant grows quickly and will mature around 25 feet high with a spread of 15 to 20 feet.

Sourwood or **sorrel-tree** (*Oxydendrum arboreum*). I'm grateful to my neighbor for planting a sourwood, which also has white blooms, below our house many years ago because the clusters of small, bell-shaped flowers make quite a show for us as we sit on our deck. In fall, it's spectacular, too, when the leaves turn brilliant orange and red. The shape is difficult to characterize because it varies from tree to tree. Although it is not the tree to plant if you are seeking the ultimate in symmetry, it does fit nicely into a more informal setting. Like rhododendrons and azaleas, sourwood belongs to the heath family and thrives in acid soil.

Shadblow or **shadbush** (*Amelanchier lamarckii*). Because it blooms when the shad are running in local rivers, this small tree, which produces white blooms in April, is a good choice for a small garden. The bark is an attractive smooth gray, and the tree can be grown with single or multiple stems. In June, the local bird population gorges on the purple, berrylike fruits.

Washington hawthorn (*Crataegus phaenopyrum*). A tough tree, which survives in city gardens and along city streets, the ultimate height of the Washington hawthorn is 25 to 30 feet, with a potential spread of 20 to 25 feet. It produces masses of white flowers in May. To some, its odor is undesirable, so you may want to plant this tree away from the house and walkways.

The indoor garden

For those with plenty of growing space indoors, clivias, which are native to South Africa, make excellent houseplants. They grow well in filtered sunlight and can tolerate overheated rooms, so long as you give them a short early-winter rest period of six to eight weeks in a location where the temperature is below 50° F. Without this rest period, the plants may be forced into premature bloom, with flower stalks failing to rise above the foliage.

During spring and summer, water plentifully, as much as necessary to keep the mixture moist, but gradually reduce amounts in fall and keep clivias almost dry during the rest period. When flower stalks appear toward the end of winter, begin a gradual increase in the quantity and frequency of waterings. Add liquid fertilizer in the growing season, beginning when flower stalks are half-developed and continuing until a month before you start to withhold water in early winter.

Periodically, the plants get infested with mealybugs, but it's easy to detect the pests against the clivia's dark green foliage, and you should be able to take care of these soft, white insects by dabbing them with a cotton swab dipped in alcohol.

As they mature, clivia plants produce offsets whose roots gradually fill the pot, and eventually you must decide between repotting the whole clump in a larger container or dividing it into several smaller lots, in either case after the annual period of bloom.

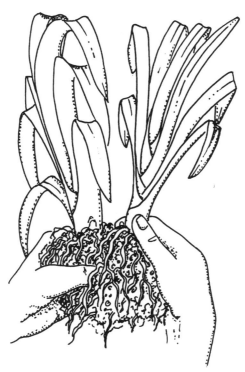

As they mature, clivias produce offsets, which can be used to start new plants. Remove plant from pot and try to detach offsets by pulling the roots apart. If this doesn't work, cut sections with a sharp knife.

Before you start dividing a clump, arm yourself with a large, sharp knife and a generous space in which to make a mess. Try pulling the offsets apart, and, if this doesn't work, move in with the knife, making sure each piece ends up with plenty of roots. Division tends to disturb a clivia's flowering habits, sometimes for a couple of years.

A favorite: Azaleas

Azaleas make excellent plantings for large public landscape areas, but also for home gardens. With the exception of the deciduous varieties that tolerate full sun, most azaleas prefer partial shade, especially in the afternoon. Well-drained, loose, slightly acidic soil is another requirement.

Azaleas have shallow roots and fail, according to one expert, mostly because gardeners plant them too deeply, suffocating those shallow roots. An advantage of their shallow roots, however, is that you can transplant them easily. When you complete transplanting or planting, each azalea should sit one to two inches above the existing soil line. By the time you add a covering of mulch, the top of the mulch should be flush with the soil line. Gardeners should not fertilize first-year plantings. During the second and subsequent years, add an acid-forming fertilizer.

Most azaleas require little pruning, but what pruning you do should be done as soon as possible after the blooms have faded. If you prune after the end of June, you will be removing the following year's flower buds. Older plantings may require drastic pruning and you'll find azaleas respond well—if you're prepared to wait several years for the plants to recover.

Here are the names of some azalea varieties, arranged by color, that should do well in your garden:

Lavender-purple. Karen, six feet at maturity; Girard's Fuchsia, double flowers, six feet.

Pink. Tradition, three to four feet; Blauw's Pink, double flowers, six feet.

Red. Hershey's Red, very hardy, blooms early; Hino-Crimson, single flowers, low-growing; Mother's Day, double flowers, six feet.

White. Delaware Valley White, four to five feet; Hardy Gardenia, large, double flowers; four feet.

White and pink. Rosebud, double flowers, six feet.

Flowering crabs

My stepdaughter wishes the homeowner who landscaped her small city garden outside Boston many years ago had not chosen a crabapple as "the" tree. By July each year, she says her terrace is covered with blackened leaves and the tree itself, almost denuded in the hottest months of the year, provides little shade.

According to my friend Steve, who runs a garden center in suburban Philadelphia, Ginny is not alone in her thoughts about crabapples. Gardeners remember the trees that "trashed" their parents' yards with diseased leaves in midsummer, then with one-inch-diameter fruits in fall. Steve points out that flowering crabs make wonderful small trees for the garden, and thanks to research over the years at several state universities, there are now crabs that don't lose their leaves and produce small fruits that not only don't make a mess of the lawn or terrace, but also provide a bonus for the birds in your area.

Crabs lose their leaves because they are highly susceptible to diseases such as fireblight, apple scab, powdery mildew, cedar apple rust, and leaf spot. If you are in the market for a flowering crab tree, specify first your desire for a type that is resistant to disease, then make your selection by size, flower, and fruit color.

Malus sargentii (Sargent crab) is an excellent tree. Its flowers are red in bud and white on opening, and the tree will be eight to 10 feet high at maturity.

The following hybrids are mostly resistant to the major diseases: Donald Wyman (pink buds, white flowers); Jewelberry (pink buds, white flowers, shrubby tree); Prairie Fire (red buds, pink flowers); and Red Jade (pink buds, white flowers, weeping form).

MAY

The Lovely Month of Color

May has to be the best of months in the garden, but it places special demands on us. Our pace must be brisk to get through the long list of activities and yet we must be patient and restrain ourselves from setting out the tender plants too early.

Some tips for early May ...

🍃 With May 15 the last likely day for a frost, your D-Day for planting many flowers and vegetables is almost upon you. (If you're in a colder area, wait a week or so longer.) As you browse in garden centers and nurseries looking for your favorite bedding plants and vegetables, look for tight, compact plants with dark green leaves throughout (passing up those with yellowing leaves or elongated stems); look under leaves for aphids and whitefly (the last thing you need to buy); and, unless you are planning for a party that same evening, look for high-quality foliage rather than lots of flowers.

🍃 Before planting seedlings grown in peat pots, tear off the top strip of each pot and then tear off pieces from around the sides and the bottoms. At least make holes in the fibrous material. If planted above ground, the top of the pot will remain dry, and if you don't break up the material on the sides, the roots will have a hard time breaking out of the pot. If your transplants are growing in plastic or clay pots, break up the roots before planting.

ᘒ If you have the appropriate place, move the houseplants outside for the summer. For those that can tolerate more light, move them by degrees into brighter areas. For most houseplants, this is prime time to repot, prune, and set them up for good growth over the summer.

ᘒ When cutting peonies for the house, cut only the blooms and leave the foliage to strengthen the plant for future years. Ants on peony buds are acting on your behalf to remove aphids, so don't try to get rid of them.

ᘒ Before putting them into the garden, harden off tender plants, flowers, and vegetables, such as tomatoes, by putting them out during the day and bringing them back inside at night. Peppers and eggplants are more cold-susceptible than tomatoes and will appreciate being kept in a warm place until the end of May.

ᘒ Seedlings will suffer less shock in transplanting if you provide optimal conditions for new roots to develop. Do not transplant in full sun. Wait until early evening and, if the sun returns the following day, shield new plantings with bushel baskets or pots. Separate congested root systems by gently pulling roots apart, and water seedlings with a diluted (one-quarter strength) fertilizer solution after planting.

ᘒ **In the vegetable garden:** Buy seeds of broccoli, cabbage, cauliflower, lettuce, spinach, and other greens now for fall sowing (garden centers often run out before you need them). ... Space tomatoes four feet in either direction. Peppers and eggplants can be planted more closely. Mix a couple of teaspoons of granular fertilizer into the soil at the base of each planting hole. Plant tomato seedlings deeply, covering the stems beyond the pair of leaves closest to the roots. Remove this set of leaves before planting. Additional roots will form at leaf nodes. Plant eggplants and peppers at the same depth as in the seedling container. Surround each plant with a cutworm collar made from a strip of cardboard or plastic. ... Cucumbers flourish in hot, humid weather and rich soil. Prepare your cucumber planting bed by adding manure (aged from the barnyard if you can get hold of it, or dried cow manure from the garden center). To warm the soil for cucumbers, melons, and other heat-loving crops, cover it with black plastic, then plant the seedlings through slits in the plastic. ... If tomatoes are on your list for planting in mid-month, assemble the stakes or cages that you're going to use to support them. It's always better to put these in as you install the plants, rather than waiting until the vines flop all over the place. ... May is the height of the planting season for the vegetable garden. If you do not have the peas in, it's too late, but it *is* the time for the first planting of snap beans. Plant subsequent rows at two-week intervals. Keep cutting asparagus and rhubarb. Thin onions as they grow and use thinnings in salads. ... For fans of Brussels sprouts, early May is the time to sow seeds indoors for transplanting into the garden in mid-June. The first time we tried growing them, we harvested tiny little sprouts in November. Their size made them just delicious, but we would have had many more wonderful meals if we had sown the seeds about a month earlier.

ᏱᎧ **For the flowers, shrubs, and trees:** In some areas, the soil may be warm enough to set out tender annuals, such as impatiens and begonias, but for most locales wait until mid-month in case there's a late frost. You can, however, set out tougher plants, such as petunias and alyssum. ... For shady areas, don't get carried away and plant annual salvias and zinnias that really do need full sun. Stick with the tried and true; impatiens, begonias, and coleus will give you that splash of color. Or try the wishbone flower, also known as torenia, which has delightful, small, deep blue and yellow flowers. Caladiums will also do well in the shade and the varieties with variegated white and green leaves are attractive. Those with red leaves can be appropriate in some settings, but the white variegation appeals to me more in summer. ... If you're a lilac fan, try a couple of smaller-growing varieties, such as *Syringa patula* Miss Kim, with purple blooms and red fall foliage, or *S. meyeri* Palabin, with lavender trusses in May. Both will grow four to six feet tall with as wide a spread. ... Sow seeds of quick-growing annuals, such as marigolds and zinnias, inside now so you can transplant them outside in early June. ... If you're planting trees and shrubs, be sure to create a "saucer" out of soil or mulch around each plant. The saucers, which hold moisture, will save hours of watering time and will cut down on the amount of water you use in the garden. ... When you plant dahlia tubers, cover each one with two inches of soil. Continue to deadhead pansies for additional blooms. ... Remove faded blooms from spring bulbs; allow stems and leaves to mature naturally. Prune early-blooming shrubs such as winter jasmine and fragrant viburnum after blooms drop.

Some tips for late May ...

ᏱᎧ If you don't already have a compost pile on your property, start one. Not only will it help you get rid of garden and uncooked vegetable kitchen waste, but it will also pay handsome dividends in years to come with compost to return to the garden.

🐛 Keep watering and fertilizing the amaryllis that flowered this winter. Come September, place the pot on its side and withhold water for about three months to allow the bulb a dormant period.

🐛 Remove faded azalea and rhododendron blossoms, taking care not to damage new shoots alongside the blooms. Azalea leaf galls are small, white protuberances that appear on azaleas in midsummer. For control, remove galls by hand.

🐛 After planting, pinch back coleus, verbena, impatiens, and begonias for lusher growth later.

🐛 Tent caterpillars will soon make their appearances, leaving a mass of crawling black larvae in a "tent" on fruit trees and many other kinds of plants. If you can reach it, remove the tent by pruning the branch over which it is suspended, then burn the branch and the web.

🐛 Pick large, central broccoli heads first to encourage development of smaller side shoots that can be harvested in coming weeks. When cauliflower heads reach teacup size, shield them from the light to keep them tender and white. Pull the long outer leaves up and over the head and secure them with a plastic-bag tie or clothespin. Leave the cover in place until you are ready to harvest the heads. Purple cauliflower varieties, such as Violet Queen, which are intermediate between broccoli and cauliflower, can be grown without tying the leaves over the heads.

🐛 **In the vegetable garden:** Basil is easy to grow in the ground or in pots, as long as you put it in full sun. Buy plants and set them out soon, or start seeds in the garden. Basil grows quickly if you plant it in reasonably good soil. You'll find varieties with smaller leaves as well as traditional large-leafed varieties. If you want the basil as a decorative edging, pick the smaller varieties, but if you want it for the kitchen, buy the standard plants so you'll get a larger and better-tasting harvest. With standard plants, be sure to pinch frequently. ... Sunny patio areas make wonderful vegetable mini-gardens. Buy a couple of large pots and grow tomatoes, eggplants, and peppers. Cherry-type tomatoes, such as Super Sweet 100 Hybrid, will provide good crops in a small space, as will Japanese-type eggplant cultivars such as Ichiban and Pintung Long. Sweet Banana and Gypsy are two good pepper cultivars for this purpose. Just make sure you give them plenty of water once it gets hot. ... To prepare for a fall crop, sow

Brussels sprouts seeds soon and broccoli and cauliflower by mid-June in small flats in the house or in a shady area outside. Chinese cabbage, lettuce, and spinach can be sown directly in the garden in August.

‮ᔕ‬ **For the flowers, shrubs, and trees:** When planting clematis, look for a site where the roots are shaded and moist, but where the vine receives at least six hours of sunlight a day. Provide a trellis or a crisscross pattern of wire or another plant to allow the clematis to climb. ... For sunny areas, plant annuals such as ageratum, geraniums, petunias, purple basil, blue salvia, vinca, and dahlias. ... Pine trees can be encouraged to grow more dense by shortening the center "candles," or growths, in every cluster, except the central leader of the tree, which should never be touched. It's better to pinch out the "candles" by hand instead of using pruning shears. ... If you're planning to prune azaleas this year, the sooner the better after the blooms fade. Pruning will stimulate new growth that in turn will produce flowers for next spring. ... Chrysanthemum growers should continue to pinch terminal buds back every two weeks until late July, then cease pinching to allow flowers time to develop for fall garden color. ... Fill in bare spots in your garden by sowing seeds of quick-growing annuals such as zinnia, marigold, cleome, and portulaca directly into the ground. Prepare the area by raking the soil. Sow seeds and cover lightly with soil, then water with a fine spray. Cover area with a layer of burlap or salt hay to help maintain moisture to encourage germination. Check daily to make sure the soil is moist. As soon as seeds germinate, remove the covers.

MAY: SO MANY TASKS, SO LITTLE TIME

A monthly overview

The gardener must establish priorities to make the most of this wonderful month. Let's start with my favorite place, the vegetable garden.

As you may have gathered, the vegetable garden is my passion, and May usually finds The Gardening Partner out in our plot, at dawn, in his pajamas, inspecting developments. Later in the summer, before I can brush my teeth, I have a full progress report and his suggestions for possible delicacies for supper.

Keep a sharp eye on the cole crops for the white cabbage butterfly that will deposit its eggs on your cabbage, broccoli, and cauliflower. The eggs are harmless, but the pale green larvae that hatch afterward can destroy a good head of broccoli in a couple of nights.

Onions are heavy feeders, so if you didn't add fertilizer to the soil when you planted, consider side-dressing them now.

The eggplant is such a favorite crop of The Gardening Partner that he practically went into mourning the year that all the plants started to droop way before frost. The culprit was a wilt disease. Tomatoes have the same problem, but breeders have produced disease-resistant varieties. With eggplant, the solution for people with large gardens is to practice crop rotation, alternating between solanaceous crops (potatoes, tomatoes, peppers, and eggplant) and crops such as legumes or plants in the cucumber family. Our garden is relatively small, so this wasn't possible, and we switched to growing eggplants in containers on our deck, grown in sterilized soil.

Eggplants play host to flea beetles, Japanese beetles, and Colorado potato beetles. You can pick off the latter two by hand, provided you can stand touching the ugly, gray larvae of the Colorado potato beetle. Flea beetles are so small that it's not possible to remove them by hand. Come early June, the worst of these invasions is almost over, so I leave my eggplants in the greenhouse as long as possible to avoid the damage. Alternatively, you can cover eggplants with a floating row cover (January, p. 169) to provide a protective barrier against the beetles.

Asparagus is standard fare in May, and our three 20-foot rows provide just enough for the two of us with the occasional visitor from mid-April through May. Committing yourself to an asparagus bed is serious business, but if you prepare the soil thoroughly, you will be repaid with years of early spring harvests. Be sure to buy varieties resistant to fungal diseases. From mid-April to mid-May is the appropriate time to plant asparagus roots.

Set aside a sunny area for the asparagus bed, allowing four feet between rows and two feet between plants within each row. To prepare a trench for the roots, remove soil to a depth of 12 inches, loosen soil below the trench, and incorporate four inches of compost. Firm the soil, lay the asparagus in the trench, spread the roots, and cover each root with two inches of soil. Gradually, as the shoots grow throughout the summer, push the soil you've taken from the trench back into it, over the growing asparagus.

Keep the bed weeded, and next spring allow asparagus shoots to develop without harvesting. The following year, invite us over for your first harvest.

Limas are worth the work

If you enjoy fresh limas, there's no better way than to grow your own. The seeds may be reluctant to germinate and the plants won't produce a crop until late summer, but I can assure you that it will be worthwhile when you finally harvest your first meal.

Bush and pole lima seeds are both available. Mr. Lima Bean, alias The Gardening Partner, thinks that the taste of the bush varieties is vastly inferior, so we stick to pole limas. Bush varieties, however, do mature earlier, so plant these if you are in a hurry.

Pole limas are space-eaters and, because of The Gardening Partner's passion, we have to devote the whole of our lower garden (about 450 square feet) to the endeavor. On account of deer, it needs to be fenced and, because limas have to grow on supports, there are six rows of poles and string inside the fence.

Some lima growers plant their seeds in hills, surrounding a tall pole. We chose cedar poles spaced at 10-foot intervals in rows six feet apart. At the top and bottom of each pole, we have strung plastic-covered wire horizontally, fastened to the poles through eye hooks. In May, The Gardening Partner puts up his "strings," pieces of baling twine that run vertically from the top to the bottom pieces of wire on which the vines will grow.

Limas need a long growing season, but because the seeds are sensitive to cold, wet ground, you can't plant them outside much before the last week in May. To get a jump start, we pre-germinate our seeds between paper towels around mid-May, then place these in zippered plastic bags to conserve moisture. Watching the seeds take up moisture and start to produce roots reminds me of kindergarten germination projects. If the soil isn't warm enough for planting the seeds when the roots are about one inch long, put the seeds in small pots to hold them until the weather warms.

The Gardening Partner and I always disagree on how many seeds should be planted per row. For safety's sake, he is generous in his planting, fearful that some will not germinate, but he also resists thinning, so when he is in charge, we end up with a thicket of limas. To my way of thinking, thinner is better because our garden is not endowed with a full day of sunlight, and I believe that too much foliage retards blooming and pod development. My goal is to end up with plants one foot apart.

Both climbing and bush limas will benefit from a heavy mulch of old leaves, straw, or salt hay. The mulch will retain moisture and eliminate the need to weed around the plants. Cultivation close to limas causes blossoms to drop.

The black-spotted orange bean beetle is a menace for both snap

Cedar poles, spaced at 10-foot intervals in rows six feet apart, create the background support for our lima beans. The vines climb on sections of baling twine, tied between pieces of plastic-covered wire.

and lima beans and will ruin your crop unless you take precautions. From late June, be on the watch for an invasion. With pole limas, it's relatively easy to check the undersides of the leaves for beetles, their yellow larvae, or the orange egg masses. It consumes time, but we pick off the feeders and destroy them in a jar of soapy water. To avoid spreading diseases such as anthracnose or bacterial blight, don't touch bean foliage when it's wet.

A final push

Finally, it's time to go all out and get the rest of the summer crops into the garden before the end of the month. Let's start with cucumbers and pumpkins.

Cucumbers are finicky when it comes to soil temperatures, and the seeds may rot if you plant them directly in the ground before the soil temperature is consistently above 70° F. For this reason, it's best to start transplants from seed in mid-April, or to buy small plants at a garden center.

Cucumbers like rich soil, so add compost or fertilizer to the planting area. If you want to push the crop, place a layer of black plastic over the planting area, covering the sides with soil to keep it in place.

If you have plenty of room, plan to let your cucumber vines grow all over the place. If space is limited, build yourself a trellis with wire or mesh netting, making sure that any wire or mesh that you use has openings wide enough to allow you to harvest the cucumbers. Plant cucumbers on 12-inch centers to allow room to spread.

Cucumbers are susceptible to wilt diseases, spread by the cucumber beetle. Most gardeners get around this disease by planting successive crops, so a later planting takes over when an earlier one succumbs to wilt.

Pumpkins, another member of the cucumber family, like really warm soil (above 75° F. for good germination), so wait until you're sure there won't be another cold spell before sowing outside. If you have seeds and want to give them a headstart, sow inside in peat pots, stick in a warm location, then transplant outdoors after 10 to 14 days.

Pumpkins need lots of water to develop successfully, and you may find the fruits bitter in drought years. Insufficient nitrogen also causes bitter fruits, so be sure to add compost or a slow-release fertilizer to these planting areas, too. Harvest pumpkins in the early fall, when the rind resists puncturing with your thumbnail.

Squash and pumpkins are closely related and will cross-pollinate if planted side by side. You won't notice any difference in the fruits this summer, but should you save the seed from either variety for next year, you may find that you've wasted your time on a plant that produces unusable fruits.

If you have lots of space, you can grow varieties that will produce pumpkins suited for exhibition, such as Prizewinner Hybrid or Rocket. For smaller spaces, and smaller pumpkins, try Jack Be Little or Baby Boo with white skin.

Don't forget the herbs

An herb garden brings pleasure to gardeners and flower arrangers, to cooks, and to lovers of good food. It can be elaborate, with parterres and flagstone paths, or it can be just a few plants by the kitchen door.

No herbs in your garden? Let's help you figure out how to get a few going for this summer. Herbs need sun, and lots of it. If there's just one little patch of sun in your garden, consider planting a few of your favorite herbs in a large pot or tub. Most herb plants have shallow roots, so it doesn't have to be a deep container, but it does have to sit in full sun.

Well-drained soil is another important ingredient for success with herbs. Perhaps you can incorporate them into your landscape on a south-facing bank. (While you search for the best location, however, bear in mind that if your primary interest is a culinary herb bed, it should be convenient to the kitchen.)

Eventually, you will build up your own list of favorite herbs, but here are a few I love. First the annuals:

Basil. Come midsummer, there's little to beat fresh tomatoes with slivers of basil. There are compact varieties, such as Spicy Globe, that make attractive additions to the flower or vegetable garden, but for kitchen purposes, I prefer the standard, large-leafed type. Sow seeds indoors starting in late April, or buy seedlings to plant outside in late May. (Basil is sensitive to cold, so don't start too early.) Throughout the season, pinch the plants regularly, above their leaf nodes, to promote branching.

Coriander or **cilantro.** Unlike a friend who finds too many foods flavored with "the big C," as he calls it, I can't get enough of this tasty herb. It's wonderful in green salads, pasta salads, salads with mayonnaise, and chicken and fish dishes. In winter, I splurge each week and buy a bunch at the farm market. Come spring, it's one of the first things I sow in the garden. Coriander goes to seed quickly in hot weather, so continue to plant several short rows in spring, then resume planting in late summer for a fall crop, which can endure a mild frost.

Dill. Some plants reseed themselves with abandon in the garden, and you spend your time trying to get rid of them. Dill is a self-sower, but it's always welcome in my garden, and the plants that grow from self-sown seed are always much earlier and more successful than any that develop from seed I sow. It's a wonderful herb for all kinds of uses, including salads, fish and chicken dishes, and for baking. If you want to introduce it into your garden, sow a row of seeds in early spring, as soon as you can work your soil. During May and June, enjoy the leaves and perhaps you will find a use for some of the seed heads if you make dilly beans. Let the rest of the seed heads mature, then scatter the black seeds around the garden where you would like to have a couple of plants. Seeds will germinate in late summer to give you a fall crop, from which you should have seeds that will self-sow for future years.

Marjoram. Mild and sweet, this oregano relative is excellent with fish. Sow seeds inside in April, or purchase seedlings to set out in mid-May.

Parsley. In some places, it's a biennial, but in my climate, I treat parsley as an annual. It's slow to germinate, so buy half a dozen seedlings to set out anytime after mid-April. Parsley will tolerate light

51

frosts, so you can count on having it for salads and garnishes through October.

The following are perennials:

Chives. Buy pots of regular or garlic chives and set them out in the garden now. Harvest your chives by cutting the tops with a knife or scissors. The soft-purple, globelike flowers are edible and decorative, so consider planting chives in your flower garden.

Mint. The leaves are great in teas, but this is an invasive plant you don't want in the flower garden. Look for a place to contain it—beside a walkway or in an old sink or washtub—because once it gets going, it spreads rapidly through underground roots.

Sage. This is not an herb I use much in cooking, but I love it for its ornamental qualities and also because the deer leave it alone in our garden. In addition to garden sage, look for purple sage and varieties with variegated leaves.

Tarragon. This is a wonderful seasoning for chicken, fish, and salads, or for flavoring vinegar. The true French tarragon is the only desirable kind and it must be propagated by cuttings. Plant 18 inches apart to allow plenty of space for the plants to spread. Unless you're going to make lots of vinegars for holiday presents, a few plants should be sufficient for any family.

Thyme. Thyme needs excellent drainage to survive our winters. Buy small plants and place them in the front of a bed. Common thyme is readily available; cooks also enjoy lemon thyme, and it's wonderful to have around just for the smell of the foliage. Variegated thymes are very decorative.

If you're not picking herbs regularly for use in the kitchen, stop by the plants from time to time and pinch the terminal shoots from such varieties as basil, oregano, and tarragon, to encourage branching.

If you're picking herbs to dry, do it before the plants start to flower because the flavor diminishes once the flowers appear. Pick the herbs on a dry day, after the morning dew has evaporated. Tie them in bunches with rubber bands and hang them upside down in a dark place with good ventilation. Once leaves are dry, crumble and place in sealed glass jars.

Preparing the houseplants

This is the time of year when my houseplants look rather jaded, many having outgrown their pots and most having lost some of their appeal during the long winter. If you have a similarly unsightly bunch, take a morning away from the outdoor garden to spruce them up as you get them ready for summer.

First, check the collection for bad infestations of scale insects or red spiders. If you see sticky exudate on the leaves or beside the plant, carefully examine the leaves and stems to see whether you can detect small, brown scale shells. Red spider infestations cause leaves to turn yellow-brown and dusty-looking. Shake the leaves over a piece of white paper to dislodge the tiny insects and confirm your diagnosis.

If you have a bad case of either problem, do yourself a favor and toss the plants in the garbage can. You will spend weeks trying to clear up the problem while you run the risk of infesting your other plants.

Now that you have gotten rid of some of the real uglies, consider whether you will do minimal pruning, heavy pruning and repotting, or propagation before discarding the old plants. Your decisions on individual plants will depend on the state of the plants and how quickly you need replacements.

With a full growing season ahead, this is the time to divide your favorites to share with friends. Many rhizomatous begonias, for example, are great candidates for novice propagators. After knocking the selected plant out of its container, shake the soil from the roots and see if you can pull the roots apart. In many cases, you'll find you have to use a sharp knife to divide the rhizomes. Save one decent-sized section with plenty of roots to make a new plant for yourself, and then divide the rest. Each small piece of rhizome should have a few roots attached to help the new plant get established. Place each rhizome section into a small pot in well-drained soil, and put them all out of direct sunlight until the roots have had a chance to develop.

With ivy or philodendron, rejuvenate the plants by removing some of the long, trailing growth. Some plants look so out of shape that it is preferable to start fresh by taking cuttings rather than trying to rejuvenate the old plant. Ivies, geraniums, and carissa (natal plum) are just three examples of houseplants that will root easily at this time of year. Select growth that is neither old and hard nor overly soft and succulent and make three- to four-inch cuttings just below a node. Remove the bottom leaves so you can stick about one inch of cutting into the rooting mixture after dipping the ends into a rooting powder.

A good rooting mix for a variety of cuttings is a one-to-one combination of peat moss and perlite or sand. Moisten the peat moss before you mix it with the perlite and place the mixture in a three- to four-inch-deep flat. I use recycled pressed-fiber market packs (in which I bought annuals) for propagation, but you can use a foil cake pan, an old milk carton, or any container about three to four inches deep with drainage holes.

Prepare your cuttings away from the sun and place the flat in good light but out of direct sun. I put my flats on a tray filled with moist pebbles to raise the humidity and set the tray back from an east-facing window. After June 1, the cuttings can be put outside in the shade. Keep the rooting mixture evenly moist but not soggy.

If you plan to make cuttings of succulent plants such as Christmas cactus and sedums, use a higher percentage of perlite or sand in your mixture and keep the mixture on the dry side.

Depending on the species of plant, the cuttings may take from a couple of weeks to several months to form sufficient roots to allow you to move them from the flat to an individual pot. After about three to four weeks, tug at the cuttings from time to time. When you get a good amount of resistance, dig gently into the medium and inspect the roots. Move each variety of plant when the roots are at least one inch long. After potting, set the plants in the shade for several days to let them adjust before moving them into brighter light.

In the flower garden

If you enjoy cut flowers in the house, try gladioli, which are easy to grow and long-lasting once picked. Choose a sunny, well-drained location for your cutting garden and buy gladiolus corms as soon as possible, to plant around mid-May.

Dig the soil to a depth of eight inches, planting corms four to six inches apart, then cover each with two inches of soil. Within a week to 10 days, shoots should appear. When they are a few inches tall, mulch the area with leaves or grass clippings to maintain moisture in the soil and to hold down the weeds.

Lilies will also need your attention throughout the spring if they are to produce abundant blooms. As shoots emerge, sprinkle a handful of a slow-release fertilizer around the base of each plant. Scratch the fertilizer into the soil, keeping it away from the leaves and making sure you do not dig into the bulb. Tall lilies will need staking. Do this when the plant is in bud, loosely tying the plant to the stake with a flexible material such as a strip of old pantyhose. Lilies are greedy when it comes to water, so plan to soak the ground if rainfall is short. As with your gladioli, mulch is a great asset to lily plantings.

Roses are a challenge to the gardener because the only way to get good blooms and attractive foliage is to monitor the plants carefully from early spring to late summer, spraying at frequent intervals.

Black spot, a fungus disease, is a very common problem. The name is descriptive and the disease goes wild on wet foliage. Powdery mildew is another enemy, spreading its white growth across the foliage and buds, weakening the plant. Japanese beetles, aphids, and thrips will also visit your roses, chewing and sucking to their hearts' content.

Good sanitation is one way to cut down on problems, cleaning up dead and diseased leaves as you garden, especially in the fall. Also, avoid watering overhead in the evening, because wet foliage is an ideal place for diseases to spread.

Ferns for the shade

Delicate-looking but tough, ferns are a good choice for shaded areas in the garden. Their airy foliage gives a lift to the shady corner, and they will appreciate the cool, moist atmosphere under a tree canopy. Here are some to try:

Christmas fern (*Polystichum acrostichoides*). If you're after an evergreen fern, try the Christmas fern, whose leathery leaves will stand one to two feet high until spring, when the fiddleheads appear and the old leaves fall down around the crown.

Cinnamon fern (*Osmunda cinnamomea).* Named for its fertile "cinnamon stick" fronds, this fern is graceful with small fronds two to four feet long.

Hardy maidenhair (*Adiantum pedatum*). Native to North America, this fern is deciduous, and the wiry stems support dainty foliage. Although it would prefer to grow in moist, rich soil, it will tolerate dry shade.

Japanese painted fern (*Athyrium goeringianum* Pictum). This fern, my favorite, grows beside the partly shaded path to our front door. It's low-growing and therefore makes a good ground cover for the front of a planting area, but its special feature is the silvery marking on the leaves.

Ostrich fern (*Matteuccia pennsylvanica*). If you're looking for a larger fern as part of a background, try the ostrich fern, which will grow taller than three feet, spreading rapidly through underground runners if planted in good soil and given plenty of moisture.

Royal fern (*Osmunda regalis*). Large and elegant, the royal fern is thoroughly deserving of its name. Like many other ferns, it will grow best in an open, shaded area with moist soil, but unlike some, it prefers acid soil.

Ferns do best in conditions that resemble their native habitat, which, for many, is the forest floor with partial shade and rich soil with plenty of organic mixture. Home gardeners can easily propagate many ferns by dividing them in early spring, taking special care not to let the roots dry out during or after planting.

A splash of color

For the gardener who wants a splash of color in the shade, there's little that can beat the impatiens, now available in a dazzling array of flower colors and in just the right height for any need, be it an edging or a background plant.

In the early 1970s, researchers on a trip to New Guinea sponsored by Longwood Gardens and the U.S. Department of Agriculture, brought home the New Guinea impatiens, now available in many garden centers with red, pink, salmon, and white flowers and often with variegated leaves.

New Guineas, like other impatiens, are succulent and tender, so you shouldn't plant them outside until all danger of frost is past. Unlike traditional impatiens, plant them in full sun. Place the plants on eight- to 10-inch centers and pinch them frequently to encourage branching so that you will get bushy, well-formed plants. They also make excellent container plants, or go well in large, hanging baskets. Red spider mites seem to be the plant's main enemies, and these are always especially damaging in hot, dry spells. To deter them, hose the plants down from time to time in hot, dry weather.

On pruning lilacs

Well-pruned lilacs produce beautiful crops of heavenly scented flowers. For the first four to five years after planting, there's no need to prune them unless you have to remove shoots that break out below a graft.

Once the plant is several years old, remove one or two of the oldest canes each year or so at the ground line after blooming, then thin out the remaining shoots to three or four well-spaced canes.

When old lilacs grow to eight feet or more with dry, brittle wood and flower only at the top, it's time to prune hard to renew these shrubs. Prune as soon as possible after the plants have bloomed. First, cut out enough lower shoots so you can reach into the plant. If you are determined to do the job all in one year, prune out all the old, rough bark-covered wood to the ground, and cut down all but half a dozen of the young canes. By fall, growth will reach above three feet on the new canes, and come spring you will want to cut them back to five or six feet. By the second spring, you should have blooms again.

Once a lilac is several years old, remove one or two of the oldest stems each year at the ground line after blooming.

You may prefer to renew the plants in stages, removing several of the older canes each spring. Start by getting rid of all canes with borer damage, and head back any disproportionately tall canes to a crotch.

It's not the acreage that counts

Container gardening can be the key to a verdant summer for anyone, from the overseer of several acres who wants something extra on the terrace to the city apartment tenant with a small terrace. The possibilities for success are limitless.

First, consider the container. Almost anything will serve—traditional pot, old bathtub or sink, wooden or plastic crate, hanging basket. The only requirement is that the container have adequate drainage holes.

The second consideration is water retention. By midsummer, if your plants are growing in full sun and their roots are well-developed, you may find it hard to keep the soil from drying out, especially if you're using terra cotta pots. Plastic pots retain more moisture, but stay away from black ones, which retain more heat; a plastic pot in a terra cotta color is attractive and will last several years if you store it in a frost-free area over the winter.

The types of plants you plan to grow should determine the depth of the container. Geraniums, petunias, and other annuals can grow nicely in a depth of eight to 10 inches, as can most herbs, while peppers, tomatoes, and eggplants need pots 14 to 15 inches deep.

If you have access to compost, use it in combination with peat moss and sand or perlite in the following ratio: two parts compost, two parts peat moss, one part sand or perlite. Alternatively, use a packaged mixture. Stay away from very light mixtures, which not only dry out quickly but also don't provide enough stability for the pot during stiff winds in midsummer, when the plants have become top-heavy. If stability is a problem, put a brick or large stone in the base of the pot before adding soil.

Adequate fertilizer is also important. When I prepare the soil, I incorporate an encapsulated fertilizer product that releases its nutrients into the potting mixture over several months. In addition, I fertilize the plants with water-soluble houseplant fertilizer throughout the summer. Some gardeners prefer to fertilize once every two weeks; others prefer to fertilize each time they water, using a very dilute solution (one-quarter the recommended rate). Feed with normal-strength fertilizer only when the soil is damp. If you apply fertilizer to dry soil, you may burn the tender feeder roots.

In keeping with The Gardening Partner's interest in plants that produce edibles, we've switched almost completely from growing flowers on our sunny deck to growing tomatoes, peppers, and eggplants. Come mid-August, it's hard to find a place to sit, with so much space devoted to the makings of a fine ratatouille.

Hanging baskets

A couple of hanging baskets can add the final touch to your May garden and, if you fuss over them periodically during the summer, they will provide you with flowers to enjoy until frost.

Wire baskets lined with sphagnum moss are the most attractive hanging containers, but you can use plastic. Stay away from clay containers because they dry out so quickly. Select a six- or eight-inch-diameter wire basket or plastic pot. Line the basket with an inch-thick layer of long-fibered sphagnum moss. Buy prepared potting soil or add perlite to the soil from your compost heap to provide better drainage. Sand, the alternative to perlite to improve soil aeration, is not as desirable for hanging baskets because of its weight.

Your choice of plants for these baskets will depend on your exposure. If you are lucky enough to have an eastern exposure with morning sun followed by filtered sunlight, you have the ideal situation for the greatest variety of plants. If your porch or patio faces south and gets lots of hot sun, or if it receives little direct sun, you will have to select plants with more care.

First, let's consider my own situation, where the sun beats down on the hanging containers from early morning until around 4 p.m. The most successful growers for continuing bloom have been, far and away, ivy geraniums. Petunias did reasonably well, but they suffered badly from drenching rains—the hanging basket's worst enemy. If you can bring your baskets under cover when a deluge threatens, you will prolong their best blooms.

A delicate plant for sunny areas is the black-eyed Susan vine (*Thunbergia alata*), which will climb up the wires that suspend the basket as well as falling down over the edge of the pot. If you think hanging vegetables would be appropriate for your balcony, try a pot of parsley or tomatoes, both of which will need full sun.

For gardeners with part sun and good air circulation, there is no more appealing plant for a hanging basket than a fuchsia. Fuchsias are almost irresistible in a garden center, but resist unless you can provide good growing conditions. These plants thrive in Maine and in my native Scotland, where the summer nights are cool. If you buy or plant a fuchsia basket, make the most of its spring blooms, then cut it back in early to mid-July and allow it to develop new shoots to bloom in early fall. Throughout the summer, water the basket generously and watch for whitefly, a major pest of fuchsia.

Several annuals make excellent plants for hanging baskets and thrive in semi-shade. Browallia is a faithful bloomer with delicate, white or powdery-blue flowers. Begonias, which come in a multitude of colors, bloom in the shade or semi-shade. Flowering vinca takes semi-shade or sun and is available in a wide range of colors.

All container-grown plants need special attention to keep them in good shape throughout the summer. Hanging baskets have the toughest time because the soil dries out so quickly once their roots are well developed. Check containers morning and evening and when you water, drench the soil until water runs through the moss or drainage holes.

Throughout the summer you must pinch and trim back the hanging plants to keep them from growing long and straggly. Do it frequently, pinching tender shoots just above a node (the location where a leaf originates on the stem). If you plan to be away in midsummer, take advantage of the time you will not have to look at the baskets and trim the plants more vigorously than usual before you leave.

Other odds and ends

There's still plenty of time to plant balled and burlapped or container-grown shrubs and trees, but the later you plant the more you must be aware of the importance of watering. Give each plant a good soaking once a week if it doesn't rain. Don't waste your time on water sprinkling daily. It's not nearly as effective as deep-watering.

To encourage a good show of bloom in future years, divide iris and other spring-blooming perennials after they have finished blooming. German or flag irises are shallow-growing plants, so they're easy to dig up and divide, which you should do every three to five years to ensure good blooms. Cut back the foliage by two-thirds first. The best divisions are double fans, with two small rhizomes growing at an angle from the larger one. Cut the fleshy roots with a sharp knife.

Plant irises in full or half-day sun, setting three new fans together in a triangle and leaving at least two inches from any edge of one rhizome to any edge of the other. The ends of each rhizome should be pointed outward. Cover with one to two inches of soil. As they develop roots, rain will wash away some of the soil, and the roots will seek their own level in the ground.

JUNE

The Good, the Bad, and the Ugly

June is the month for roses, the first peas, and lots of fresh lettuce. But it's also the month for the flea and Colorado beetles, and a few other hazards. As you enjoy the bounties, look carefully for the marauders and try to catch them before they do too much damage.

Some tips for early June ...

❧ Transplanting young plants is easy in the spring when the temperatures are cool and the rainfall is usually abundant, but as summer comes on, you need to be more cautious. If possible, wait for a cloudy day but at least wait until the sun has gone from the piece of garden you'll be working in. By planting late in the day, you give the plants the benefit of a cooler night, followed by several cool hours after daybreak. Once the sun heats up the following day, cover each plant with an old basket or flower pot. Make sure that plants have adequate water after transplanting.

❧ Get your houseplants outside for the summer. This is the time they will grow best, so give them ample water and fertilizer to help them take advantage of the warm temperatures and good light. Shade-loving plants will enjoy an area on the north side of the house. Succulents and other sun-tolerant varieties eventually will be able to take full sun on a deck or patio, but move them into full sun gradually or the leaves may burn.

ᴥ While you're moving your houseplants, take a good look at all of them. A couple could probably benefit from repotting to allow their roots more room to spread during the summer. Do it now, rather than waiting for fall, when the plant will not rebound as quickly. Throughout the summer, fertilize houseplants regularly, using either a dilute solution (such as a quarter measure) each time you water or a full-strength solution every 10 to 14 days. Reduce levels as the nights get longer and cooler in September. Check regularly for insect infestations.

ᴥ Water as you go when installing trees, shrubs, perennials, and annuals, rather than praying that it will rain when you've finished. It rarely does. Before you know it, a full week has passed before you get out to look at the poor, suffering transplants.

ᴥ Annual vines are effective in covering bare walls and fences. Plant seeds of morning glories or the hyacinth bean (*Dolichos lablab*), which produces beautiful, pealike, pale-purple flowers, then rich purple-colored pods. Both need full sun.

ᴥ June is a good month to work on yews, junipers, Japanese hollies, and other hedge plants. As you prune, remember to keep them narrower on top than at the base so the lower foliage will get light and remain healthy.

ᴥ Do not place ashes from the charcoal grill in the garden. Many products contain chemicals, and ashes invariably contain fat and perhaps pieces of meat that are welcomed by rodents and other pests. If test results show that your soil needs potassium, fireplace ashes are a good source.

ᴥ **In the vegetable garden:** When rains are lighter, sow seeds slightly deeper and cover with burlap, a newspaper, or salt hay to keep the soil moist as the seeds germinate. ... There's still time to plant lima beans, but not much. ... Pile on anything you can find that will serve as mulch to keep the weeds down and retain moisture. If your mulch supply is short, start with a layer of newspaper, then put the leaves on top to make the garden look more attractive. ... Vegetable crops such as kohlrabi and leeks will benefit from side-dressings of fertilizer now. ... For fall crops of broccoli, cabbage, and cauliflower, or for extended crops of tomatoes, sow seeds inside or in a seedbed outside before mid-June. ... Your first crop of string beans should be on the dinner table within a month. Sow more rows at biweekly intervals between now and late July for late-summer harvest.

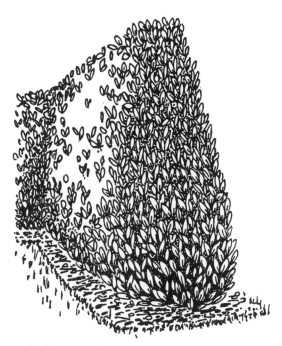

When you prune a hedge, remember to keep it narrower on top than at the base so the lower foliage will get light.

Sow fresh batches of cucumber seeds to replace plants hit by wilt diseases. Watch for gray larvae of the Colorado potato beetle on potatoes and eggplants and remove them by hand. ... Herbs lose some of their flavor once they begin to flower, so if you're planning to dry them for kitchen use, do it sooner rather than later. ... If you don't have the tomato stakes in place, get them in quickly and start training your plants. Tie the central leaders to the stakes with a strip of soft material, such as old bedsheets or pantyhose. ... Complete asparagus and rhubarb harvests soon and side-dress both crops with fertilizer to encourage growth throughout the summer.

For the flowers, shrubs, and trees: There's still time to plant seeds of quick-growing annuals to fill in the gaps that inevitably arise in the flower garden. Plant zinnias and marigolds in a small seed bed. With the warmer temperatures, the seed will germinate in just a few days. Thin the rows gradually until plants are large enough to move into the garden. ... Another excellent choice, particularly for the back of the bed, is cleome, also called spider flower, which produces airy, pink and white blooms. At maturity, the plants will be three to four feet tall and two to three feet across, so leave plenty of room for them to spread. As with many annuals, they'll do best in

63

full sun. ... Houseplants with fuzzy leaves, such as African violets, will do better inside throughout the summer. Cacti and succulents will benefit from the higher light outside, but be careful to let them adapt gradually from the lower light on your windowsills.

Some tips for late June ...

₰ Keep the amaryllis growing by providing the foliage with good light and adequate water. Fertilize the plants on the same schedule as you would houseplants. If it's convenient, put them outside for the summer in a semi-shady spot; if you can place them in a sunny window, they'll do fine inside the house. Come fall, force them into dormancy by withholding water.

₰ Those annuals and vegetables in pots on your deck or terrace will need more and more water as their roots fill their containers. If the morning is overcast, but the forecasters expect it to clear up later, don't take a chance. Water before you leave for work. There's nothing sadder than wilted plants when you get home. In some cases, they'll revive, but that period of wilt will leave its mark and the plants will be less resistant to pests and diseases. Containerized plants also need more fertilizer.

₰ Slugs hide in dark, damp places during the day and feed at night, so capture them under flower pots and destroy them each morning. If you use commercial slug bait, keep it away from children and pets.

₰ Orange spots on the undersides of ash tree leaves indicate ash rust, a disfiguring but rarely destructive disease.

₰ Consider the end of June your last chance to do all those things you have been planning to do since May. Fertilize the azaleas and rhododendrons and prune the hedges.

₰ Promptly remove deadheads from annuals, and stake vegetables such as tomatoes, peppers, and eggplants now—before they snap in a storm or the heavy fruit weighs down the branches.

₰ Midsummer is a good time to sow perennials from seed. Young plants will be sturdy by fall and can be overwintered in a protected spot such as a coldframe.

₰ **In the vegetable garden:** It's tough to grow lettuce in the heat of midsummer, but it can be done if you can provide a partly shaded location, such as under old window screens propped up on bricks or concrete blocks. If your house is cool, start the seeds indoors, where they will germinate better.

🦃 **For the flowers, shrubs, and trees:** Reproduce your favorite African violets by making leaf cuttings. Remove a leaf with a one-inch-long petiole from the "mother" plant and stick it into damp vermiculite, sand, or perlite. Keep in shade until roots are one inch long. ... When your lilies fade, remove the blooms unless you want them to set seed, then keep the plants in good shape throughout the balance of the summer by watering when it's very dry and keeping them surrounded by a good layer of mulch. The better you treat the plants in the coming months, the more nutrients they will store in the bulbs to produce even better flowers in subsequent years. ... Pamper those potted geraniums, petunias, and impatiens throughout the summer, removing deadheads where necessary. Water copiously and fertilize regularly. ... If your geranium flowers are being consumed before you can enjoy them, they're probably victims of larvae of the geranium plume moth, which are small, yellow-green or reddish caterpillars. Handpick regularly, and spray with *Bacillus thuringiensis* ... Continue to feed and disbud chrysanthemums. ... Try to finish pruning the evergreens in the next couple of weeks. If you prune after mid-July, you risk having the new growth nipped by an early frost. Unless it's a formal hedge, leave the shears in the house and work instead with hand pruners, removing branches here and there rather than clipping the poor plant into the shape of a ball or box.

To reproduce your favorite African violet, make a leaf cutting and root it in damp perlite or vermiculite.

65

JUNE: ENJOY SOME DIVIDENDS

A monthly overview

June is the month to enjoy perennials, late-flowering trees such as the Chinese dogwood, peas and strawberries, and the asparagus, lettuce, and rhubarb that have been so welcome throughout May.

Pruning and feeding shrubs after mid-July encourages lush growth that can be easily damaged the following winter. June is therefore the month to complete your tasks on the shrubs. Hedges of Japanese holly, yew, or privet can be pruned now after the first flush of spring growth. Old lilacs should be pruned to encourage bloom next year. Remove all dead and diseased wood and if plants are crowded in the center, cut old branches to the soil line to let air and light into the plant.

By the end of the month, the strawberries will require attention as they finish fruiting. Some gardeners are brave enough to run a rotary mower through their strawberry patch. I prefer to go through with clippers removing all old, diseased leaves and excessive runners. After weeding, fertilize the plants and mulch with straw or chopped leaves. Weeds such as chickweed and oxalis can ruin a strawberry patch. Mulching will help control them, but you will also need to weed periodically throughout the summer to keep them in check.

By mid-June, stop cutting asparagus and rhubarb to allow the plants ample time to revive for next year's harvest. Fertilize both, then repeat in mid-July and again in mid-August, scratching the fertilizer into the soil with a trowel. As with strawberries, keep after the weeds.

A productive garden rarely has empty spaces, so after pulling up spent pea vines, plant additional rows of green beans. Late in the month, prepare a couple of rows to plant carrots for harvesting in the fall. Spring carrot plantings are frequently ruined by the carrot fly whose larvae destroy the roots, but by planting after June 15, you generally avoid this pest and by mulching generously after frost, you'll be able to harvest fresh carrots throughout the winter.

Gardens and passions

A special word about broccoli.

Once in a while, The Gardening Partner gets passionate about a vegetable and before I know what's happening, he's advocating that we grow almost nothing but this one crop. Then you hear him singing its praises in the bank, in the post office, on the phone to his friends, and even to his mother-in-law.

This happened one year with broccoli. We had grown broccoli before many times, although he apparently had not noticed. But that year, he could hardly leave it alone. Each morning, he would dash into the garden to see if there would be another head of broccoli for supper, and he continually chastised me for not growing enough. Needless to say, I got my sowing orders for the next year—to have enough of the stalky green vegetable to satisfy the world's biggest broccoli fanatic.

Broccoli is just one of several vegetables that will give you a wonderfully productive fall garden, and this is the time to plan how it's all going to come together. Right now, the garden probably looks as if you cannot cram another thing into it, but within a few weeks you will find spaces opening up that you can get into production for late summer. For instance, what were you planning to sow after the peas? Or the first string beans that will be finished by early July?

Let's start with members of the cabbage family because seeds for these plants must be sown first. Start seeds of Brussels sprouts in late May or early June, then plant the cauliflower, cabbage, and broccoli no later than June 20. You can sow them in a corner of the garden, in a coldframe, in flats on the deck, or in the basement. The same principles apply as when you are sowing seeds in the spring—keep the soil moist but not soggy and keep the containers out of the sun until the seeds germinate. If you sow them in the garden, cover seeds to keep the soil moist.

Once the seedlings have their first true leaves, which are easily distinguished from their seed leaves, transplant them into more spacious quarters. If you put them in individual containers (plastic, clay, or peat pots or recycled paper cups with holes punched in the bottom), they will be easy to transplant later. About four weeks after sowing, the seedlings should be ready to plant in the garden. If you still don't have free space, move them into larger pots to hold them over.

Chinese cabbage is another member of the cabbage family that does especially well in fall. Seeds can be sown directly into the garden in early August for harvests starting in October.

Propagate by cuttings

June is the month to make softwood cuttings of deciduous shrubs, such as forsythia, weigela, viburnum, lilac, and spirea. The exact moment will depend on the variety of plant, but the cuttings will root best when the wood snaps as you bend it. Take the cuttings in early morning, when the stems are not weakened by a day in the hot sun, and place them immediately into a bucket of water or a plastic bag with a damp paper towel. The sooner you can place them in the rooting medium, the better.

The scale of the plant will dictate the size of the cutting, but for most of the larger shrubs, four to six inches is appropriate. Strip the lower leaves and dip the end of the cutting into a rooting hormone. Your rooting medium must be well-drained and you can choose between vermiculite and peat moss, or perlite and peat moss, in equal quantities. Wooden or plastic flats, or recycled pots will work well as containers, provided you allow about two inches of rooting medium and drainage holes.

Humidity is essential to prevent the cutting from wilting during the rooting process, and although some days in June may seem sufficiently humid for most purposes, it's not consistently humid enough for rooting cuttings. Create a mini-tropical environment by covering containers with polyethylene plastic and setting them out of the sun. To prevent the moisture on the plastic from sitting on the cuttings, support the plastic above them. Coat hangers often work well if you are using large flats, or prop the plastic up on bamboo stakes.

Think ahead on roses

June is not only the month to give your rose bushes a little care and attention, but it's also the time to plan a fall crop of blooms. The flowers of June—visible in planter boxes, tire urns, and neatly edged beds everywhere—will, sadly, fade soon. If you get busy now, you could coax a few more blooms from your roses throughout the summer and certainly see a crop of September flowers.

The key to summer rose care is deadheading. Under normal circumstances, plants produce flowers, set seeds, and then either die if they are annuals or prepare for dormancy, as is the case with roses and other perennial plants. By removing each rose as it starts to fade, you delay the onset of dormancy and encourage additional blooms to form.

Remove spent blooms or flowers for the house by making a clean, slanted cut a quarter inch above a mature leaf with five leaflets. Immature leaves are immediately below the bloom and have only three leaflets. Cutting the rose stem just above immature leaves encourages development of weak shoots and poor blooms. Make your cut with a sharp pair of pruners above a bud that points to the exterior of the plant to encourage shoots to grow outward. If you cut above buds facing inward, you will end up with a jumble of crisscrossing canes that hinder good air circulation.

Continued removal of dead flowers and foliage throughout the summer will not only encourage additional blooms but will also help combat powdery mildew and black spot, two fungus diseases present on most rose bushes.

One more tree

Oaks, ashes, and sycamores are the giants of our landscape, providing shade for houses, parks, and streets. The dogwoods, crabapples, cherries, and other smaller trees provide an essential midsize dimension to the garden. If your garden needs another small to medium-sized tree, summer is a good time to decide what would be appropriate to plant in the fall. Look around your neighborhood and visit gardens and arboretums before making your selection.

In addition to the trees I mentioned in the April chapter, here are a few others to consider:

Carolina silver-bell (*Halesia fetraptena*). In mid-May, the silver-bell produces a mass of graceful white flowers that hang down under the leaves. The branching habit is also graceful, and the only thing the tree lacks is good fall foliage color.

Fringe tree (*Chionanthus virginicus*). Late May is the flowering time for the fringe tree, and around Memorial Day it is clothed with long, white fringes. The leaves are late to appear, so be patient with it in spring and don't panic and assume it is dead. Plant the fringe tree in a place with plenty of good soil.

Korean stewartia (*Stewartia pteropetiolata* var. *koreana*). A member of the tea family, this wonderful medium-sized tree blooms at the end of June. The flowers are white, similar to those on a camellia, with yellow stamens in the center. The tree is upright and narrow, and it is perfect for the corner of a house, or for a small garden. In fall, the foliage is striking, and in winter you will enjoy the mottled bark. Plant this tree in a location with good soil. It's not a tree for a dry, tough area.

Paperbark maple (*Acer griseum*). Most of the maples we enjoy so much, the red and the sugar, are large-scale trees. The paperbark maple is a smaller model, which has an upright shape not unlike that of the stewartia. Its main attraction is the marvelous satiny, orange-brown bark that gleams throughout the winter, but its narrow shape and fine foliage should suggest it as an excellent small tree. It's hard to propagate, and therefore you may find it expensive to buy.

Growing vines

Walls and fences can be beautiful by themselves, but they frequently look even better if they're partly covered with vines. Vines can also be useful in camouflaging an unsightly area. If you're making a new garden this spring and need fast cover, consider planting an annual vine that could still give you lush growth this summer and fall. You could plant a more permanent vine nearby for future cover. For the gardener who has run out of space on the ground, vines offer an excellent way to increase the diversity in the garden.

Climbing hydrangea (*Hydrangea petiolaris*). This is a hardy, perennial vine that produces white flowers in mid-June and will do a good job covering a shady wall. Don't get discouraged if the plant seems to make little progress in the first couple of years because it will make up for it with heavy growth later.

Hyacinth bean (*Dolichos lablab*). This annual, which grows very rapidly in the summer, is a member of the legume family. The flowers are white and purple, but the plant really looks its best when it produces large, purple pods in late summer. There's also a variety with white flowers and green leaves, but I find this rather dull compared to the attractive, many-shades-of-purple display. Again, plant seeds in full sun.

Morning glory (*Ipomoea*). Morning glory is the most rambunctious grower in many parts of the country, if you plant it in full sun. Sky blue is the color we usually associate with morning glories, but you'll also find seeds of white varieties, such as Pearly Gates, and red, such as Scarlett O'Hara.

Porcelain vine (*Ampelopsis brevipedunculata*). This is a tough, perennial vine that produces fall berries that turn from yellow to lavender, and finally to bright blue.

For a sunny wall looking for a hardy vine, there's nothing more satisfying than a clematis. When you poke around in the garden center, you'll find a bewildering selection, but here are suggestions for three types that I have grown with success.

First to flower is the montana group, the most common of which is *Clematis montana* var. *rubens* with numerous small, pink flowers that start in May. This variety will grow rapidly.

In the second group are many hybrids with large flowers in colors ranging from white to pink and deep purple, such as the easy-to-grow jackmani, which produces deep purple flowers in May. These plants grow more discreetly.

The sweet autumn clematis (*C. paniculata*), the third type, is a rapid, rambunctious grower with small, fragrant flowers that cover the vine in late August and September.

All clematis grow best in full sun with their roots shaded. To climb, all require a trellis or some other form of support to which their tendrils can cling. Many gardeners, especially in Britain, plant clematis at the base of a tree or shrub and let it clamber all over.

Pruning clematis is a topic that requires discussion. When you plant a vine, immediately cut it back to two or three pairs of buds. If you have a weak plant, prune back to a single pair. To prune any kind of clematis, you must loosen the clinging leaf tendrils. After pruning, use strips of soft cloth to retie the remaining tendrils to the supports.

The time of bloom will determine how and when a specific species or cultivar should be pruned. After the first year, prune hard all late-flowering varieties in late winter and early spring. When the growing season starts, they will put out new growth on which the following summer's flowers will develop. Unless the plants get out of control, do not prune early-blooming clematis.

Ground coverings

Ground covers can be a real boon to the gardener, filling in awkward spots or creating large, attractive landscape areas that will be relatively easy to maintain after the first few years following planting.

Many of the most successful perennial ground covers are readily propagated by division, from cuttings, or by layering, and will spread quickly. Search among your friends for desirable varieties and persuade them to give you a few divisions now so you can plant them in a nursery bed at home to develop sizable plants for planting in fall or next spring. Alternatively, you may wish to buy a few starter plants from a local nursery, establish them in your own nursery, and let them grow until they are large enough for division. Low-growing shrubs also make good ground cover.

Soil preparation for this ground-cover bed can be done in the summer when you can pick away at it, a little at a time, in preparation for fall planting. Plan to incorporate a two-inch layer of organic material, such as peat moss, compost, or rotted leaves, into the growing area.

Your selection of ground covers should be guided by the situation of the planting bed. Is it on the south side of the house in full sun where soil will dry out rapidly, or under a canopy of high trees with good, moist soil? First, a few shrubs for sunny areas:

Barberry. These may not be the most delicate of plants, but they certainly are practical, especially in gardens where deer—and other animals—present a never-ending challenge. In the back of my house

I have a deck, then the ground slopes sharply to the lawn below. Railroad tie steps get us from one level to the other. The plantings on either side have always been a problem because the site is in full, baking sun and the dogs rush down the slope in pursuit of, no, not deer, but squirrels, sometimes smashing plants as they go. The low-growing Crimson Pygmy barberry (*Berberris thunbergii* var. *atropurpurea* Crimson Pygmy) has been a real trooper on this site. One plant grows slightly in the shade of a hemlock, and the difference in foliage color is evident. So plant Crimson Pygmy in full sun. To keep the plants small, I prune them back to about six inches every year in late winter and some years I take them all the way down to small stubs.

Cotoneaster. This is a semi-evergreen shrub. Its different varieties lose their leaves at different times throughout the winter. Be prepared for the invasive habit of most cotoneasters because they spread very rapidly and require a great deal of pruning unless you allow ample space or select a slow-growing variety. They are also hard to kill. On one bank, we planted a juniper-cotoneaster combination and later I wanted to remove some of the cotoneaster to make way for the expanding junipers. Because I was not strong enough to remove the cotoneaster roots, I figured I would get rid of them by pruning the plants back to the ground. Wrong. They sprouted up again. Actually, in their reduced size, the plants were once again in keeping with the rest of the planting, so I left them alone and kept pruning hard in future years. Before you make your cotoneaster selection, specify to the nursery the ultimate desirable height and spread for the planting. *Cotoneaster dammeri* is one of the neatest, growing into a small mound with lots of red berries in fall.

Deutzia. The standard form of deutzia has made a good low hedge in my garden, growing to about four feet over a couple of decades with minimal pruning. In April, it produces masses of small white flowers. *Deutzia gracilis* Nikko grows into a smaller, mounded shape and does well as a ground cover.

Forsythia. Most forsythias are too large to be considered as ground covers, but the low-growing *Forsythia viridis* Bronxensis will work well.

Junipers. These are usually dependable plants for sunny slopes, most of them growing quickly despite tough, dry conditions. One of the lowest varieties is *Juniperus horizontalis* Wiltonii, and within the Sargent juniper group you will find gold, green, and blue forms in a range of heights.

Spirea. *Spirea japonica alpina* is an excellent choice for very dry, sunny areas. I planted three under a roof overhang facing east in front of a large window. The shrub is deciduous and has clusters of pink flowers in early June. Each year, as soon as they have finished blooming, I trim the plants back to remove the dead flower heads and to encourage new growth. It is too time-consuming to trim each shoot with a pair of pruners, so I use hedge shears, clipping unevenly to avoid a boxy shape. Some years, I trim the plants to four to six inches above the soil line in early spring.

Several perennials, including daylilies, sedums, and snow-in-summer, will serve as good ground covers in full sun. Select lower varieties of daylilies if you are planting a bank.

Sedum. *Sedum acre* is a low-spreading sedum, about two inches high with yellow flowers. *S. kamtschaticum*, or gold moss, will bloom in late June and grow to about six inches, with deeper yellow blossoms. Of the taller sedums, *Hylotelephium telephium* and *H. spectabile* will bloom in late summer.

Snow-in-summer (*Cerastium tomentosum*). This has become a favorite with city gardeners, growing abundantly and providing endless divisions, with white flowers in May.

When you move into the shade, your choice of ground covers expands dramatically to include all sorts of delightful woodland plants.

Crested iris (*Iris cristata*). This plant will produce sapphire-blue blooms for a short period in May, and if we get enough rain the foliage will look good until early September. *I. cristata* var. *alba* has white flowers.

Epimedium. Happy to grow in sun or shade, epimedium, or bishop's hat, faithfully produces wiry stems and heart-shaped leaves each spring. It, too, will bloom in May with pink, white, or yellow flowers, depending on the variety.

European ginger (*Asarum europaeum*). This is one of the true winners in my garden because it looks good all summer long. Its leaves are rounded and shiny, and the deer never seem interested in it.

Ferns. Here's an excellent group of plants for shady sites. Choose a low-growing species such as the Japanese silver painted fern (*Athyrium nipponicum* Pictum).

Foamflower (*Tiarella cordifolia*). This is the star in my collection in May, blooming profusely around low-growing rhododendrons. Foamflower is native to the northeastern United States, growing in woodlands.

Hostas. These are my favorite plants for ground cover in the shade, and every season there's something new available in this genus. The lighter the shade, the better results you will get with the variegated varieties such as Gold Standard.

Lilyturf. This has narrow, thin leaves and spiky flowers in late summer. *Lirope muscari* has blue flowers; *L. muscari* Monroe's White has a good combination of white, spiky flowers with deep green foliage. There are also varieties with variegated foliage. All benefit from being divided from time to time.

Sweet woodruff (*Galium odoratum*). This delicate plant competes reasonably well with the shallow, rocky soil in a bed under an ash tree in my garden. Originally, I managed to make a few large holes to accommodate the plants. Now it has spread three to four square feet, producing white blossoms in early June. When sweet woodruff starts to emerge each spring, gently remove last year's leaves.

Variegated bishop's weed (*Aegopodium podagraria* Variegatum). Here's a plant that some garden centers will recommend as a ground cover. Having watched friends try to remove this from their gardens, I suggest you resist the temptation to get it started.

Yellow archangel (*Lamium galeobdolon* Variegatum). This is the plant to use when you're desperate and have found that nothing else will grow in a particular spot. In my garden, it grows under a small tree with a mass of surface roots, solving a difficult landscaping problem. Spotted dead nettle (*Lamium maculatum*), similar to yellow archangel, is much more reserved in its growth habits. There are many attractive cultivars with variegated leaves. Beacon Silver and White Nancy are two suggestions.

Two views of composting

There's just nothing like having a good argument with your gardening partner. Of our many points of difference, I think our compost discussions are the best. They go on all summer as we each lay claim to the products of our joint labor.

If The Gardening Partner had his way, all the compost would end up on the beloved vegetables. I, on the other hand, contend that the vegetables can get along with a combination of chopped leaves and fertilizer but that the houseplants and the perennial garden deserve nothing but the best. Others with established compost piles probably behave as we do and argue just as hotly about the disposition of the glorious pile.

If you are not composting, start this summer. Not only will you have developed another item for polite discussion with your gardening partner, but you will also have a ready supply of organic material, which is hard to come by without paying an arm and a leg.

The authorities have written copious texts on the art of composting. But before I get halfway through any of them, I already know that my own pile will never be as perfect as the author's. The instructions are so complicated, recommending a little of this and a layer of that, a dose of this activator, a dab of that fertilizer. It seems that anyone who follows the instructions to the letter would probably never have time for other gardening activities.

Many years ago, we built an elaborate structure to contain our first compost pile. In all innocence, we used a material recommended by one of the "perfect-pile" people—concrete blocks. It was fun to build but unnecessarily expensive. The next year, we realized that the pile inside the concrete blocks would never rot down before we were ready to start adding to it again. Obviously, we had to have another pile. This time we made the enclosure with four-foot-high turkey wire supported by four five-foot metal poles. It worked so well that we built another enclosure the following summer.

For our garden, three seems to be the ideal number of compost piles, allowing one section for a pile of partially rotted compost (that will be fought over later in the summer), a half-full pile, and one empty spot from which we withdraw soil for a multitude of jobs. Having three piles means we do not have to turn them in the recommended fashion because they have plenty of time to rot. I do periodically add limestone but never any compost activator. If you have a shredder or suitable lawnmower, it helps to shred the debris before you put it on the pile. Smaller pieces naturally decompose faster.

If you put all your garden debris on the pile, you must be prepared for plenty of weeds in the finished compost. It seems unavoidable because, unless you maintain a "perfect" pile, it is unlikely to develop sufficient heat to kill the weed seeds. I consider the rotted product too valuable for me to worry about the weeds. If plants are diseased, I dispose of them rather than spread the infection by putting them in the compost pile.

Kitchen waste is a good source of compost material as long as you stick with vegetable waste and do not add fats or meats. I add all citrus and vegetable peelings and wilted salads but never eggshells, salads with dressings, or any of the other items mentioned above for fear of attracting rodents to the area.

When I start a new pile, I place a 12-inch-thick layer of wood-chips at the base to help improve the air circulation, then add an eight-to-10-inch layer of garden waste and cover this with soil from another pile. I continue to construct the pile in this fashion, keeping the sides high with a dip in the middle to catch the rain and maintain, where possible, a damp pile to speed decomposition.

If you do not have ready access to extra soil to layer between garden debris, buy a load of topsoil to get started. Plants contain only a small percentage of the microorganisms necessary for decomposition. Garden soil, on the other hand, is loaded with them, so your pile will decompose more readily if you add a two-inch layer of soil for every eight to 10 inches of garden debris. In the fall, add leaves to the pile in moderation. When you reach the top of the wire enclosure, cover the pile with soil, still maintaining an indentation to catch the rain, and let the debris decompose during the coming year. A pile completed one fall will probably be ready for use at the end of the following summer.

Some gardeners eschew the pile method and do their composting on site, adding debris directly to the garden bit by bit.

Pruning

Like composting, pruning is another vital gardening fundamental. Those overgrown yews, rhododendrons, azaleas, and junipers can loom large, obscuring windows, blocking walkways, and gradually taking over your garden. In some cases, there is little recourse but to yank out the old-timers and replant. Such a drastic measure is expensive, and it will be many years before you recapture the mature look in that area of the garden. So instead, consider heavy-duty pruning. With a sharp pair of pruners, a pair of loppers, and a pruning saw, you can tame these monsters.

Correct timing is essential to give the plants ample opportunity to put out new growth and to mature before heavy frosts arrive. If the shrub produces flowers, then you also want to make sure you are not destroying next year's show of blooms. Prune flowering shrubs—azaleas, rhododendrons, mountain laurel, and andromeda, for example—within a month of the completion of the current year's blooms, before the flower buds set for the next year. If you can get to the task within a couple of weeks after the blooms fade, it will be even better.

With evergreens—yews, junipers, Japanese holly—prune at almost any time other than late July, August, and September. Pruning in these months will stimulate new growth that will not have enough time to harden off before frost. If it's a holly tree you must tackle, wait until December; then you can prune the branches with berries and enjoy them for the holidays.

How do you deal with a plant that is blocking your walk or window? Let's suppose you have an old, six-foot-tall azalea blocking your dining-room window. Because it's almost as wide as it is tall, it's also covering half the front walkway. Before you start cutting, stand back and study the shrub's current shape and figure out how you want it to look when you are finished with it. The plant most likely has an exterior framework of green foliage. Toward the interior, the limbs probably are bare because insufficient light reaches in to encourage new growth. With many plants, you can only prune back to a point on the stem where you see green foliage or buds. Azaleas, however, are equipped with adventitious buds on what appear to be bare stems. Once you prune, you stimulate these buds to produce foliage, allowing you to prune heavily, knowing that within a few weeks of cutting there will be new signs of life.

So here you are, equipped with the pruning tools, and here is the azalea, equipped with its buds. Cut away until you have the shrub reduced to the desired shape and size. Let the plant grow for a couple of years, then start pruning to develop the new character. Spreading yews and Japanese hollies can also take hard pruning. Rhododendrons, mountain laurel, and other evergreen flowering shrubs should be treated with a little more caution, maybe removing one-third of the wood every other year over several years.

Shrubs or trees with strong central leaders, such as hemlock, will never look the same if you remove the top. But quick-growing shrubs with multiple stems, such as forsythia, weigela, and cotoneaster, will usually rebound even if you cut them to the soil line.

After heavy pruning, feed the victims with a slow-release fertilizer. Spread a couple of handfuls of fertilizer below each shrub, then mulch heavily, using woodchips or leaf mold. If the summer turns dry, water those plants you have pruned heavily once a week, using at least a couple of gallons for medium-sized shrubs. A hard winter may produce some dieback on the new growth. Prune it back to good wood early next spring.

Be sure you make clean cuts, rather than leaving jagged edges that will take longer to heal. Keep your tools sharp and well-oiled. Wipe them off before you put them away. When pruning plants that exude resin, such as pines, remove the residue from the blades with turpentine before you oil the tools.

On watering

With the hot weather about to settle in, it's a good time to talk about watering. The frequency with which I've had to face summer drought restrictions has helped me realize that the clear liquid that flows so easily from our taps is a precious gift and that it's our responsibility to use it wisely. To ensure that every drop that leaves the tap makes it to the plants, replace broken washers and leaky faucets.

When watering a small number of plants, let the water dribble from a hose into the rootball of one plant for, say, half an hour. Then move it to another plant. For vegetable gardens, where the rows are straight, and for some areas with shrubs or perennials I have greatly benefited from using black porous or "leaky" hoses that deliver water slowly to the root zone.

Water at a sensible time of day. Early morning is best. Although it may be just as cool in the evening, overhead watering will encourage diseases to spread by leaving foliage wet overnight.

When you water, do it thoroughly, soaking the plants so the water goes deep into the soil. If you water superficially, you encourage plants to send out surface roots, making it even harder for them to tolerate a drought. Water the plants, not the landscape. Overhead watering may seem easy because all you do is haul the sprinkler into place and turn on the hose, but you waste an unconscionable amount of water through evaporation and runoff—or simply by watering a sidewalk that is in the sprinkler's path.

JULY

An In-Between Month

As you cruise around your garden on a July morning, look at it with an eye to next year. Look at the blooming combinations, recording them before you forget them. Mark down the gaps you might want to fill in. And note the perennials to be divided to encourage additional bloom in the future.

Some tips for early July ...

ᘒ Just a few basil plants will provide you with enough of this wonderful herb to make pesto for the whole block, plus some leftovers to freeze for an easy winter meal. It's not too late to pick up a few plants and plant them in a sunny place. Even if you don't get around to using many leaves, keep pinching the plants so they don't produce flowers and set seed.

ᘒ Dill should be in flower by now. If you don't plan to use the seed heads for dilly beans, leave them on the plants and let the seed scatter around your garden. You'll get another crop this fall and most likely additional crops in subsequent years. Having purchased one packet of dill seeds, there's no reason why you should ever have to buy another.

ᘒ If you let a potted plant or hanging basket dry out to the point of wilting, remove it to the shade and soak the whole plant—pot and all—in a bucket of water until bubbles stop coming to the surface of the water.

꿎 Remove suckers from the base of trees with a pair of sharp pruners. Complete pruning of evergreen shrubs shortly, then hold off additional pruning until mid-October.

꿎 Make sure you're watering effectively. For such plants as peppers and tomatoes, remove the bottoms of several large tin cans, and sink them halfway into the soil in a ring around the root system. When you water, the moisture will penetrate into the root zone, instead of running off between rows.

꿎 When you go on vacation, move all houseplants to the north side of the house or garage. Or sink the pots into the ground under a tree. Water all thoroughly before leaving. Also, cut back the annuals, give them a dose of fertilizer, and water them heavily to stimulate new growth and bloom for your return.

꿎 **In the vegetable garden:** July and early August are the months for onion harvesting. When the onion tops turn brown and start to wither, dig them on a sunny day and lay them in a dry, airy place for a couple of weeks to allow thorough drying before storage. … The seeds you sowed in mid-June for cabbage, broccoli, and cauliflower will be ready for transplanting into the garden by mid-July. If you can, wait for a cloudy spell. If not, transplant in the evening, then shade each plant with a large flower pot for a couple of days to give them a good chance of success in the summer heat. Water each one with a dilute fertilizer solution after transplanting. … The bugs of July include the squash vine borer, the tomato hornworm, and the Mexican bean beetle. Early detection is your best defense, so check your crops once a day and handpick eggs and larvae as they appear. … Don't wait until your snap beans are the size of those available in the grocery; pick them when they're small and thin. … If squash vine borers don't get the zucchini plants, the harvest no doubt will get ahead of you, but pick them small, too, rather than letting them grow into monsters that are suitable only for zucchini bread. … Blossom-end rot, common on tomatoes, is a physiological problem caused by alternating dry and wet soil. Mulch and regular watering will help control this by ensuring consistently moist soil. … With the strawberry crop over for the season, remove those plants that have produced for three years and trim or mow the rest. If you use a mower, set it at four to five inches. Rake leaves and burn or bag them to avoid the spread of diseases.

꿎 **For the flowers, shrubs, and trees:** The flowers you cut from your own garden are far more precious than any you might purchase from a florist, so treat them with special care. Pick them as early as possible in the morning. If you miss in the morning, wait until the sun is off the garden. Make your cuts with a sharp knife, not with pruning shears, which bruise the stems. As soon as you get them into the house, recut the stems on a slant, remove all leaves that will be below the water line, and put the flowers into a deep bucket or vase filled with warm water. Leave them there for several hours or overnight to soak up water, then create your arrangements. ... As perennials fade, remove deadheads and diseased foliage and cover bare spots in the garden by planting potted annuals that will gradually fill the empty spaces. ... Consistent deadheading of annuals and perennials will lengthen bloom and save plants the energy necessary to produce seeds. In some cases, you can shear whole plants back in midsummer to encourage new growth for the cooler days of late summer. ... Summer care for newly planted trees and shrubs should include deep waterings between periods of good rain. Let the hose drip slowly into the rootball for several hours, rather than spraying the plants more frequently.

Some tips for late July ...

❧ Bulb catalogs are starting to arrive in the mail. Order your fall selections now.

❧ Houseplants summering outdoors are vulnerable to red spider mites, so continue to check them regularly as you water for yellowing leaves and stunted growth. As a precaution, dunk them from time to time in a pail of rinse water saved from the bathroom or kitchen sink or hose with a strong spray of water.

❧ The Mexican bean beetle is out in full force. This pest can be controlled with handpicking but you must search for it every day, destroying adults, eggs, and larvae, many of which will be found on the undersides of the leaves. Pinch late-flowering mums one last time before allowing them to go ahead and bloom.

❧ **In the vegetable garden:** If you plant them before the end of the month, you should be able to get one last crop of snap beans to mature before frost. As the days get shorter, you'll find that the beans take longer to produce pods. ... If you have spaces left from spring crops, get the ground ready in preparation for planting leafy vegetables in August. ... Sow seeds of Chinese cabbage directly into the garden; look for seedlings of cauliflower and cabbage in local nurseries. Cover all cole crops with horticultural fabric to deter cabbage moths. ... Check tomato plants in the evening for the tomato horn-worm caterpillar, a large, bright green larva that can defoliate a large plant in a couple of days. Destroy unless it has the white eggs of the parasitic wasp stuck to its back. If eggs are present, leave it because the wasp larvae will eventually kill this hornworm and in the future, as an adult, the wasp will produce more eggs and eventually kill more destructive larvae. ... When planted in early spring, carrots are often consumed by the carrot rust fly. Instead, by planting every two weeks from mid-July through early August, you should get a good harvest with little damage from this pest. ... If you have a shady area in the vegetable garden, plant lettuce seeds to get an early fall harvest. Sow thinly, water well, and cover soil with newspaper or another material to reduce evaporation. As soon as germination occurs, remove the cover. ... When summer-bearing raspberries are finished, prune out the spent canes to make room for the development of the new canes that will provide your crop for next spring. Old canes are tan-colored; new canes, green.

🐦 **For the flowers, shrubs, and trees:** If your petunias look shaggy, cut the plants back and give them a dose of liquid fertilizer. Water

When the summer-bearing raspberry crop is over, remove spent canes to ground level.

periodically, and you should have a new crop of blossoms within two to three weeks. The drier the soil, the more gradual your watering of all plants should be for maximum effect. ... If you have a greenhouse, this is a good time to empty it and wash windows to ensure maximum light penetration next winter. ... Most daylilies will bloom more freely if you divide the plants once every three to four years, saving the extra divisions for a new planting area or for your friends. After they bloom, water the plants well and cut back the tops to six to eight inches above ground before you lift each plant. Once a plant is out of the ground, remove enough soil so that you can see what's going on, then try to pry roots apart. You may have to resort to cutting the sections apart with a spade. Replant the more vigorous sections and discard the older central pieces. ... Sow seeds of the biennial forget-me-not (*Myosotis sylvatica*) now and you'll have those beautiful, delicate blue flowers all over your garden come spring. Sow inside in a small flat, transplant into pots in early fall, then keep outside in a sheltered spot throughout the winter for planting in the garden early next spring.

JULY: VACATIONS, ODD CHORES, NEXT YEAR

A monthly overview

With vacations just around the corner, it's time to talk about some steps you might take to ensure that you'll be greeted by something other than a mass of weeds and dead plants on your return.

First, let's see what you can do with all those houseplants. If you can, put them outside in reasonably heavy shade and sink the pots into the soil or cover them with a mulch, such as woodchips or leaves. Fertilize each one with a water-soluble fertilizer, then soak the surrounding soil or mulch before you leave.

If you plan to leave the plants in the house and ask a neighbor or friend to water them, make life as simple as possible for the waterer. A color-coded label system has produced good results for me. Those with yellow labels got watered every day, those with blue labels every three days—and so on.

Before you leave, check plants for insects such as aphids, white fly or scale, or red spider mites. If you detect an infestation, isolate the plant. In fact, consider disposing of it.

As long as you won't be home to look at the flower garden and the pots on the terrace, cut back the annuals before you go. My geraniums, for example, get this treatment once a summer and are much better for it when I return. Use a sharp pair of pruners and cut to just above a leaf node (where the leaf joins the stem) to encourage new shoots to develop below the cut.

Cushion-type plants, such as ageratum, will not benefit from such pruning, but petunias, impatiens, and begonias, to name a few, will respond vigorously. As with the houseplants, fertilize all the annuals before you leave.

I use the same fertilizer for my potted plants as on the houseplants. For the garden annuals, I scratch a little fertilizer around each plant and then water thoroughly. Alternatively, soak soil with a water-soluble fertilizer.

In the vegetable garden, my pre-vacation watchword would be to mulch as heavily as you can so your weeding chores are minimized on return. Also, encourage your neighbors to enjoy the crops while you are gone.

Whether it's you or a deputy picker on the job, by mid-July keeping up with the vegetable garden harvest will be essential to maintain production. If *you* cease picking, the *plants* will cease producing. Check summer squash plants daily, and pick fruits when they are six to seven inches long. Eggplants are at their best when their black skins are shiny. Harvest will depend on the individual variety (usually four to six inches long), but if you don't pick them in the shiny stage, you will find the fruits bitter and full of seeds.

Peppers are the least demanding because the fruits remain in good shape for several weeks as they turn from green to red or, in the case of varieties such as Sweet Banana, from yellow to orange and finally red. Leave fruit on the plants until you are ready to use them rather than storing them in the refrigerator, where the taste will deteriorate.

On your return from vacation, check out the vegetable garden for insect damage. If you see that the tomatoes have lost many leaves and upper stems, you can be sure the monstrous tomato hornworm is in town. Search for the beast in early morning or at dusk.

If you have beans—snap or lima—you may already have seen skeletonized leaves, evidence of the Mexican bean beetle. The adults have orange bodies with black spots; the yellow larvae are the ones that do the damage, feeding on the undersides of the leaves. Remove as many as you can by hand and kill them in a jar of soapy water.

And speaking of pests, squash growers never fail to encounter the squash vine borer once each season. The key to control is to monitor your crops closely for wilting of vines and also to inspect plants

Spring

Prunus x Okame, a fast-growing cherry that produces masses of pink blooms in early spring, is a good tree for home gardeners. *(The Pennsylvania Horticultural Society Gold Medal Award Program)*

Daphne caucasica, the Caucasian daphne, is a deciduous shrub, 4 to 5 feet high, whose spring flowers are delightfully fragrant. *(The Pennsylvania Horticultural Society Gold Medal Award Program)*

Crabapples are excellent trees for small gardens, provided disease-resistant cultivars are selected, such as *Malus* Donald Wyman. *(The Pennsylvania Horticultural Society Gold Medal Award Program)*

Bleeding heart *(Dicentra spectabilis)* has lovely rose-red flowers in late spring. Its gray-green foliage may die down in midsummer. *(Derek Fell)*

Unlike herbaceous peonies, tree peonies do not die to the ground each winter. The massive flowers come in vivid and pastel colorings and appear in May. Shown here are *Paeonia suffruticosa* Canary (above) and *Paeonia suffruticosa* Red Moon (below). *(Derek Fell)*

In my parents' garden in Scotland, *Clematis* Nelly Moser was a favorite; it grows just as well in and around Philadelphia, provided its roots are shaded and the vines are grown in full sun. *(Derek Fell)*

The hybrid flowering dogwood *(Cornus* Ruth Ellen) has shown resistance to dogwood anthracnose that has devastated plantings of *Cornus florida* in gardens and woodland areas. *(The Pennsylvania Horticultural Society Gold Medal Award Program)*

This low-growing form of slender deutzia *(Deutzia gracilis* Nikko) flowers profusely in May and would do well as a groundcover on a sunny bank. *(The Pennsylvania Horticultural Society Gold Medal Award Program)*

Fragrant white spring flowers, smooth gray bark, and a nice spreading habit are just a few of the characteristics that make yellowwood *(Cladrastis kentukea)* a good choice for gardeners in search of a medium-sized shade tree. *(The Pennsylvania Horticultural Society Gold Medal Award Program)*

Sweetbay or swamp magnolia will grow in areas with wet soil, producing fragrant white flowers in June and July. *Magnolia virginiana* is a small tree, often with multiple stems. *(Derek Fell)*

Stewartia pseudocamellia has masses of white flowers with yellow centers in late June. *(The Pennsylvania Horticultural Society Gold Medal Award Program)*

Summer

Butterfly bush is true to its name and come midsummer its blooms will be covered with butterflies. Plant *Buddleia davidii* in full sun and prune to the ground in early spring. *(Derek Fell)*

Hostas are among the most adaptable of perennials, with cultivars for shaded and sunny sites. Plants are easy to divide in early spring or fall. *(Derek Fell)*

Hydrangea quercifolia Snow Queen can grow in shade, even in dry soil. Leaves of oakleaf hydrangea turn wine-colored in fall. *(The Pennsylvania Horticultural Society Gold Medal Award Program)*

The flowers of Snow Queen are white and appear in large clusters in late June and July. *(The Pennsylvania Horticultural Society Gold Medal Award Program)*

Daylilies grouped in masses in sunny areas make an excellent groundcover. (*Derek Fell*)

Hundreds of cultivars developed by commercial daylily specialists and hobbyists offer the homeowner an endless variety of sizes, bloom times and flower colors. (*Derek Fell*)

Crape myrtles may die back to the ground over a cold winter, but the masses of long-lasting summer flowers on *Lagerstroemia indica* make up for loss of growth. *(Derek Fell)*

Caryopteris x *clandonensis,* the bluebeard, grows into a low mound and produces masses of blue flowers by late summer if plants are sited in full sun. *(Derek Fell)*

For growing in containers, there's little to beat eggplant Ichiban, an Asian variety with long, slender fruits. *(Derek Fell)*

The hardy begonia *(Begonia grandis)* is a great plant for a shady border. In late summer its red-tinged stems produce masses of pink blossoms that last until frost. *(Derek Fell)*

Tomato hornworms are large, green caterpillars that consume leaves and stems of tomatoes and peppers. The white protuberances on this hornworm are larvae of parasitic wasps, which will eventually kill the hornworm. *(Derek Fell)*

The elegant green and black swallowtail caterpillar larva can destroy parsley, carrot and rue foliage. *(Derek Fell)*

The author outside The Gardening Partner's lima bean garden in midsummer, with Candy. *(Laura Lewis)*

Larvae of Mexican bean beetles feed on undersides of leaves of lima beans and snap beans. *(Derek Fell)*

The bounty of summer from a Pennsylvania garden includes tomatoes, peppers, blueberries, raspberries, and peaches. *(Derek Fell)*

Fall/Winter

Malus Jewelberry is a dense, shrubby crabapple with pink buds that open into white flowers, followed by glossy red fruit in fall. *(The Pennsylvania Horticultural Society Gold Medal Award Program)*

Plant amaryllis bulbs in fall for a colorful array of blooms in early winter. *(Vicki Valerio, The Philadelphia Inquirer)*

Paperbark maple *(Acer griseum)* makes an excellent small shade tree. Its bark is appealing year round, and especially in winter. *(The Pennsylvania Horticultural Society Gold Medal Award Program)*

The bark of stewartia ranks with that of the paperbark maple as one of the best for winter interest in the garden. *(The Pennsylvania Horticultural Society Gold Medal Award Program)*

for telltale signs of the borer: brownish, sawdust-like material on the ground, or eggs on or near a stem. The squash vine borer is a clear-winged orange and black moth that lays eggs on a stem. Once they hatch, the white, brown-headed larvae tunnel into the stems, eventually causing the stems to wilt. Some gardeners suggest wrapping a nylon stocking at the base of each stem to prevent the moths from laying eggs. Others wait for signs of trouble, then slit the stem to reveal the sawdust-like material and remove the borer. As with cucumbers, it's a good idea to make successive plantings so the later ones can take over if you don't get around to killing the borer larvae before they do too much damage. Butternut, which has a solid stem, is not bothered by squash vine borers.

Ambivalence

My feelings about the garden are divided in July. In some ways, I love it for the first beans, for the early tomatoes and eggplant, but sometimes I wish it wouldn't cry out for help on the hottest days of the year. There's a bonus in those hot days, however. They force the gardener out of bed early on the weekend to beat the heat, and I, for one, relish the quiet early mornings with just the dogs and birds as my companions.

As you cruise around your garden early on a July morning, look at it with an eye to next year. Look at the blooming combinations, recording them before you forget them as the season progresses. Mark down the gaps you might want to fill in this fall or early next spring, during the prime planting months. And note the perennials that should be divided this fall to encourage additional bloom in future years.

In the vegetable garden, keep a record of how things worked out this spring. Did you have an abundance of lettuce that started to go to seed at the end of June? As you go through the next few weeks, watch for the favorite vegetables and remind yourself to plant more of them next year.

After completing your note-taking, it's time to answer the pleas of plants that require deadheading, of those that would like a midsummer shot of fertilizer, and of woody plants that should be pruned.

The plants that require your closest attention are those in containers, because frequent waterings allow nutrients to leach out of the pots more rapidly than they would if the plants were set in the ground. Liquid feeding is the easiest for most home gardeners. If you have lots of plants, consider buying a watering wand with an addition to which you can add fertilizer.

For the gardener planning a good crop of fall vegetables, July and August are active months. If you planted leeks, continue to hill the soil up around the plants. This darkness will produce long, white stems, which are much tastier than the green leaves. If you run out of compost or soil, I've found that rotting leaves work well.

Favorite trees

In spring, we become rather blasé about tree blossoms as cherries, crabs, magnolias, and dogwoods compete to steal the show. In July, blooms are not as common, so I treasure every one that comes out, such as the following:

Golden rain tree (*Koelreuteria paniculata*). This medium-sized tree has yellow flowers that grow in upright clusters and later develop into brown pods. My only caution is that the wood is weak, so this is not a tree that will last as long as others. Grow it primarily for its summer display.

Japanese pagoda tree (*Sophora japonica*). If you are looking for a slightly larger tree, this one may fit your bill. At maturity, it will grow to about 60 feet tall, and in August it's covered with creamy white flowers. The leaves are delicate so the shade it casts isn't too heavy, and one of the great virtues of this tree is its ability to withstand city conditions.

Sweet bay magnolia (*Magnolia virginiana*). This could be called the perfect tree. In summer, it produces fragrant, white blooms with shiny leaves. It will grow well in damp soils and its small stature makes it a great addition to smaller spaces, such as beside an entrance door, in a courtyard, or as part of a shrub and perennial planting. In addition, unless pruned otherwise, it has multiple stems, which gives it an excellent shape.

Yellowwood (*Cladrastis lutea*). Native to the east coast of North America, this tree has attractive gray bark, which resembles a beech tree. The long, white, pendulous flowers appear in late May or early June. Trees may get to be 40 feet tall with almost as wide a spread. Yellowwoods can be planted in either spring or fall. Take a stroll in a local arboretum some time this month to check out their blooms and shapes and sizes so you can determine which would be suitable for planting in your garden.

Shrubs for summer bloom

Hydrangeas, fashionable in Victorian days, have recently reappeared on the list of "in" plants, and for good reason—they do their thing in summer. Their flowers, if taken individually, are small, but because they grow in clusters, they can make quite a show. Many flowers are white; some blue or pink. The hydrangea you buy at the florist for Easter or Mother's Day is most likely not hardy in this area, so stick with cultivars of *Hydrangea macrophylla, H. paniculata,* and *H. quercifolia.*

The macrophylla hydrangeas have big, fleshy leaves and require at least partially shaded sites. In hot, dry areas, and even in dry shade, the leaves wilt in midsummer. The soil should be moist, with plenty of organic matter. Some cultivars produce flowers that are stable in their flower colors, but in general, if the soil is acidic (with a pH of less than 7.0), the flowers will be blue; if it's alkaline, the flowers will be pink. (That's why my mother, in Scotland, could never get her hydrangeas to turn blue; the soil pH was just too high, no matter how much sulfur she dumped on it.)

To get the best blooms, prune mature plants after flowering, removing one-third of the stems to the ground. Prune back the remaining stems to one-quarter or one-third, making each cut just above a pair of strong buds. Hydrangeas bloom on mature wood, so if you prune all stems to the ground, it will be two seasons before you get more bloom.

Bigleaf hydrangeas are divided into two groups, lacecaps and hortensias. Following are suggested cultivars, starting with the hortensias: Forever Pink; Heinrich Seidel (purple flowers); Mme. E. Mouillere (white); Nikko Blue; Nigra (grown for its almost black stems); and Pia (pink flowers on a small plant that matures at around two feet tall). Among the lacecaps, you will find cultivars such as Blue Billow and Quadricolor, with white and green variegated leaves. The hydrangea with white flowers in August, often growing 15 to 20 feet high, is the old-fashioned PeeGee hydrangea (*Hydrangea paniculata* Grandiflora).

For dry, shaded areas, the oakleaf hydrangea is a wonderfully tolerant plant. Its ultimate height is about six feet, and its peeling bark is attractive, as are the deep green leaves that turn shades of orange, red, and purple in fall. *Hydrangea quercifolia* Snow Queen, which has larger panicles of white flowers, is an excellent variety.

Finally, there's a vining hydrangea, *Hydrangea petiolaris,* that's a great addition to a shady wall, where it will support itself by clinging to the masonry. Prune it from time to time to make sure it doesn't get out of control.

Beyond the hydrangeas for summer flowers, I have become enamored with butterfly bushes. Not only do they bloom in midsummer, but they do attract lots of butterflies, and so far the deer haven't touched our white-blooming plant over several years.

Butterfly bushes (buddleias) bloom on new wood, so in late winter or early spring, cut the plants back to stubs just above the soil line and stand back while they grow five to eight feet, even in the driest of summers. During bloom time, prune away the old blossoms so the new ones can look their best. Besides the white-flowered varieties, you will also find those with pink flowers; lavender flowers, such as Lochinch, which may grow even taller than eight feet; and Black Knight, with dark purple flowers. If you want to propagate your own buddleias, they root easily from cuttings taken from June through August.

Caryopteris, or bluebeard, is another summer-blooming favorite. It has silvery green leaves and spires of blue flowers that bloom on new growth, so treat the plant as you would buddleia and cut the stems to the ground in late winter. Nurseries offer several cultivars of *Caryopteris* x *clandonensis,* which range from pale blue flowers to those of Longwood Blue, developed at Longwood Gardens in Kennett Square, Pa., which are deep blue. Plant bluebeard in a sunny site with well-drained soil.

Annuals

July is the month to enjoy the blooms on annuals, and it's worth checking around to see if there are some different varieties to try next summer. Consider these possibilities:

Canna. Here's a plant for the heat of summer. Grow them from tubers, which must be stored inside over winter. Place at the back of the border because most varieties will grow five to six feet by summer's close.

Cuphea. You used to find cuphea offered only as a houseplant, but now it's available for summer bedding. The flowers may not be as big and brassy as zinnias or marigolds, but the combination of dark green leaves and fiery red flowers is effective.

Globe amaranth. This is a good flower for drying, and the cultivar Strawberry Fields, whose flowers really are strawberry-colored, is good for the front of the border. Grown in full sun, they can take dry soil.

Ornamental peppers. At any one time, you might find pale yellow, orange, and deep red fruits on varieties such as Fiesta and Treasure Red. As with peppers for the kitchen, grow these in full sun.

Purple heart. Here's another plant you may have grown indoors, perhaps in a hanging basket, but it will work just as well outside in a flower bed. The purple leaves of *Tradescantia palida* will keep their strong color if planted in full sun. It's easy to propagate purple heart from cuttings, so take some at the end of winter and you will have a whole bed of plants by the end of the summer.

Salvia. Many summer plantings include the firehouse red *Salvia splendens*, which is valuable for its ability to withstand poor soil and lack of water, but the color can be hard to combine with more delicate shades. *S. coccinea* Lady in Red has carmine-colored flowers, which go well with pink and blue combinations, as does *S. farinacea* Victoria Blue, which has brilliant blue flowers that last until frost. This plant is of medium height and not as tender as some annuals. Some years I left the summer plants in place and after a mild winter found the roots pushing up stalks the following year. Another bonus of both Lady in Red and the blue salvia is that they will come back in future years by reseeding.

Verbena bonariensis. This plant may be tall, but its wiry stems make it the perfect annual to put near the front of the border because you can see through the stems and small, purple flowers to the plants beyond. Like some of the salvias, it will reseed so come spring take care not to remove the seedlings as you weed.

Vinca. This annual gets the blue ribbon for being the most adaptable. Its shiny leaves and pink, white, or lavender flowers are a real plus in any garden or in containers, including hanging baskets. The plant seems to withstand dry or wet conditions, full sun or part shade. The only caution is to be patient with it in spring because it takes hot weather to get it going.

Again, think spring

If you have space in your garden for some shasta daisies, globe thistles, alyssum, and other varieties of perennials, you could start them now from seed and have a show of blooms next spring. All you need to get into production is some potting soil—or a spare corner of the garden—and the seeds. Garden centers and nurseries may still have perennial seeds in their racks or you will find them in catalogs.

If you plan to do your planting outside, choose a well-drained area where the light is good but where the plants will not be in full sun. Cultivate the soil, incorporating compost and sand or perlite to improve the drainage. Those with raised gardening beds can make these into wonderful seed beds.

Sow the seeds in shallow furrows, six to eight inches apart, then cover them with soil to three times the depth of the seed. Planting too deeply usually results in poor germination, so be sure not to cover the seeds with too much soil. Some seeds require light to germinate; in these cases, just sprinkle them on top of the soil. After sowing, soak the area with a fine spray and cover it with newspaper or burlap to retain moisture.

If you want to sow the seeds in a flat or pot, cover the container with a plastic bag and set it out of the sun in a location that you pass frequently so you can keep checking to see if the seeds have germinated. As soon as you see green leaves starting to appear, remove the plastic bag and set the container in a well-lighted area. With both inside and outside seedlings, you must never allow the soil to dry or the plants to wilt. Water in early morning.

If you have a coldframe, this is an ideal place to start perennials from seed because you can place a light lath or screen over the frame to shade the seedlings.

When the seedlings have at least one pair of leaves in addition to the seedling leaves, transplant them into larger quarters. As with all transplants, try to do it on a cloudy day or in late afternoon and water the plants well several hours before you transplant. Be very cautious in lifting the seeds from the germination medium, holding them by their leaves rather than by the delicate stem.

Set the plants six to eight inches apart, shade them for a couple of days following transplanting, and keep the soil moist, watering with houseplant fertilizer a couple of weeks after you transplant them to their new facility.

It is probably better to delay transplanting the young plants to their final locations until early next spring, allowing them the fall to develop strong root systems.

Some perennials, such as delphinium, columbine, and candytuft, need cool temperatures (60° to 70° F.) to germinate and should be sown earlier in the year. Many others, including the following, should germinate readily in midsummer:

Basket of gold (*Aurinia saxatilis*). With yellow flowers in April, this plant looks great in a rock wall. Do not cover the seed. Like many other plants with gray foliage, basket of gold should be planted in well-drained soil.

Globe thistle (*Echinops ritro*). This plant will produce blue flowers that can be dried in July for winter use. Set young plants 24 inches apart in well-drained soil.

Shasta daisy (*Chrysanthemum maximum*). Do not cover the shasta daisy following sowing. It prefers light shade in the hottest part of the day and good soil.

Snow-in-summer (*Cerastium tomentosum*). Another plant with gray foliage, snow-in-summer will grow almost anywhere, as long as the spot is hot and dry.

White marguerite (*Chrysanthemum frutescens*). Several chrysanthemums are easy to grow from seed. The white marguerite will grow to three feet in full sun and produce white flowers with yellow centers.

Yarrow (*Achillea micrantha*). With bright yellow flowers, yarrow blooms in June and is very tough, surviving in dry soil. The seed is fine and needs light to germinate, so it should not be covered.

Propagation 101

When I took my first summer job, as a gardener in 1976, I wasn't sure what to expect. After all, since I had had only one year of horticulture in college, it would have been reasonable to confine me to the mulch pile or the pot-washing detail. Sally, my employer, had other ideas and gave me a wonderful introduction to practical gardening. One of her passions was propagating plants, so over the summer we sowed hundreds of seeds and also made hundreds of cuttings. Since July is a good time to make cuttings, I offer some of her helpful hints for home propagators.

Azaleas are not only popular plants for home gardens, but they're easy to propagate with a minimum of equipment. Once you have mastered the techniques for azaleas, you can try your hand with rhododendrons, which are usually trickier to root.

If you have a greenhouse equipped with a mist system, you will have no trouble achieving success with your cuttings. A homemade mini-greenhouse, however, will assure similar success. To make the mini-greenhouse, use a wooden flat and cover it with a sheet of clear polyethylene plastic. Support the plastic over the cuttings with two pieces of wire—coat hangers bent straight, then shaped into a Quonset frame will serve well. As alternatives to the wooden flat, use clear plastic shoeboxes or an old aquarium to create a propagating box. Use a polyethylene cover for these containers also; polyethylene "breathes" and allows oxygen to enter the chamber.

Next, consider the rooting medium for your cuttings. A mixture of equal parts sand and peat moss is best for azaleas. If you do not have sand, use perlite, available from hardware stores and garden centers.

July and August are good months to make softwood cuttings of cotoneaster, deutzia, forsythia, hydrangea, andromeda, viburnum, and of azaleas that hold their leaves throughout the winter. In the fall and winter, concentrate on evergreen trees and shrubs, such as arborvitae, box, euonymus, holly, juniper, pyracantha, and yew.

June is the best time to take cuttings of deciduous azaleas that lose their leaves in fall. To test the readiness of the plant for rooting, break off a stem. If the wood snaps, it's time to start taking the cuttings. If the stem bends limply, keep testing until it's ready.

Prepare the propagating box ahead of time. Mix the sand and peat moss thoroughly, cover the bottom of the flat with a double layer of newspaper to retain the mixture, then place the medium in the box, water it well, and allow it to drain overnight. When you plant, your soil mixture should be damp but never soggy. Plan to take your cuttings early in the morning.

Arm yourself with a sharp pair of pruners to make the cuttings and keep them moist until you get them into the rooting medium. If you're taking cuttings in a friend's garden, place them in a plastic bag with some wet paper towels or a few drops of water, then place them in a cooler until you get them home.

The length of cutting you take will depend on how much pruning you want to do. From shrubs that have extensive spring growth, prune severely, then trim the cuttings to three to four inches from the top before sticking them in the medium. For smaller-growing plants you will want to remove less stem, and the eventual size of your cutting will be smaller.

To prepare the cuttings, use a sharp penknife or a single-edge razor blade and trim each piece to just below a node at a 45-degree angle. Then strip a thin outer layer from either side of the cutting, slicing about one-half to one inch up the stem from the cut. Remove enough bottom leaves from the cutting so you can place one-half to one inch of the stem into the rooting medium without having the remaining leaves touch the damp mixture. After removing the lower leaves, you should have a rosette at the top—if the leaves are large, bunch them together and trim away about 30 percent of the leaf area with a pair of scissors.

In these preparations, you are wounding the base of the stem to encourage root development and reducing the leaf area to reduce transpiration. Rooting hormones, which are available in many garden centers, also will promote root development.

Once you have each cutting in place, firm the mixture around the stem to ensure contact between stem and rooting mixture. When all the cuttings are in place, spray the leaves with a fine mist and cover the cuttings with the sheet of clear polyethylene, securing it on all sides of the wooden flat with push pins. If the plastic touches the cuttings, adjust the wires to create a taller tent.

Set your propagating box on the north side of the house or in good shade under a tree. Under no circumstances should direct sun-

To prepare cuttings, use a sharp penknife and trim each piece to just below a node at a 45-degree angle.

light hit the plastic. The cuttings will remain in the box until early fall. Leave them alone except to ventilate the tent, if condensation seems excessive, and to pick out dead leaves. Try to open the tent as infrequently as possible, but do remove the debris because diseases will spread easily among rotting leaves.

After six to eight weeks, open the tent and tug a couple of cuttings to see if they have rooted. If they resist, dig one out carefully with a spoon or fork to inspect the root system. Roots should be at least one-half to three-quarters of an inch long before you move cuttings to the next stage.

To get the healthiest plants, move cautiously, trying to avoid giving the cuttings a dramatic shock, such as a change of environment. Remove the tent from the box gradually over two weeks, then pot the cuttings, each one in a three-inch clay or plastic pot, using the same potting mixture. Place the cuttings in the shade for a couple more weeks, then gradually move them into brighter light.

Store cuttings in a coldframe or a cool greenhouse during the winter. Alternative storage areas would be a shaded window well covered with plastic, a sunporch, or a cool room where the temperature stays below 50° F. Here again, it is important to have good light but no direct sunlight.

Come January, start fertilizing the cuttings, using a half-strength solution of houseplant fertilizer every three weeks. When you see new growth, pinch it back from time to time to produce a bushy plant. Once all danger of frost has passed, sink the pots into the soil in the garden. The following winter, bring them back into the cold-frame, then plant them in the garden after the second winter under shelter. Make sure that they don't dry out in summer and feed them once a month, from May 1 to July 1. After the first summer, feed just once a year.

Sally the Propagator taught me that evergreen azaleas root better after the new growth has hardened. Take these cuttings after the first hard frost, using the same flat and tent, and place it in a cool north window throughout the winter. Bottom heat is always helpful in promoting rooting, but be careful not to get the soil too warm.

Try taping a six-foot length of heating cable to the upended bottom of a wooden flat with packaging tape, then set the flat with the cuttings on top of the cable. If you set the flat on a radiator, put a board or a layer of newspapers between the radiator and the flat. As before, place your box out of direct sunlight. Leave the cuttings in the propagating box until late January or February, then give one the tug test. If the roots are long enough, remove the heat source, reduce the humidity by gradually lifting the plastic, then pot the cuttings as you would in the late summer.

If you don't succeed the first time with your propagating endeavors, try again. The first time I tried it, a few years before I met Sally, I took my direction from a television program, but I didn't take in one critical fact. I covered my box with black plastic, not realizing that the cuttings need light to put out new roots!

There's no escape

With the garden come the weeds.

Each weekend brings a new growth of them and, depending on the time of year, there is usually an outstanding variety or two. The cool weather of April brought onion grass. There was chickweed in May, oxalis in June. Now in July, purslane and lamb's-quarters are beginning to spread rapidly.

There are the vines as well—honeysuckle, bittersweet, and poison ivy. Turn your back on a planting area for a couple of months and you will surely find it smothered by one or all of these.

Weeding by hand and hoe are old and effective methods. Pull by hand when the ground is damp so you get as many roots as possible. If you use a hoe, do it before a couple of dry days so the plants will wither and die rather than reroot. Once you have removed the weeds, you can debate with yourself endlessly whether to add the weeds to your compost pile. Some gardeners say that if you add them to the pile you will have worse problems with weeds in years to come. In our case, since The Gardening Partner and I have so many weeds as it is, I don't think it makes any difference whether we generate a few more seeds from the compost pile, so I pile them all on.

Mulching is a wonderful way to control weeds. Not only do the weeds not grow through the mulch, but you also add organic matter to improve soil structure. On shrub beds and under trees, woodchips or pine bark are appropriate. In the garden, grass clippings, salt hay, composted leaves, even newspapers or black plastic are alternatives. Mulch after a heavy rain, rather than when the soil is dry. If you use fresh grass clippings or woodchips, sprinkle fertilizer on top to encourage bacterial decomposition without robbing the plants of nitrogen. Also, if you are using herbicide on your lawn, I suggest not using these clippings on the vegetable garden.

Herbicides are a way to control weeds in your garden, but before you treat weeds with chemicals, learn as much as you can about the weeds and the chemicals because misapplication can lead to disaster. There are preventive chemicals that kill seeds before they germinate, and there are other applications that kill weeds once they are up and growing. Correct timing for both is important. Read product directions carefully and if you are required to dilute the concentrate, do it as specified, using a sprayer exclusively for applications of weedkillers.

Do not, under any circumstances, reuse the same sprayer for insecticides. Even if you wash out the container, all the weedkiller will not be removed. Just one short blast of spray can severely damage plantings.

AUGUST

Enjoy the Harvest, But Look Ahead

The summer's bounty of tomatoes, peppers, and zucchini makes it tempting to concentrate on the harvest and forget about the potential for late-summer and fall crops. But remember: If it's a year with an extended summer, time spent fighting weeds and hot weather now will bring ample rewards later.

Some tips for early August ...

๛ Continue to deadhead annuals, perennials, and plants such as geraniums that are growing in pots on decks or patios. If they look straggly, cut them back severely and continue to fertilize every 10 to 14 days with a water-soluble fertilizer. As you've been doing, continue to check houseplants you've placed outdoors for the summer for insect or disease infestations. Frequent hosing with a strong stream of water will help control aphids and red spider mites.

๛ Keep amaryllis growing for another month to six weeks, treating it as you would any houseplant. Then force the plant into dormancy by gradually withholding water. Once the leaves turn yellow, remove them, and place the bulb in a cool, dry spot for a rest period.

๛ Fall webworms, whose damage is similar to that of the tent caterpillars of the spring months, will make cocoons and can completely envelop and defoliate branches and large sections of trees. In many cases, they are too high up to reach, but if you can get hold of them, snip off the branch on which the web is growing and dump it in a bucket of soapy water.

❧ Summers with abundant rainfall will bring masses of millipedes and earwigs, but these are more annoying than damaging, so don't worry about them.

❧ Green, pineapple-like galls on the tips of spruce are caused by Cooley spruce gall adelgid or Eastern spruce gall adelgid. To control next year's brood, prune out the galls before they turn brown and open over the next few weeks.

❧ Order a soil test kit from the agricultural extension service. Early next month marks the optimum time of year for lawn renovation, so be sure to do your test this month.

❧ **In the vegetable garden:** Cole-crop seedlings (cabbage, cauliflower, and broccoli) should be planted for fall harvests. Plant in early evening, and shield seedlings from the sun for a couple of days until they have a chance to develop new roots. And there's still time to plant seeds of radishes, lettuce, and Chinese cabbage. Select quick-maturing varieties, plant seeds slightly deeper than you would in spring, and be sure to keep the seedbed moist to assure good germination. … As empty spaces develop in the vegetable garden, sow a cover crop to hold the soil from erosion and also to provide extra nutrients. Winter rye is the most practical crop for this area because it will germinate in the cool nights of late fall. If you sow it late, the seeds will germinate early the following spring. … If you didn't get around to removing the spent canes from summer-blooming raspberries, do so now. Cut the canes to the ground. Save those of at least pencil-thickness, leaving one new cane every six inches within a row. … To test an eggplant for ripeness, press your thumb into the flesh. If the dent stays, the eggplant is ready to harvest. If the flesh springs back, try again in a couple of days. Eggplants need plenty of water. If the fruits are bitter and full of seeds, you've probably let the plants dry out and wilt.

❧ **For the flowers, shrubs, and trees:** Quit fertilizing roses to avoid stimulating late-season growth that may be killed by early frosts. … Cut dahlias in full bloom in early morning before the sun hits the flowers, slicing the stems diagonally with a sharp knife. Place the flowers in a clean vase immediately.

Some tips for late August ...

𝜘𝒐 Late August and early September are good times to transplant evergreens, allowing three to four months before hard frost for root development. Water plants well several days before moving them.

𝜘𝒐 An economical way to spread your ground covers is to divide the plants in early fall. If you plan to develop new ground-cover areas, prepare the beds this fall. Come spring, ask friends if you can take a few divisions from some of their favorites to get new plantings underway. Later, you'll be able to divide these plantings, too.

𝜘𝒐 If you don't have one, start a compost pile. It can be fancy with lumber and wire, or it can be simply a pile in some out-of-the-way spot, but it will pay enormous dividends in years to come. I have found three heaps to be the perfect number, so there's ample time for maturity. Add all garden waste except diseased plants. Also add uncooked vegetable waste from the kitchen, but do not add cooked foods or any kinds of fat.

𝜘𝒐 If early tomatoes, squash, and cucumbers are done, remove the vines rather than letting them get moldy in the garden.

𝜘𝒐 Late August and September are the best weeks of the year to do minor and major lawn repairs—dethatching, reseeding, or even redoing a lawn entirely with sod or seed. If you were planning renovations next spring, speed up your schedule and do it this month. The results will be much better. Cooler temperatures and more even moisture will foster seed germination, and since few weeds germinate at this time of year (compared to spring), your grass seed will get a good start with minimal competition.

𝜘𝒐 **In the vegetable garden:** If you planted garlic last fall or this spring, August is the month to harvest it. When the stems no longer have any trace of green, the tops will most likely bend over. If they don't, push them gently. Pry the plants from the ground with a fork and let the bulbs dry in the sun for a couple of days. If it's going to rain, bring them under shelter. Store them in a net bag in a cool, dry place. ... You may also have planted potatoes, which can be harvested when the tops die down. Dig gently to avoid piercing them, because damaged potatoes rot first. Leave on top of the soil to dry for several hours, then store in mesh or burlap bags in a cool, dark place. If left in the light, potato skins turn green and these are inedible. ... Summer squash are producing faster and faster. Let a couple of days go by without picking and you will have massive monsters on your hands. If even your friends are tired of zucchini, pick them anyway and put them on the compost pile.

❧ **For the flowers, shrubs, and trees:** Continue feeding chrysanthemums until buds show color. ... Take four- to six-inch cuttings from outdoor bedding plants such as coleus and impatiens for color indoors in winter. Cut below a node and remove bottom leaves and any flowers. Dip in rooting hormone and place in vermiculite or perlite. Cover with plastic and place in a location with good light but no sun until roots form. ... Impatiens don't root as well from flowering stems, so cut the plants back and wait until they produce new stems. Then take cuttings before flower buds appear.

AUGUST: IT'S HARVEST TIME

A monthly overview

A visit with my family in Scotland has reminded me how Scottish gardeners can count on using their ground only once a year while I can plant spinach and lettuce in March for harvest in May, then plant tomatoes and eggplants in the same spot for summer harvest. In another section of the garden, I can plant peas, followed by a fall crop of carrots or turnips. And despite the potential for growing beautiful perennials in Scotland, there is just one other problem with the climate: It is totally unsuited for lima beans, which ensures that The Gardening Partner and I will not move to Scotland.

August in the vegetable garden is a busy time. The tomato harvest is in full swing and we're making endless pots of sauce and soup. In early July, we removed the remaining pea vines and early this month is the time to turn over the soil for late-summer plantings.

And if you remove crops but don't plan to replant with vegetables, do not leave the soil bare. That encourages erosion. Sow a cover crop, such as winter rye, to hold the soil throughout the winter. Early next spring, you can turn it under as a green manure.

Frost can be expected in my area as early as the first two weeks of October, but most of the fall vegetables I've mentioned are capable of tolerating light frost. As you plan your fall garden, remember that you probably will have to water to ensure good germination. Also, plan to side-dress each row of vegetables with fertilizer when the seedlings are two to three inches tall.

In the flower garden, this is a good time to divide perennials that have bloomed, such as Japanese iris and daylilies, allowing them ample time to grow new roots before the cold weather. It will be quite a challenge to dig up the well-established perennial roots, but you will get better blooms if you divide most perennials every three or four years.

In addition to making the divisions, the gardener should at the same time improve the soil by adding compost or leaf mold before replacing the plants. Cut the plants back to within six to eight inches of the ground, lift up each plant with a spade, and divide the sections by placing two forks back to back in the middle of the plant to separate the roots. Dividing perennials can create large piles of debris, and I hope that by now every gardener has adequate composting facilities to handle the load.

Later in the month, stop by the garden center and pick up a few chrysanthemums to give added color for September and until frost comes. Mums are a wonderful value and you can get just the right effect if you wait until the buds show color and you can choose the touch you want to add to your color scheme.

On a final note, order yourself a couple of attractive bulb catalogs to ponder throughout the month. In September, local nurseries and garden centers will have excellent selections of bulbs for forcing and for planting in the garden.

Enjoying the bounty

Above all else, August is for harvesting, hoarding the bounty, and hoping for rain so that you don't have to haul those hoses around.

Harvest your vegetable crops at the peak of their flavor. Wait until the tomatoes ripen on the vine instead of picking them ahead of time and letting them ripen on the kitchen counter. Cut eggplants from the plant with a pair of pruning shears when the fruit is full and still shiny. Once eggplants turn dull, they are over the hill and may be bitter.

Continue to harvest onions. Wait until most of the tops shrivel, then gently push over those that still stand tall and green. Once all the tops have shriveled, lift the bulbs and spread them in a single layer to cure in a dry, well-ventilated location for about a week. Good ventilation is the key to this process. Old screens make excellent curing trays. Once the bulbs are cured, clip off the dried tops, leaving about an inch of stem on each bulb, then store them in well-ventilated containers such as net bags in a dry place.

Look ahead, too

While you are trying to figure out what to do with what I hope are your bountiful summer crops, turn your thoughts ahead to fall. Now is the time to make sure you have everything in place for extending your harvesting season into October and November.

Leafy crops are a wonderful source of late-summer and early-fall salads, and, as I've said before, there's still time to plant lettuce, spinach, and other greens, such as mustard.

Germinating seeds at this time of year is a challenge because the conditions often are far from ideal, with lack of moisture and hard, crusty soil. Prepare a small area by turning over the soil and then raking it to remove large stones so you can use this as your seedbed. Later, you can transplant the lettuce seedlings into other places, filling up spots vacated earlier in the summer. If possible, locate the seedbed near a water source.

Sow the seeds a little deeper than you would in early spring, water the ground thoroughly, and then spread burlap, a board, or damp newspapers over the area. Your goal is to keep the soil shaded to reduce evaporation and drying. As soon as the seeds germinate, however, you must be sure to remove the cover to give the plants plenty of light.

A small bed works well for lettuce because you can keep on thinning and transplanting, gradually adding plants in various parts of the garden. Sow spinach seeds in a permanent spot and thin the plants if they seem too crowded. Chinese cabbage is also a speedy grower and will do better if you sow the seeds in a permanent spot instead of transplanting. Because an early fall is always possible, try to get the seeds sown without delay.

In addition to Chinese cabbage, there are several other cole crops that really provide better harvest in fall than in spring. Cabbages, cauliflower, and broccoli have all done well for us, and you should be able to find transplants in some local garden centers. Again, get them in as soon as you can.

Be prepared to deal with cabbage looper larvae and cabbage-worm caterpillars, which can make mincemeat of cabbage and related crops. The caterpillars are green, and their color is so close to that of the cabbage that sometimes you will be able to see only the holes in the leaves. *Bacillus thuringiensis*, a nontoxic pesticide, will help keep this problem under control, but it has no residual power, so you must spray every four or five days and always after rain.

Lawn repairs

Ever since we moved into our house, the lawn has been a source of aggravation. In the early years, I spent days removing weeds and seeding, assuming that was all I had to do to produce a lush, Scottish-style lawn. It took me much too long to realize that the builder probably dumped all the subsoil from our basement out back, leaving us with a lousy bed on which to grow grass. To compound the problem, this area of the garden faces east and when we have a hot, dry summer, the "lawn" burns to a crisp before midsummer. Irrigation would help, but we have a well and there's no way The Gardening Partner will let me endanger his shower by taking care of the lawn. Consequently, it's a sea of crabgrass. The front of the house has better grass because the area is shaded, but in many areas, the grass struggles to compete with roots of oaks and maples.

In a nutshell, The Gardening Partner and I are much more interested in tomatoes and lima beans than we are in lawns. The guidance I offer below is general. If you want the best lawn in the neighborhood, you're going to need more help than I can give, and one of the best sources is your agricultural extension agent.

Early fall is the best time to do repairs on a lawn or to seed a new one. Cooler temperatures and more even moisture will foster seed germination, and since few weeds germinate at this time of year, compared to spring, your grass seed gets a good start with minimal competition.

Before you do anything, test your soil for pH and fertility, then retest every three or four years to keep pace with changes. The pH level governs the soil's ability to take up fertilizers, so unless you have the pH correct, you could be wasting time and money when you add fertilizer. The printout you will get from the soil-testing lab will specify the current pH and the amendments needed to bring it in line with your plans for seeding. In many gardens in this region, the pH may be as low as in my garden—around 4.5. Lawn grasses prefer a pH of 6.0 to 7.0.

To reduce compaction and weeds, aerate the lawn once a year. Core aerators can be rented for this purpose. You may also want to rent a thatching machine to remove buildup of living and dead roots growing laterally at the soil surface. In future years, you may be able to reduce thatch buildup by using an organic fertilizer. Chemical fertilizer encourages thatch by releasing water-soluble nutrients at the surface. Organic fertilizer breaks down thatch naturally by feeding beneficial organisms. You can also remove thatch with a stiff rake and lots of muscle power.

Your choice of grass seed will have a lot to do with the success of your lawn. Grass seed mixes are blends of different types of grasses, and for most lawns in this area, it's best to use a fine-leafed, turf-type tall fescue blend. The particular blend will depend on whether you are planting in shade, partial shade, or full sun. Besides the fescue grasses, the blends will probably contain perennial and annual rye grass. In addition, you should look for endophyte-enhanced grass seed, which has been inoculated to make it less appealing to the insects that bother turfgrass, such as chinch bugs and sod webworm grubs.

Your best defense against weeds is a strong stand of turf. If you have large areas of annual grass weeds, such as crabgrass, these can be controlled with preemergence herbicides, which should be applied prior to weed seed germination in early to mid-spring. Best results will be obtained by applying these herbicides between mid-March and mid-April. In addition to keeping the blades on your mower sharp, it's important not to cut the grass too short. Taller grass shades roots and chokes out weeds. Set the mower at three inches and leave clippings on the lawn to provide nitrogen.

When establishing a lawn, the seed and seedlings will require at least one inch of water per week. If you have an overhead sprinkler, stick a coffee can within its drip range and figure out how long it takes for one inch to fall, then use that timing for future waterings. With a lawn, the worst thing you can do is to spritz it a little each night, never providing a good watering. When it's really dry, lawn grasses are better off if you allow them to go dormant (and an ugly brown) until the rains of the fall are sufficient to revive them. By watering a little here and a little there, you trick them into remaining in a vegetative state, which in turn makes them more susceptible to drought.

Crape myrtles for summer color

Crape myrtles often get a bad rap. Because they are at the edge of their hardiness range in this area, they may die to the ground in unprotected sites following a tough winter. But from late July into early September, they make up for this lack of hardiness with wonderful white, pink, and lavender blooms. And their excellent fall foliage color is not to be missed.

The late Dr. Donald Egolf, a researcher at the National Arboretum in Washington, introduced about 25 hardier crape myrtles, all with American Indian names. Here are a few of Egolf's best introductions for planting in full sun and well-drained soil:

Hopi is a low-growing shrub (six to eight feet at maturity) with pink flowers and bright-red fall foliage. Zuni is also semi-dwarf and multi-stemmed with lavender foliage. Acoma, also small, has white

103

flowers. If you want larger plants, look for Muskogee, with lavender flowers, and Natchez, with white flowers and the best bark of them all. Both will grow to 15 feet if they make it through several winters.

If you buy plants in fall, make sure they were dug in the spring because they don't move well at the end of the growing year. Crape myrtles leaf out very late, so keep your pruners away from your plant even if you don't see leaves until the end of April. Once leaves start to come out, prune out dead wood. If the limbs still appear dead by early May, cut the plant to the ground and perhaps it will grow again from the roots. If you choose to grow crape myrtles as very low shrubs, prune them to the ground each year in early spring.

Evergreens are good neighbors

Evergreen trees can make the best of neighbors—if you plant them in the right place and take care not to block the sun from the next-door vegetable garden or terrace. Now is the time to start planning your fall plantings so the new roots will have adequate time to expand before winter.

Size is the most important factor in selecting the right evergreen. Many of the best-known evergreens—the white pine, Norway, and blue spruce—are forest giants and you must be sure you have adequate room for growth. One of my garden mistakes was planting a white pine too close to our vegetable garden. Now, The Gardening Partner hardly lets a month go by without reminding me of its already gigantic proportions.

If you decide that the white pine is too big for you, consider alternatives in the same genus. The lacebark pine (*Pinus bungeana*) is a beautiful tree with long needles and, eventually, loose growth. This is not a small tree. It will eventually be about 60 feet tall with a spread almost as wide, but it's not as massive as the white pine and it grows more slowly. In addition, it forms a clump and tends to retain its lower branches, making it an excellent screening plant.

The limber pine (*P. flexilis*) has more of an upright habit and will not grow as large as the lacebark. The needles are short and the branches are flexible, which means this species loses fewer branches in heavy storms and snowfalls than does the white pine.

P. cembra, the Swiss stone pine, is even more modest in size, rarely exceeding 30 feet. It grows slowly and is, at first, upright, later opening up to become flat-topped with spreading branches. This pine is not for impatient gardeners who want to screen the neighbor's barbecue pit overnight, but rather for those who want an attractive, slow-growing tree. *P. densiflora umbraculifera*, the

Tanyosho pine, is as beautiful as its name; it has a flat top, many stems, and spreading branches.

What of the spruces? Many years ago, I wanted to plant a blue spruce. No thanks, said The Gardening Partner, and he was right; it would not have been appropriate in the setting. We do have one Norway spruce (*Picea abies*), the survivor of several plants given to us by old friends as a wedding present. At first, we planted them much too close, but fortunately, when they were still small enough that we could remove them ourselves, I began to see how large they might become at maturity, so we removed most of the planting.

Now our surviving spruce is more than 25 years old and perhaps 40 feet tall, with wide spreading branches. Since it's in an open spot, it has retained its lower branches and makes an attractive screen. But be warned, Norway spruces can grow much taller.

Another excellent spruce for the Mid-Atlantic region is the Serbian spruce (*P. omorika*). Eventually, it will grow to about the same height as the Norway spruce, but it has a more slender, ascending habit and grows more slowly.

P. pungens is the scientific name for the Colorado or blue spruce. If you love this tree, use it carefully in your landscape because the foliage color can be too obtrusive.

If you find, as we do from time to time, that the plants we placed so carefully—even just a few years ago—have thoroughly outgrown their allotted space, fall is a good time to move them around. Water them a couple of days ahead if the weather has been dry, and dig the new hole before you dig up the plant. Make as generous a ball of earth as you can so you can save as many roots as possible. Plants sink as the soil settles, so plant the tree or shrub slightly higher in the new location than it was in its original planting.

Backfill halfway with soil, and fill the hole with water. Return later to add remaining soil, then construct a saucer with soil or mulch surrounding the plant and fill this with water. Later waterings will be easier if you leave this saucer in place.

105

SEPTEMBER

A Learning Experience

This is a month for evaluation. Stroll around your garden with a notebook and mark down what has done well in a particular spot, noting, if you can remember, the best varieties and how you treated them. Did you try a new variety, a new mulch, or a different fertilizer? With what results? Note also ideas from other gardeners that you can implement next year.

Some tips for early September ...

❧ Toward the end of September, you should bring house-plants back indoors, so start checking them now for insects and diseases and removing straggly branches. If a plant has appeared sickly outside, do not bring it back inside where it will probably only get worse and infect other plants as well. Expect some leaf drop when you bring the plants inside—this is a natural adaptation to a less favorable environment.

❧ Once you get the plants back indoors, go easy on the fertilizer until late winter. With the lower light indoors and poorer growing conditions, you'll only weaken them by adding fertilizer.

❧ Early fall is the best time to move most conifers, allowing them time to produce new roots before frost. If you're moving deciduous plants, hold off until the leaves drop.

ॐ Weed trimmers, those miracle workhorses that save hours of trimming, may be damaging your trees. Although tree bark may seem tough and durable, the outer tissues, which transport the water and nutrients that trees need to prosper, are highly sensitive to injury—especially when this occurs regularly. Save your weed trimmers for fences and the base of buildings.

ॐ I'll make the point again: If you're not already doing it, become a composter. My rules are very simple: only uncooked vegetable waste—no fats and no meat—and I add skinny layers of soil between thick layers of green matter.

ॐ Pick gourds before frost, leaving two-inch stems. Leave them on the ground to cure in the sun, then dry, wash, disinfect, and paint or varnish for fall decorations.

ॐ **In the vegetable garden:** When you remove crops from the vegetable garden, sow winter rye as a cover crop to hold the soil and provide additional organic matter to be turned next spring. ... There's still time to sow lettuce seeds now for midwinter salads. Sow them indoors for a quicker start, or directly into a coldframe, if you have one. If you can find transplants already started in a nursery, buy a few for your earliest crop.

ॐ **For the flowers, shrubs, and trees:** Plant fall flowering bulbs as soon as you can find them in garden centers. They will soon have a full stock of bulbs for fall planting. Buy early to make sure you get exactly what you want, and be sure to include some varieties for planting in pots to force into bloom early next spring. Dwarf iris and daffodils, crocus, and grape hyacinths are excellent for forcing, and most bulb displays mark the varieties recommended for forcing. ... Hold off fertilizing trees and shrubs until late fall. If you fertilize now, you may stimulate late growth that will be damaged by frost. ... Gardeners with cold porches or greenhouses where winter nighttime temperatures range between 40° and 50° F. should pot freesia bulbs as soon as they are available for fragrant blooms in midwinter. ... If you've been taking care of them through the summer, your amaryllis should have lots of long, healthy leaves. Now it's time to give the plants a rest. Water less and less, gradually allow the foliage to die down, then don't water the bulbs for six weeks. After the rest period, remove brown foliage and repot bulbs in fresh soil, then resume watering and fertilizing. ... The cooler nights of September will encourage blooms on roses, annuals, and perennials if you do your bit by continuing to deadhead and keep plants free of insects and diseases.

Some tips for late September ...

🐛 Fall is an excellent time to change your landscape as it gets colder. If you're working with deciduous plants, those that lose their leaves in winter, water them heavily a couple of times several days apart, then transplant them shortly after the leaves fall. The sooner you move them after leaf drop, the more time the roots have to develop before the ground freezes. Most root growth on woody plants occurs between 40° and 90° F., with the most active root development at the lower end of the scale.

🐛 If you left pruning undone during the spring and summer, do it either later in the fall or early next spring. If you prune now, new growth will be stimulated by late summer rains, but it may be killed by winter frosts.

🐛 Let perennial foliage die back naturally so that it can continue to feed root systems.

🐛 This is the prime time of the year for repairing lawns. See the previous chapter for a fuller explanation.

🐛 **In the vegetable garden:** For late-summer frosts, have old blankets and other covers handy to throw over the tomatoes, peppers, eggplants, and other tender crops. Often we'll have a glorious late summer, and you'll reap a glorious late harvest by taking precautions on those few cold nights. ... Carrots, parsnips, leeks, and beets all seem to taste better after a couple of hard frosts, so leave these plants in the ground as long as possible. If you still have some left by Thanksgiving, cover the plants (leaves and all) with a six- to eight-inch layer of leaves (shredded if possible), and mark the rows to make sure you can find them after a snowfall. In most winters, you'll find that the soil won't freeze under the mulch and you'll be able to harvest fresh vegetables throughout the winter. ... Leave winter squash on the vine until the skin is hard and resists pressure from your thumbnail. ... After turning the garden over, sow a couple of small rows of spinach. To speed germination, soak the seed for 24 hours in water. The tops will die during the winter, but the same plants will produce a spring harvest much earlier than anything you can plant in early March. ... As long as the weather is not too cold, pumpkins will keep well if left on the vine in the garden. When harvesting pumpkins, cut stems carefully with pruning shears. If the stem tears from the fruit, it may rot.

❧ **For the flowers, shrubs, and trees:** If you've set yourself an ambitious goal for bulb planting this fall, start with the daffodils, which need more time to establish good root systems. Then plant the early-flowering varieties—crocus, snowdrops, grape hyacinths, and scillas. Tulips can be left until last because they can make do with less time to put down roots in the fall. Try to get all bulbs planted by early November, in case there's a short autumn. ... Lily of the valley can be separated and transplanted now. Select strong crowns and plant them just below the surface of the soil, about three inches apart. Repeat every three or four years.

SEPTEMBER: THE BEST TIME FOR A LOT OF TASKS

A monthly overview

The Gardening Partner doesn't know it yet, but there's an awful lot of work to do around our place in September. Once he gets through freezing lima beans and making tomato soup, tomato sauce, and tomato everything, we must revamp the perennial bed and bring in the houseplants. Toward the end of the month, there will be shrubs to transplant and bulbs to plant, and before long the leaves will start to fall. Labor Day should be just the beginning of an active month for gardeners everywhere.

If you didn't do it in August, September is the month to attend to the lawn. Don't delay, because there will never be a better season to patch and seed as the nights turn cooler.

Clean up in the vegetable garden as plants start to look straggly and cease to produce. Put only the reasonably healthy debris on the compost. If you include heavily diseased plants, you will create problems in future years. Once you have cleared a space in the garden, sow a cover crop as soon as possible. We use winter rye as a green manure cover crop because of its speedy germination and frost resistance. Even planting it as late as October has produced some growth in the fall. During winter, it will lie brown and dormant and will come to life again in early March, often making considerable headway before we dig it into the garden in April to provide additional organic matter. Buckwheat, oats, and clover also can be used as cover crops. In addition to increasing the organic content of your soil, cover crops prevent erosion during heavy winter rains.

Consider sowing spinach in the middle of the month for harvesting in the spring.

109

The insects of the month will probably be the white cabbage butterfly and cabbage looper, whose larvae will hatch in your fall broccoli, cabbage, and cauliflower. Check periodically for green caterpillars that quickly ruin a fine head of any cole crop. *Bacillus thuringiensis*, an organic pesticide, will combat these invaders, as long as you spray regularly. Once a week should do it, but if it rains frequently you may have to do it more often.

Sometimes in early spring, you're just itching to get out and plant, but the ground is too wet to work over the whole garden. Designate a small area this fall for your earliest plantings, turn it over thoroughly before winter, rake it, and lay leaves on top to prevent the soil from freezing too hard. Situate the early planting spot near the edge of the garden, so you can get to it without having to tread over the rest of the plot. Spinach, lettuce, and early peas are among the hardiest vegetables and are well suited to very early planting.

September is probably The Gardening Partner's favorite month because he's reaping the harvest from his beloved lima beans. Each day, I am subjected to the bulletin from the lima bean department with reports on number of bean beetles squashed, moisture content of soil, bumble bee activity, and other pieces of pertinent information. Toward the end of the month, he's anxiously crossing his fingers for warm weather to swell the flood of small pods that always seem to appear at the end of the season.

In the rest of the garden, I am fretting over the crops he ignores when the Dr. Martin limas claim his attention. The carrots, for example, are prone to attack from a brilliant green-and-black swallowtail butterfly caterpillar that can consume enormous quantities of foliage within a few days. The gardener must make a daily check and remove the insects by hand.

Shrubs and trees, with few exceptions, can be planted in the fall. Plant broadleaf evergreens such as rhododendrons, hollies, mountain laurel, and andromeda as soon as possible. Needle evergreens such as pines, spruces, and firs can be planted later.

If they are to be freshly dug, deciduous trees and shrubs such as red maple, dogwood, hawthorn, tulip-tree, sweet-gum, magnolia, oaks, lindens, cherries, and other stone fruits will do better if you wait and plant them in early spring. Plants that were dug and burlapped last spring in a nursery have compact balls and are suitable for fall planting.

Begonia grandis is the only begonia hardy in our area, but what a star. Its leaves are lush and deep green with pinkish stems, and although they are small, the pink flowers are a welcome sight in September. The plant that a friend gave me years ago died in the spot I chose for it under an ash tree, but seeds migrated to a shaded corner of the vegetable garden, where it has flourished and expanded over the years. If you plant one in your garden, be sure to remember the spot because the hardy begonia is slow to come up in spring and it's too easy to dig over the seedlings.

A transplanting strategy

If you transplant trees and shrubs on your own property, plan your strategy before you get out the shovel. In the absence of a good rainfall, water the plants that are to be moved. Soak each one thoroughly a couple of days ahead of digging. Before you start on the roots, tie up the branches to provide easy access to the soil.

The height of the plant will determine the size of rootball you must dig. For example, an 18- to 24-inch plant will require a 10-inch ball; six to eight feet, a 16-inch ball; 10 to 12 feet, a 24-inch ball, and so on. The depth of the ball should be at least two-thirds its diameter.

Mark the circle of the ball on the ground and excavate a trench on the outside of the ball, using a flat-bladed spade. Following exca-

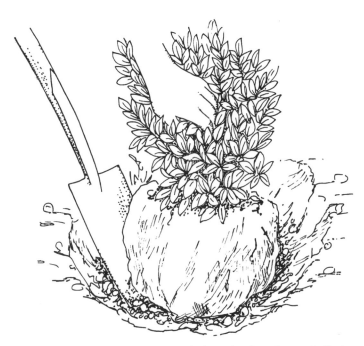

When planting or transplanting, prepare a hole wider than the rootball, then loosen soil at bottom of hole. Set plant in hole so top of rootball is slightly higher than in original site.

111

vation, wind a rope around the ball at several levels or tie a piece of burlap around the ball and secure it with rope and nails to keep the soil firm around the roots.

Prepare a hole wider than the rootball of your transplant. Loosen the soil in the bottom of the hole and set the plant so the top of the rootball is slightly higher than it was in the original site. More plants are killed because gardeners plant them too deeply. As the soil settles, plants sink, so start them with the rootball at a slightly higher level.

Fill the hole halfway with soil and water thoroughly. When the water has disappeared, cut the ropes and fold the burlap back into the hole. Add the balance of the backfill and water again.

Divide the perennials

Sooner or later comes the September when you can no longer ignore the perennials. I remember the fall when it had been four years since our perennial bed had been planted, and few of the plants had been divided since then. They had bloomed well, but after three years, many perennials will bloom less profusely if left undivided. Exceptions to this general rule are peonies and poppies, which should be moved as infrequently as possible.

Lifting and dividing perennials can be a hefty job, especially if you have several clumps of daylilies. If possible, divide and replant on a dull day following a rain. If it has been dry, soak the soil a couple of times a couple of days before you start. Damp but not soggy soil is a lot easier to dig, and transplanting damage will be less severe if plants are not under stress from lack of water.

Aim to complete transplanting by month's end so your plants have adequate time to make new roots before heavy frosts. Before replacing the plants, improve the growing conditions. If the soil is poorly drained, add a combination of sand or perlite and organic materials such as peat moss or leaf mold. All soils benefit from additional organic matter, so if you have a compost pile, mix some in. Spread sand and organic materials on the bed, and incorporate thoroughly.

Generally, the rule to follow in making perennial divisions is to divide spring bloomers in the fall and fall bloomers in the spring. But because there is so little time in the spring, I try to divide as many plants as possible in September.

Daylilies, hostas, yarrow, beebalm, and other perennials that have finished blooming are in ideal condition for division now. Members of the daisy family, such as coreopsis and aster, are still in flower,

Some perennials can be separated by pulling apart the roots.

and with these plants you will want to wait and divide them next spring. Fall-blooming sedums and anemones are also too attractive to disturb at the moment.

Cut back the plants you intend to divide to six to eight inches from the soil line. Discard all foliage to remove potential sources of disease for the following year and dig the plant out of the bed with a spade.

Place two gardening forks (some call them spading forks) back to back in the center of each plant and make your division by forcing them apart. Matted roots, such as those on a daylily, will be hard to pry apart and you may have to use a spade to cut the plant into sections. Ideally, however, you want to separate the roots as gently as possible so as to cause minimal root damage.

Separate plants into the appropriate number of divisions, and discard the old, woody centers, saving only the strong outer sections for replanting. If you want to increase a small clump quickly for sharing with friends or to establish a new clump in your own garden, use a sharp knife to cut divisions off plants that remain in the garden. This technique can also be used on plants such as astilbe, when new shoots appear in early spring.

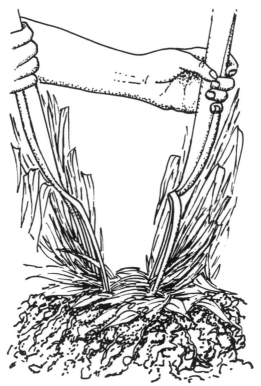

For other perennials, you will need to force the roots apart with a couple of forks.

Fall divisions must also be watered after planting and kept moist until frost. Create a basin to hold water around each plant and plan to soak plants thoroughly once a week if rainfall is scarce.

If divisions are made in early September, plants should be well established before the first frost. After several such frosts, you may want to protect perennials by covering them with a mulch of salt hay or evergreen boughs. With the mulch, your goal is not to keep the soil warm but to keep it frozen as long as possible. Alternate freezing and thawing subjects plant roots to considerable upheaval and damage as the soil expands and contracts.

Tree peonies, which are shrubs (as distinguished from herbaceous peonies, which die down to the ground in winter), should be planted in September or October. Fall-set plants, if large enough, will likely flower the following spring, and certainly every year thereafter.

The tree peony is not actually a tree; rarely do they get more than four feet tall, but their May blooms are exquisite. Their blooms are large, perhaps six to eight inches across, and the petals resemble

114

crepe paper in texture, with bright yellow anthers in the middle of the surrounding darker petals.

This is one of those special garden plants that you should place where you can enjoy it without disturbance for years to come. Choose a site where you can enjoy the blooms every day, a place with several hours of sun per day, preferably in early morning or late afternoon, and where the plant will be sheltered from high winds. The soil should be well-drained, with plenty of organic material and with a pH of about 7.0—considerably higher than most soils in this area, so you may have to add lime. Set each plant with the point of the graft about four inches below the soil level. After planting, remove dead wood with shears. In subsequent years, there will be little need for pruning, other than removing stems that detract from the shape of the plant.

Spring bulbs

Before September's over, I expect to visit my local garden center armed with a short list of such basic items as perlite, peat moss, and plant labels. When I emerge after an hour or so, my bag may bulge with parcels. Spring-blooming bulbs are my downfall, and now that bulb distributors advertise their wares with glamorous color photos and good cultural information, I am even more likely to make additional impulse purchases.

Bulbs now come in a wonderful range of hybrids, colors, sizes, and shapes. Most, however, have similar cultural requirements, easily met in most gardens. High on the list for early consideration is good drainage. Bulbs will not flourish in wet situations, so select your planting spot with care. Plant them on a slope rather than in a flat valley, and if the soil appears heavy, improve it with sand or perlite and organic materials such as peat moss or compost.

Most bulbs prefer a nearly neutral soil with a pH of 6.5. (There's the value of that soil test again; there are just so many times when you need to know your pH.) If you have to add lime to raise the pH, dig this in when you loosen the soil for planting.

For best effects, use at least 12 bulbs of each variety and prepare the soil for a whole clump at one time instead of digging each bulb in separately. Plant bulbs in drifts and clumps rather than as single units. Stay away from areas with surface-rooting trees, such as maples, and closer-growing ground covers, such as pachysandra, ivy, and creeping euonymus. Vinca roots, on the other hand, do not form such a dense system, and bulbs can be planted in combination with this ground cover.

Depth of planting will depend on the size of the bulb. Plant large bulbs such as daffodils, tulips, and hyacinths six to eight inches beneath the surface of the soil. Smaller bulbs such as scillas and crocus should be planted three to four inches deep. If in doubt about planting depth, use three times the height of the bulb as your guide. Place bulbs in the ground, noses up, cover with half the soil, water well, then replace the rest of the soil before watering again.

Before you go to the garden center, get a rough idea of the varieties and numbers of the bulbs you require. Plant large bulbs six inches apart, small bulbs two to three inches apart. Select your bulbs to get a range of blooming times and styles. The larger bulb groups, such as daffodils and tulips, are usually labeled according to variety with a note regarding blooming times. Think also about fragrance; Geranium, Louise de Coligny, and Erlicheer are among my favorite fragrant daffodils. For smaller gardens and rock gardens, look for hybrid miniatures such as Tête-à-Tête, Sundial, Hawera, Beebee, and Minnow. Tiny daffodils, such as *Narcissus bulbocodium conspicuus,* are harder to grow but well worth the effort if you can provide a very well-drained site, such as a rock garden.

If the smaller daffodils intrigue you, look for some minor bulbs to complete your display. For new gardeners, crocuses, snowdrops, scillas, and grape hyacinths are sure bets for spring displays. *Crocus tomasinianus* may be the first thing to bloom in your garden. In a mild winter, they can bloom in early February.

Snowdrops will also bloom very early, and it is hard to resist these in combination with the yellow-flowered winter aconite (*Eranthis hyemalis*). Dwarf iris (*Iris reticulata* and *I. danfordiae*) made a wonderful show one spring in our garden but never bloomed again. Tiny blue scillas, on the other hand, are faithful bloomers, appearing year after year in March or April. Grape hyacinths, which produce leaves in the fall and flowers the following spring, have a wonderful fragrance when they bloom in April.

Tulip lovers have endless possibilities for dramatic spring displays, provided you are not plagued, as I am in my garden, by squirrels and rabbits. If the animals had stuck with the flashy, large-flowered tulips I would not have minded, but when they went for the small, early *Tulipa kaufmanniana* with its beautiful, mottled foliage, I gave up the tulip battle.

Geranium patrol

If you want to hold some of your favorite geraniums for next year, take cuttings as soon as possible. Select new growth, rather than the older, woody stems, and make your cut just above a node (where the leaf joins the stem) with a sharp knife. For standard geraniums, the cuttings should be four to five inches long; for smaller varieties, you will be working with less stem.

Use a container three to four inches deep with drainage holes to hold your soil mixture. Geraniums will root best in a well-drained mixture, so you can use all perlite or vermiculite or a two-to-one ratio of perlite to peat moss. Fill the container with the mix, water it well, and allow the excess to drain for 15 to 25 minutes before you stick in the cuttings.

Bring the cuttings into the shade, strip the leaves from the lower part of the stem, and recut each stem with a sharp knife just below the last node. The new roots will come from the node; the excess stem will simply rot and increase your chances of losing the whole cutting. Dip the stem ends in water, then in rooting-hormone powder, and stick the cuttings in the mixture so as to cover at least one node.

If the internodes are short, you may end up with two to three nodes beneath the soil line; often it's only one. Firm the rooting mixture around the cutting, and place your container in an area with good light but not direct sun. Mist the leaves lightly as soon as you have the cuttings in the soil, and repeat once a day for a week or

To hold geraniums over the winter, make cuttings in early fall and root them in damp perlite.

so. Water the rooting medium when it dries out on the surface, and promptly remove any diseased or dead leaves.

After three weeks, tug gently at the cuttings. If they resist, they have probably rooted and you can dig down gently with an old fork or spoon, pull up the cutting, and inspect the root system. Make sure roots are one-half to three-quarters of an inch long before repotting into a well-drained potting soil in four-inch pots—again with drainage holes. To hold the new plants throughout the winter, place them in a well-lighted area where the temperature is cool.

Think about perennials

Remember that September is more the time for garden evaluation than for dwelling on the approaching winter. So while you're in the flower garden, consider the color schemes of the summer past. Was the bright red salvia really just what you needed next to the purple petunias? Mistakes like this occur in my garden when I wax too enthusiastic over the seed catalogs in midwinter. Come spring, I never have time to plant as many as I had anticipated and then, when the time comes to transplant the seedlings, I find I have not grown enough of the softer colors to offset the bright dazzlers.

This month, before you pull up the garden and relegate the plants to the compost pile, make notes of these situations and mark open spaces for planting early-blooming bulbs. Note also the fall-blooming perennials you may want to move and divide next spring.

September is the month to plant the peony, the queen of perennials and one of the longest-lived flowering plants in the garden. For years, breeders have experimented with flower color and size among peonies. I prefer single rather than double blossoms because they hold up better in wet weather. In addition, I favor those with fragrant blossoms. Garden centers frequently stock a selection of potted peony roots in spring and bareroot plants in fall. If you can't find the variety you desire locally, check a catalog and order roots to plant this fall.

Choose the spot for peonies carefully because once they're planted, it's better not to move them. Select a location with good air circulation. Ideally they should be planted in full sun. They will survive in light shade, but the flowers will be fewer and the chances of disease greater.

Dig a large hole (two feet across by 12 to 18 inches deep) for each root, then shovel some of the soil mix into the planting hole to create a mound on which to set the peony root. Placement of the root is crucial because, if it's planted too deep, you will end up with all foliage and no flowers. The pink buds on the root should be covered with about two inches of soil. Water well after planting, and mark the location of each bulb with a stick. It's easy to forget such things in the hustle and bustle of fall, and it would be fatal to start digging around on top of your new planting.

A preference for pansies

I admit to a distaste for those ornamental cabbages that have become so popular in home and commercial plantings in recent years. They look chipper and colorful until a couple of frosts turn their leaves soggy and floppy, by which time the maintenance crews have moved their attention to tree work and snow removal and ignore the miserable state of the smelly cabbages.

I would rather see a planting of pansies. Their dear little nodding heads are delightful and, even if they look somewhat limp after a snow, if you treat them right, they will perk up again as soon as the weather turns warm. You can plant pansies from Labor Day until mid-October, but the sooner you plant them, the more roots they will put down, and more roots will mean better bloom the following spring. Good drainage is also essential for repeat bloom in spring.

Minor bulbs such as grape hyacinths, scillas, and miniature daffodils make an attractive combination with pansies. Plant the bulbs, then the pansies, then finish off the bed with a light covering of mulch.

Bring the plants in

Even with the best intentions, I rarely achieve my goal of bringing our houseplants indoors well ahead of the first frost. A sudden change of temperature at the end of September catches me off guard, and I rush home one evening to stuff them all into the greenhouse, the porch, the bathroom, the kitchen, or wherever else I can find space. Naturally, they resent this unplanned change of location and react poorly to the new conditions. On some the leaves turn yellow, and within a couple of weeks, formerly beautiful specimens will be partly leafless and unattractive.

There is a better way. The key to success is careful planning. Start your preparations in early September, before the nights turn cool, and get the plants and their indoor locations in tiptop shape before you make the move.

First, let's consider the plants. Inspect each one carefully for pests. Red spiders often take hold during hot summer months and will spread readily throughout your collection if you bring them in on one plant. Inspect upper leaf surfaces for tiny white specks that indicate mites are feeding on the undersides of the leaves. Hose plants with a strong shower of water and wash foliage in warm sudsy water at weekly intervals.

Scale can be a very discouraging pest because its coverings protect it well. Inspect plants thoroughly and frequently for small, brown, translucent bodies on the undersides of leaves and on the stems. Sticky exudate on stems or leaves is usually a clear indication that you have either scale or aphids. If the culprit is scale, scrub leaves and stems with a soft toothbrush or cotton swab dipped in soapy water to dislodge insect bodies. If you have a bad case, discard the plant rather than risk infecting your others.

Mealybugs, which look like bits of cotton in the forks of stems or in the crown of a plant, can be removed with a cotton swab dipped in rubbing alcohol. Aphids will cause leaves to curl, new buds may be deformed, and as with scale, a sticky substance may be present. Once again, that weekly shower under good pressure, or spraying with an insecticidal soap, will help keep the aphids at bay.

Having labored over these preparations, don't delay. Bring the plants indoors before the cool nights start to affect the tropicals. Plants that can survive cooler temperatures, such as azaleas, camellias, and citrus, can stay outside for a couple more weeks.

The soil is everything

Better plants come from better soil, so gardeners should develop the best soil possible. At the risk of belaboring the point, late summer is a good time to send soil samples to your local extension service for testing. The test will determine the soil's pH, or acidity/alkalinity level. Many soils in this area have a low pH, meaning a higher acidity. Soil that is too acidic can be made more neutral by adding lime, which can be spread in the fall. Soil test results will indicate the amount of lime needed.

Vegetables, many annuals and perennials, and fruits such as raspberries and strawberries grow best in a soil with a pH of 5.5 to 6.5. Acid-loving plants such as dogwoods, azaleas, hollies, and blueberries prefer 4.5 to 5.5. Lawn grasses do best when the pH is 6.0 to 7.0.

OCTOBER

Out with the Warm, in with the Cold

Cleanup is the name of the game right about now. Clean up after the spent summer crops. Clean up in the flower garden, removing faded annuals but leaving perennials until after a hard frost has blackened the foliage. And think spring by planting bulbs. Keep up with leaf removal. And there's still time to finish transplanting shrubs.

Some tips for early October ...

🐛 If you're planning to develop a new flower or vegetable garden in the spring, get out the spade and turn it over now so the sod can break down over winter.

🐛 Leaf raking is upon us. For the next several weeks, the wearisome task will be there for the doing anytime you choose. Mound the leaves in a pile to make mulch for use in the garden next year. Building a mulch pile is easier than bagging the leaves, and it will give you the feeling that the boring task has a worthwhile purpose.

🐛 Continue addressing the low indoor humidity on behalf of the houseplants you brought in. Spraying once or twice a day isn't really a good solution because the relief is only temporary. Instead, keep the house cooler and group your plants together on a tray of moist pebbles.

🐛 As you build a compost pile with garden debris, add sprinklings of lime to reduce the acidity of the final product, and also add soil to stimulate bacterial activity and hasten decomposition. Keep a depression in the center of the pile to trap water.

In the vegetable garden: If you have winter squash to store, keep them around 50° F. in a dark place. Before putting them into storage, wipe away all the dirt, and spray the skins with Lysol to deter fungal problems. … Vegetable gardeners should be cleaning up the debris and digging over the garden in preparation for winter. It's not a good idea to leave old tomato vines, rows of beans, or other summer crops sitting around on the soil all winter because the vegetation provides a resting place for insects and diseases. Put diseased materials in the trash, and save the rest for the compost heap. … Harvest sweet potatoes before heavy frost.

For the flowers, shrubs, and trees: After the first hard frost, dig up gladioli, cut their stems two to three inches above the corms, and store after drying spread out in a cool, dry location on a wooden flat. … In addition to planting major bulbs, such as daffodils and tulips, plant smaller ones, often called minor bulbs, such as grape hyacinth, snowdrops, scillas, and chinodoxa. Plant them close to walkways, on rock walls, or in other places you pass daily. … If you have bulbs waiting to be planted, store them in cool places. If they're packed in plastic, remove them from these containers and put them in open trays or paper bags to avoid mold and deterioration. … Remove annuals when they have been blackened by frost. … After frost kills the foliage, cut perennials to a couple of inches from ground level. If some perennials need dividing, do it now, then water the plants well so they can set down new roots before winter. … Leave ornamental grasses and flower heads or plants such as sedums that will provide interest in the garden throughout the winter.

Some tips for late October …

If you provide them with the right conditions, cyclamen can flower indoors for three to four months at a stretch. To get the most satisfactory results, give them good light and cool temperatures, especially at night. Fertilize once a month with houseplant fertilizer.

Bring in hoses, watering cans, and rain gauges to avoid winter damage.

In the vegetable garden: Prune everbearing raspberries (those that bear in summer and fall) after the fruits are over but before winter. If you want crops in both June and fall, remove only dead and diseased canes and fruiting tips. If you prefer to omit the June crop and wait for a large fall crop, prune all canes to within two inches of the ground. ... Though it's better done in September, if you are just getting around to cleaning up the vegetable garden, it's not too late to plant a crop of green manure to keep the soil from eroding in winter and to provide organic matter when you turn the crop under next spring. We use winter rye, which germinates very quickly and is available in garden centers. When pruning blueberries, remove dead twigs and branches and those that reduce air circulation by growing toward the interior of the plants.

For the flowers, shrubs, and trees: Prune diseased and dead branches from trees and shrubs before leaves fall, while it's still easy to tell them from healthy ones. Prune without leaving stubs. ... If you're debating whether there's still time to plant shrubs and trees, go for it. Get them into the ground as soon as possible, and add a two- to three-inch layer of mulch to retard frost in the rootball area and allow as much time as possible for the plants to put down new roots. ... As a precaution, rake all rose foliage from beds and destroy it to prevent possible spread of disease. Thyme and sage can be pruned through the early winter as you use the leaves for cooking. ... Sedums make wonderful perennials and now, when many are in bloom, is a great time to find out which ones you like. Among my favorites are *Hylotelephium* Autumn Joy and *Hylotelephium* ssp. *maximum* Atropurpureum. ... As white pines shed their old needles, rake them and use as a mulch on acid-loving plants, such as azaleas, rhododendrons, and andromedas. ... Don't neglect newly planted shrubs and trees if it turns dry. A plant that goes into winter with dry roots is going to have a tough time making it when the ground freezes and the winter winds dry out the tissues.

OCTOBER: RESPECT WINTER, THINK SPRING

A monthly overview

Cleanup is the name of the game right about now.

Many of the activities that *need* to be finished this month *could* have been done last month, so you might flip back a chapter and review. By the time October ends, you'll want to have cleaned up after the spent summer crops, giving reasonably healthy plants to the compost heap and diseased plants to the trash. Dig over the vegetable garden and sow a crop of green manure, such as winter rye, to hold the soil over the winter. And sow a row of spinach for an early crop in the spring.

Cleanup is the word in the flower garden, too. Remove faded annuals, but leave the perennials until after a hard frost has blackened the foliage. Think spring by planting bulbs. Keep up with leaf removal from lawns and flower beds. And there's still time to finish transplanting shrubs.

If you have tree work to do, make plans now so your tree surgeon can survey the property while trees are still in leaf. The surgeon will probably choose to do the work later in the winter, when the leaves have fallen.

Dahlia tubers will not survive winter in open ground. It's easy to dig them, but it's often difficult in modern houses to find an appropriate storage location. My friend Ed, a horticulturist who gardens in New Jersey, digs his tubers after frost, cuts off the stems and leaves, then lets the tubers dry in the sun for a couple of days. One year, he stored them in his unheated garage. Obviously, the garage was too cold, because the tubers did not sprout the following spring, so now he stores the tubers in his basement, where the temperature is a fairly constant 50° F. His storage container is a five-gallon steel drum and he lays the tubers between layers of dry vermiculite.

Check the tubers a couple of times during the winter to make sure they are not shriveling. If they look very dry, dampen the vermiculite slightly. Excess moisture will cause the tubers to rot.

The thing to remember about all these tasks is that if you put them off until spring, they will get lost in the fever of planting.

Closing out the vegetable garden

August is great for harvests around our place, but October is almost as good. We are into the last of the summer vegetables (tomatoes, peppers, and eggplants) and are usually still picking The Gardening Partner's favorite, lima beans. Finally, after years of experimenting with trellis arrangements and spacings, we have learned that the experts really *do* know what they're talking about when they recommend not planting beans too close together.

Before we wised up, we used to plant our beans in rows four feet apart, and by late August we had to scramble through a tunnel formed by vines from one row growing over to twine with those in the next. Harvesting was a nightmare. One fall, huffing and puffing, The Gardening Partner dug up most of the heavy posts and reset them so the rows of beans would be six feet apart. Things have improved greatly.

In addition to the limas, October gives us string beans, planted in early August, plenty of lettuce, and delicious broccoli, Chinese cabbage, and arugula. Yields from the fall garden somehow seem even more of a bonus than those in midsummer, and we still have the carrots and leeks to look forward to during the winter.

Rhubarb is not a favorite with The Gardening Partner, but I could eat it several times a day, and it is one of the garden's easiest and most reliable plants. If you would like to start some and hear a friend extolling its virtues, ask for a division this fall. Failing that, you'll find plenty of plants in the garden centers next spring.

We let our plants go many years without division, contrary to the advice of some gardeners to divide rhubarb every four to five years. But the plants always produced well, with the addition of a fertilizer in early spring and again in late June, after I harvest for the last time. Space plants at least four feet apart to allow for spreading, and plant enough so you can freeze some for the winter. Once stewed, it freezes well, and it makes a great mid-January breakfast fruit. Don't harvest any stalks the first year after planting. In the second year, harvest modestly, and after that, pick as much as you want from spring through June. When picking, pull the stalks, rather than cutting them, then remove the leaves, which are poisonous.

If a light frost is threatened, use the trick I talked about last month, covering your last tomatoes, eggplants, and peppers with old bedsheets and towels in early evening so that if a few weeks of warm weather follow those early frosts, you'll continue to harvest the vegetables. But if the forecasters predict heavy frosts, pick as much of the crop as possible. Peppers and eggplants can be stored in the refrigerator. We lay our surplus tomatoes in a cool room, out of the sun and on a tray covered with newspapers. If you're overwhelmed with green tomatoes, make some green tomato chutney.

I'm reminded of something else for late in the vegetable season. One spring, we covered our first sowings of lettuce, mustard greens, spinach, and Chinese cabbage with low plastic tunnels. The effect on all crops was dramatic, and we were able to harvest those vegetables reared under plastic a full two weeks ahead of the row we had not covered. So I've adapted the same approach to October, using the same plastic over late lettuce and Chinese cabbage. Leave the plants uncovered as long as possible, because if the weather turns unexpectedly warm you may need to remove the plastic to prevent foliage burn. Remember, too, that you'll have to water the plants beneath the plastic. If you have a soaker or drip hose, run it along the row before you put the tunnel in place.

Deciduous trees such as dogwood, maple, and ash will soon enter dormancy and shed all their leaves, after which you can transplant them with little fear of losing them. Evergreens such as pine, hemlock, and spruce will also go dormant with gradually decreased activity.

"Evergreen" is a misleading term because conifers do not actually hold the same set of needles forever. Every year, each tree will replace some of its needles. The white pines usually shed in the fall, hollies in the spring.

By the way, pine needles make excellent acid-forming mulch for azaleas, rhododendrons, and blueberries. Spread the needles beneath your plants later in the fall, after the ground has frozen and after the mice have found alternative nesting sites; doing it now may encourage them to nest among your azaleas and blueberries. Later in the winter, when food is scarce, they may feed on the bark of your shrubs. By mulching later in the season, you may avoid this destruction.

Autumn is for lilies

Fall is the time to plant lily bulbs, and local nurseries and mail-order sources will have ample supplies available during October and November.

Plant the lily bulbs as soon as you receive them because unlike daffodils and tulips, lilies never go dormant. So don't let them sit around on the garage shelf and dry out. If you order late-blooming lilies from Oregon, they may not be shipped until next spring. When they arrive, get them into the ground as soon as possible so they can develop a good root system before flowering.

For successful lily culture, it is essential to plant the bulbs in well-drained soil. If your soil is heavy, this will mean building up the planting bed or planting on a gentle slope, then adding sand and humus to your planting mixture.

Excavate a 12-inch-deep hole for each group of bulbs and mix the soil with equal proportions of sand, compost or leaf mold, and peat moss, adding a handful of ground limestone and a tablespoon of fertilizer per hole. Replace a few inches of the soil mixture in the bottom of the hole, settle the bulb in, and place four to six inches of soil on top of the bulb, pressing firmly. Water thoroughly to eliminate air pockets. Label each planting of one variety. Within a group, leave 12 inches between small bulbs and 18 inches between large bulbs.

There's a wide range of lilies available, starting with the Asiatics, which grow easily in our area, are generally unscented, and come in a variety of colors. Enchantment, with red flowers, and Connecticut King, with yellow flowers, are two popular choices. If you're in search of fragrance, buy Oriental lilies, such as the beautiful white-flowered Casablanca or Stargazer, with white and crimson flowers, that grows to four feet tall. The Trumpet or Aurelian lilies are tall growers that will be happy in full sun or light shade. In this group, Regale, the regal lily, has white pendant, trumpet flowers on tall plants, and can grow to five or six feet. Martagon hybrids are good too, especially because of their resistance to disease.

Forcing hardy bulbs

Forcing bulbs is a wonderful autumn activity for the gardener who would otherwise face the bleak prospect of months without flowers. Forcing hardy bulbs requires no fancy equipment or structures. The biggest challenge is finding a location with the right temperature to encourage root development. When you put the bulbs in storage this month, temperatures will be conducive to root formation. As it gets colder, you want to make sure that the bulbs are well insulated so that they continue to form roots. When it gets really cold after Christmas, your insulation must keep the soil in the pots from freezing.

I force my bulbs in a coldframe, leaving the cover off until December. Some gardeners have a window well, or a partially heated garage or attic, where the temperature is around 40° to 45° F. in December and January. An old refrigerator or a spare corner in your regular refrigerator are also convenient places to store small pots. But wherever your pots are, they must be in the dark. In the refrigerator, cover them with foil or put them in a shoebox. You also can dig a trench in the open ground and bury pots under 10 to 12 inches of soil, later covering them with an 18-inch layer of insulating mulch, such as chopped leaves.

October and November are the months to pot the bulbs and settle them into winter storage. Be sure the container has a drainage hole. Bulb pans are the most practical containers because they are shallow and easier to sink into the storage area. In addition, they require less soil than a regular pot.

Give your bulbs every chance to put on a superior performance by potting them in a soil mixture with plenty of air spaces. I use equal parts compost, peat moss, and perlite. A bagged potting soil will work as well. Mix the ingredients thoroughly before potting, and place a piece of broken pot over the drainage hole before you fill the container.

The planting depth for each type of bulb will determine the amount of soil you put below the bulbs. With standard daffodil bulbs, you will hardly have room for more than a shallow layer. With these large bulbs, your goal is to have the tip of each bulb just showing above the soil and to have one-half inch of space between the soil line and the rim of the pot to allow for adding water. With smaller bulbs such as scillas and crocus, it is best to cover the bulbs completely with a half-inch layer of soil. Pack the soil carefully between the bulbs, because they may get pushed up as the roots form below.

Before you sink the bulbs into storage, water each pot thoroughly. Later in the fall, if the ground in the storage area is dry, be sure to water again. If you bury your bulbs in a coldframe or open trench, cover each pot with a generous layer of perlite or sand before adding soil to protect the shoots as they emerge. If you have extra pots available, turn these upside down and place one over each bulb pan.

Most bulbs require at least three months in storage to develop good root systems. Some daffodils require a full 16 weeks. To get the most out of these midwinter treats, plan your forcing schedule so you can bring a few pots into the house every couple of weeks starting in late January.

If this is your first attempt, stick with varieties recommended for forcing and try different types of bulbs to see which are best suited to your house. For example, I grow only a few pots of the larger daffodils because these look best on the floor or on a very low table, and I have limited floor area on which I can place pots without damaging the carpets.

Tender bulbs

If you don't have ready access to a cold storage area, try forcing tender bulbs into bloom. Paperwhites are very easy to do, but you can also have great success with hyacinths, amaryllis, and freesias.

First, let's consider hyacinths and paperwhites, which will bloom in a bowl of pebbles and water. You can also bloom a single hyacinth bulb in a hyacinth glass, one that has a special lip on which to suspend the bulb.

Plant hyacinths at two-week intervals from October through mid-December in a container four to five inches deep. Three good-sized bulbs will do nicely in a four-inch bowl. Fill the bowl about two-thirds full with pebbles, place the bulbs pointed end up on the pebbles, and surround the base of each bulb with more pebbles. Be sure to add these extra pebbles, because if you just set the bulbs on top of the pebbles, their roots are apt to push the bulbs out of the bowl. Add enough water to touch the base of the bulbs.

After planting, place the bulbs in a cool (50° to 55° F.), dark storage area. Check the water level periodically. If planted in early October, hyacinths should be ready to be moved from the storage area in early December and should bloom about three weeks later. Direct sun and high temperatures will shorten the life span of these and other bulb flowers, so keep them cool and in bright light.

Paperwhites, which can also be grown in pebbles and water, will bloom even more quickly. Plant them in mid-October and you should have blooms by Thanksgiving. For Christmas bloom, plant in mid-November. The yellow-flowered Soleil d'Or will also bloom in pebbles and water, but they may take a little longer than paperwhites.

Estimate the number of pots you want to bloom throughout the winter and buy the bulbs soon, shortly after they arrive at the garden center. By storing them in a cool, dark location, you'll give them better conditions than most stores can provide. If foliage grows tall and spindly and blooms are small or nonexistent, the plants have probably been too warm or have made insufficient root growth before being moved into full light.

Both hyacinths and paperwhites are fragrant, but freesias win the prize among bulbs for the most exotic, pervasive fragrance. Be warned, however, that you need a location where the light is bright and the nighttime temperature low, say 50° to 55° F. I have experimented with many varieties of freesias and have decided that I get the most pleasure from planting the mixed tetraploids. The stems and flowers are much stronger and the variety of colors brings joy in the dark days of late winter.

Freesias can be planted from September through November to provide a sequence of bloom. Plant bulbs as close as you can in well-drained potting soil in azalea pots, which are deeper than bulb pans, and cover with one inch of soil. Place in a cool, dark location until leaves appear, then move them into full sun with a nighttime temperature of 50° to 55° F. A greenhouse, sun porch, or large plant window provides the conditions needed for freesias.

Freesia leaves and stems are fragile and will definitely need staking, unless you grow bulbs in a hanging basket. Place bamboo stakes in pots as soon as leaves start to appear, then build a "cage" with black or dark green cotton thread to contain leaves and stems. As plants develop, encourage leaves to grow within the bounds of

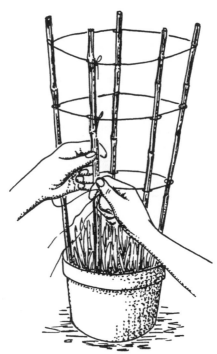

To support freesia stems and leaves, use bamboo canes, then build a "cage" with dark green or black cotton thread.

the strings. Staking later, when leaves are fully developed, is not as satisfactory.

The beauty of mulch

I am a mulch person, much to the chagrin of The Gardening Partner, who has long since tired of my never-ending search for organic matter. In the fall, I try to convince him that leaf-raking is a jolly, fruitful experience and that he should consider the leaves as bounty to be carefully collected and regarded with respect. With reluctance, he wields the rake and we haul the leaves up to the leaf pile. By late autumn, we have a pile about six feet high and 20 feet in diameter.

The following year, as soon as the spring crops of peas and lettuce have been harvested, I start hauling the leaves down the hill to add them to the vegetable garden as mulch. By this time, they are damp, smelly, and soggy, and the tannins have a way of staining your clothes, marking you forever as a leaf scavenger.

After hundreds of trips up the hill, we finally have every unplanted inch of garden covered with leaves, and at this point The

Gardening Partner can relax and enjoy the benefits of our labors. These benefits are considerable because we almost never have to weed the garden after early July, and the four- to six-inch layer of rotting leaves greatly reduces the need to water. Come fall, after we have removed the dead plants, The Gardening Partner readies his spade and turns the soil over, incorporating the decaying leaves.

This homily on leaves is intended to turn you into a leaf scavenger this fall. If you can find chopped leaves, so much the better because your pile will be neater and the product superior. If not, collect what you can and use them generously in your garden next summer. Leaves of oak and maple trees are acidic, but you can adjust the pH by adding lime when you turn the garden over in the fall after you use them as mulch.

Good garden soil is in itself almost a contradiction because you want it to be well drained as well as to have good water-retentive properties. Organic matter, with its large-surfaced, water-retentive particles, provides you with the latter property, and these same large particles provide air spaces for good drainage. Sand also increases the air spaces and therefore improves the drainage.

Winter foliage

Preserved leaves make wonderful fillers for holiday decorations or for dried and fresh flower arrangements. You can even arrange them by themselves and stage them against a blank wall or in a tall vase in the corner of a hall or living room, where their shadows create interesting patterns.

If you want the foliage to last for several months, drying the leaves is not just a matter of cutting the branches and bringing them indoors. If dried this way, the leaves will shrivel and fall from the branch quickly. To preserve the leaves, you must place the stems in a solution of glycerin and water, and wait until the solution has made its way up the stem and to the end of each leaf.

The success of this preserving technique depends on using the leaves from appropriate trees and shrubs. The stems and leaves of some, such as dogwood, maple, and tulip tree, shrivel before the glycerin solution has a chance to penetrate the leaves. The leaves of oak, beech, laurel (both cherry and mountain), skimmia, sarcococca, and rhododendron have worked beautifully for me and made long-lasting arrangements. If you are lucky enough to have access to the Southern magnolia (*Magnolia grandiflora*), you will find that these leaves will dry very successfully.

On the whole, the most suitable species have tough, leathery

131

leaves. Look around your garden for alternatives with such characteristics—leucothoe and andromeda are two other possibilities.

Buy glycerin in a drugstore. It is expensive, so choose your branches carefully, selecting a variety of leaf sizes and cutting branches that fit the size of the vase you plan to use. A small table arrangement would be appropriate for stems of shrubs such as skimmia, whereas branches of oak and beech are better suited to larger settings.

Cut branches of deciduous trees such as oak and beech before the leaves start to drop. Evergreen branches can be cut later; I have always had better luck by doing it before Thanksgiving.

Before you cut the stems, prepare the glycerin solution (one part glycerin to three parts warm water) and assemble your containers. Tall vases with wide necks are best for soaking large branches. If you find the container to be top-heavy, put a three- to four-inch layer of gravel or pebbles in the bottom.

Cut the branches, a few at a time, with a sharp pair of pruning shears, making your cuts just above a node. Remove leaves that would otherwise end up submerged in the solution. To allow the stems to absorb the glycerin mixture more quickly, smash the bottom three inches of each stem with a hammer before you place the branch in the vase. Fill the vase with the glycerin solution, and place the container in a cool room out of direct sunlight. As the mixture is absorbed, add more liquid so the cut ends are covered at all times. To avoid distorting the natural shape of branches, do not crowd them in the vases.

Gradually, the glycerin mixture will penetrate the leaves, making them supple and creating a branch that may be used in arrangements for several years. Oak and beech leaves will take four to six weeks to complete. Southern magnolia may take up to two months. Once the leaves have absorbed the glycerin solution, you can place the branches in a container without water.

Magnolia leaves turn a rich brown, beech a sandy brown, and oak a dark brown, closer to the color of the magnolia leaves. If you get tired of your dried arrangements by next spring, remove the branches from the vase, cover them with a plastic bag, and store them by hanging them upside down in the garage or attic. Leave open a slit at one end to discourage mold or mildew from forming. Next fall they should be in good shape and ready to use for another season.

NOVEMBER

The Best Time for a Lot of Chores

If you leave your garden cleanup too long, you'll be tempted to just wait until the spring. That would be a mistake, so do it now and avoid creating a home for garden pests. And your vegetable harvests need not be finished for the year— not if you pay attention to the later vegetables.

Some tips for early November ...

- If you're planning to add lime to a garden or lawn, spread it in winter so it can gradually work its way down into the soil in the next few months as the ground heaves and resettles with frost.

- Assemble mulch for covering overwintering vegetables such as carrots, leeks, and beets.

- Get out and rake the leaves. If you let them lie over winter on the lawn or in flower beds, they'll eventually form a dense, soggy mat that weakens grass and other plants. In wooded areas, on the other hand, let the leaves stay where they fall. They make an excellent mulch.

- **In the vegetable garden:** Plant lettuce and spinach in coldframes for early harvests next spring. ... Remove debris from the vegetable garden as quickly as possible. If you leave it on the ground, you're encouraging pests to overwinter in your garden.

❧ **For the flowers, shrubs, and trees:** There is still time to pot daffodils, tulips, scillas, grape hyacinths, and other bulbs for early spring blooms. Water pots well and store in a dark, cool location (40° to 45° F.) for 12 to 14 weeks. ... Remember to remove summer plantings of caladiums, cannas, and gladioli from the ground and to store the tubers and corms in a cool, dry place over winter. If your storage area is plagued by rodents, place the tubers in a metal can. ... If your plans for the holidays include buying a live tree, prepare its planting site this month before the ground freezes. Then you'll be able to plant the tree even if the ground is hard on the surface. Store the backfill where it won't freeze, and make sure you have some mulch handy to cover the exposed area after planting. ... Cheer up those window boxes and planters on your patio or deck by planting small evergreen shrubs. But remember to keep the soil moist throughout the winter. ... With garden mums over for the season, trim the plants back to six inches from the ground. Early next spring, you can dig up the clumps and separate them for another season's growth. ... Daffodil bulbs should be in the ground by now, but if yours are still sitting in the garage, get them in as soon as possible.

Some tips for late November ...

❧ Inspect houseplants frequently for insects—whitefly will rise in a cloud when you shake plants; white mealybugs, looking like cotton, nestle in leaf axils; aphids, which may be almost any color, cluster on tender new shoots sucking juices; scale insects, one of the most difficult varieties to defeat, have hard, brown shells. Spray with insecticidal soap mixed with pyrethrins.

❧ Jerusalem cherries make attractive holiday plants with their dark-green foliage and bright-red berries, but you'll find their berries won't last long unless you keep the plant in a cool nighttime location.

❧ Check your tools before winter. Wipe blades clean with a solvent, such as kerosene, to remove sap residue. Before storing, wipe each with oil to keep it rust-free. Drain gasoline from gas-powered equipment.

❧ Cacti and succulents can take full sun in a southern or southwestern window. Many can go from October to March with no water if the nighttime temperature in the growing area drops to 50° to 60° F. In warmer temperatures, you may have to water once a month.

🐚 Remember to check the bulbs you stored in the closet, the refrigerator, or outdoors. Make sure the soil is moist. Those stored in self-defrosting refrigerators are likely to dry out first, and the blooms will be less than satisfactory if you forget to water them.

🐚 Don't forget to drain garden pools and turn off and drain all outside water connections, after one final watering of newly planted landscaping.

🐚 **For the flowers, shrubs, and trees:** In the absence of rain during the next couple of weeks, soak newly planted trees and shrubs thoroughly once or twice more before the ground freezes. If you have time, do the same for established large-leaf evergreens such as rhododendron, laurel, skimmia, and andromeda. Within reason, the more moisture plants have at their root zones, the better equipped they are to withstand the pressures of frozen soil, drying wind, and winter sun. Small cyclamen, purchased this month, will flower until March or April if kept in a cool, brightly lit spot. … Now that growth has slowed down with the cooler weather, it's a good time to prune, just as long as you stay away from shrubs such as azaleas and rhododendrons that bloom in spring. Do these next spring, right after the blossoms fade. … Paperwhite narcissus make wonderful holiday gifts. Start them now in a dish of pebbles, then fill the dish with water up to the neck of the bulb. When you see green shoots emerging from the bulbs, place the pots in a bright, cool window.

NOVEMBER: A RACE AGAINST COLD WEATHER

A monthly overview

Gardeners will be busily involved in cleaning the summer's debris away from their vegetable gardens and moving it onto the compost pile. Try to get this done now before the cold weather sets in, when you will be tempted to leave the decaying vegetation on the ground until next year. Both flower and vegetable debris provide an excellent winter home for insects and diseases, placing them in a prime spot to develop rapidly in your garden next spring.

This time of year usually gives us wonderful crops of fall vegetables. The Gardening Partner is particularly pleased with the broccoli, lettuce, and spinach, and I am raving about the celeriac (celery root), Chinese cabbage, and turnips. The cauliflower is coming along, though it's always a race between getting decent-sized heads and a big frost. All of these vegetables will be listed in the seed catalogs, which should start to arrive in late December, and I commend them to your attention for next fall.

Frost will turn asparagus plants brown—your signal to remove the ferns. I cut mine almost to the soil line, leaving just enough stubble to mark the rows so I can fertilize the plants before new growth starts next spring.

Rhubarb plants will die down completely after a few hard frosts. Mark plant locations with stakes to avoid disturbing roots before growth begins next year.

If you still have carrots in the garden, plan to leave them in the ground for harvesting throughout the winter. After a couple of hard frosts, usually in late November and early December, cover the ground with a thick (18 to 24 inches) layer of leaves. Harvesting will be easier if the leaves have been chopped with a mulcher or mower because they won't pack down into a solid mat. Be sure to wait until the ground freezes before adding the leaves. If you add them earlier, you'll just encourage mice to settle in for the winter, making it extra convenient for them to nibble on your crop.

Over the years, I have experimented with various storage methods (lifting the carrots and storing them in the garage in sand, or freezing them) and have found that root vegetables keep best in the ground if I don't jump the gun on the mulching. As you dig throughout the winter, be sure to mark your progress down the row with a stick—one good snowfall makes it hard to find the winter's bounty.

Soil erosion is a problem every gardener should consider when putting the garden to bed. We try to alternate bare spaces where the soil might wash away with winter crops, such as carrots and leeks, and the spinach that was sown in September. The spinach tops may die down, but there are still roots to hold the soil. I also try to get the garden cleaned early enough so that the winter rye will germinate before the soil gets too cool—every root will hold another particle of soil during heavy winter rains. Some sections of the garden I dig over and leave bare and ready for planting the first crops in March—peas, lettuce, and more spinach.

The indoor garden

Amaryllis bulbs, available now in local garden centers, will bloom for the December holidays if you pot them up around Thanksgiving. Choose a deep pot, clay or plastic, with a diameter one inch larger than the widest part of the bulb. Use a basic houseplant potting mixture (equal parts soil, peat moss, and sand or perlite by volume, or a prepackaged mixture) and plant the bulb so that two-thirds of the neck rests above the soil line—which should be one-half inch below the rim of the pot to allow room to water. Amaryllis bulbs have long roots, so the easiest way to get the correct potting depth in the container is to hold the bulb in position and pour the soil around the roots that dangle below.

Water the soil thoroughly after packing it round the roots, then do not water again until you see signs of growth. Once the shoots start to appear, put the pot in full sun and water generously whenever the soil appears dry. Amaryllis are perfect apartment plants because they like warm temperatures—60° F. at night and 70° during the day. My house is considerably cooler, and the amaryllis eventually flower, but they take much longer than in a warm room. When the plant is in blossom, move the pot out of the full sun into bright light to prolong the life of the flowers.

Holiday cactus

Schlumbergera is their botanical name, but most of us call them either Thanksgiving or Christmas cactus. Their blooms are bright and, if you treat them right, you can bring the plants into bloom year after year. Large plants grow successfully in hanging baskets, or place a regular pot on an inverted pot so the stems can cascade down the sides.

Schlumbergera truncata flowers first, most commonly around Thanksgiving, with pink to deep red flowers. An easier name, claw cactus, will help you distinguish it from the Christmas cactus. Look for the deep notches on the stems. *S. buckleyi* has more rounded stems and blooms in December.

Both these cacti come from the tropical jungle, where they receive only filtered light. At home, keep them out of direct sun in summer, but in winter they can tolerate conditions in a south-facing window. The trick is to get them to flower in successive years. In early fall, flower buds start to form, and full flowering is initiated by the restricted light of shortening days. Once you see buds forming, remove the plants from rooms where the lights burn in the evening, or cover them with black plastic when the lights are switched on.

Unlike most cacti that prefer dry soil year round, keep the potting mixture for these varieties moist all the time, except for the winter months after flowering. As soon as you see new growth starting to appear in spring, resume heavier watering.

Trees and shrubs: There's still time

If you're behind with fall planting, there's still time to get trees and shrubs into the ground—if you do it before the ground freezes and you take a couple of precautions.

After planting, add a thick layer of woodchip or bark mulch to delay freezing of the ground around the rootball. That will give the roots as many days as possible to develop.

Now is also a good time for the trimming—for example, pruning rampant ivy from a wall—that was put aside when there were more pressing garden chores.

If you're overwhelmed by the leaves and can't get around to raking all of them as quickly as you'd like, try to remove those on the lawn and in ground-cover beds where they can do the most damage. Each year, I collect enormous piles of leaves in an out-of-sight place at the top of the garden. Over the winter, they mat down and in midsummer I haul them down to the vegetable garden, where they make wonderful mulch for The Gardening Partner's pole limas. In this setting, they're fine, but for my taste they're too coarse for flower beds, so we invested in a machine to chop them into a more refined mulch. The results are wonderful and I recommend such a machine for small gardens.

A good time to prune

With many leaves gone from trees, winter is a good time to prune because your cleaning chores are lighter and you can better see the structure of each plant.

Large trees are better left to a professional arborist, but with pole pruners, hand pruners, a small saw, and a pair of loppers, the home gardener can tackle many smaller jobs. I'm particularly fond of my folding saw and a pair of ratchet loppers, which make it possible to easily remove branches up to one inch in diameter.

On small trees and large shrubs, such as dogwoods and viburnums, you'll probably notice water sprouts, those long, skinny, upright branches. Remove them, along with branches that are obviously crossing and rub against each other.

When you prune, don't make your cuts flush with the branch. If you study tree structure, particularly the way one branch meets another and the way trees heal after pruning, you'll begin to notice natural collars forming around the cut areas. As you prune, try to leave these collars intact. If you cut flush to the stem, the healing process will be slower, and the possibilities for infection greater.

Tree wound paint may make you feel better because it covers up the pale-colored scar, but recent research shows that this, too, hinders healing.

Tackling the larger trees is an expensive proposition, but it's one of the best investments you can make in your property. Well-pruned and fertilized trees not only have longer lives, but you're in less danger of having to call the arborist in an emergency after a storm. More thoughts on that later in this chapter.

Winterizing

Probably the single most important thing you can do now is to make sure your plantings go into winter with ample moisture around their roots, especially if it has been a dry fall with ground moisture low and plants under stress.

When the soil freezes, what moisture there is becomes unavailable to the roots. Later, strong winds and late winter sun cause severe leaf burn and dessication. Broadleaf evergreens are especially susceptible to this kind of damage, as are new plantings with less developed root systems.

When you water, use a drip hose or add a water breaker to your hose, and run the water very gently until the rootball is thoroughly soaked.

Poor drainage is often the cause of winter damage. In poorly drained areas, moisture from heavy rains or melted snow lingers around the roots, then freezes. If you notice low spots where plants tend to die for no apparent reason, try improving the drainage there next year.

Fertilize in late fall so nutrients are available to the plant as soon as growth starts next spring. Commercial operators inject a liquid fertilizer into the root system of trees, but the gardener can spread fertilizer on top of the ground around each plant.

Many broadleaf evergreens, such as holly and rhododendron, may suffer structural damage from the weight of a heavy snowfall. Boxwood is especially fragile. To prevent this breakage, loop a rope around each of your most precious evergreens before mid-December to keep them pulled together and better able to withstand additional weight.

If a plant is small, you can wrap it in burlap. Never wrap plants in plastic, which acts as a greenhouse and can cause severe burning when the sun hits the plastic. For valuable broadleaf plants, especially those with a southwestern exposure, spray with an antidessicant to prevent water loss. Follow directions on the label and spray once in November and again in December. Apply the material only on warm days when the temperature is above 40° F.

Rodents can cause severe winter damage by chewing the bark at the base of a plant, eventually girdling it and cutting off circulation. Mulching close to plants encourages rodents to nest among them, so leave several inches around stems and trunks. Salt hay is especially appealing as a nesting site, so don't use this as a mulching material for woody plants. Salt hay is, however, ideal for perennials because it allows ample air circulation. Wait until after the soil is frozen before you spread the hay.

Garden resolutions

As I cleaned the garden one recent fall, I made a bunch of resolutions. Most likely, I'll get around to fulfilling only a few, but that will be progress. These are some of them:

Seeds. In mid-October, with temperatures in the 70s, I was longing to plant another row of spinach to mature in the spring, but my seed supply was exhausted. Local garden centers had long since returned their unused seeds, and for my Scottish soul it would have been too expensive to order just a couple of packets from a mail-order house. In future years, I'm going to make sure I order extra in spring.

Summer labor. The fall garden will be only as good as the time and effort you put into planning it in the summer. This means sowing seeds for broccoli and other cole crops in late June and doing the same for leafy vegetables toward the end of August. Let it slide, figuring you can always hustle to your local garden center to buy some transplants, and you'll probably find the shelves empty. I was once delighted to find some lettuce and broccoli, but my delight was premature. The leaves were off-color, and the plants obviously stressed. I bought them anyway because I was desperate. Each of the lettuces developed into a bitter plant and quickly went to seed. The broccoli fared better, but only slightly. The resolutions: Remember to sow my seeds and not to buy over-the-hill transplants, no matter how desperate I am.

Fall herbs. Coriander and chervil can both flourish in the fall from Labor Day sowings, and, with a little protection from a floating row cover (January, p. 169), there will be fresh pickings through this month. Dill is also spectacular in fall. The best way to get a good crop is just to let a couple of spring plants go to seed. Once the seed heads mature, scatter them where you'd like to see them grow later in the year.

Late harvests. Cover plants if it turns cold in September. Many years, we experience some cold nights, maybe even some frost, in late September. Some gardeners listen to the forecast dutifully, then pull out the old blankets, cover their tomatoes and peppers, and go on to enjoy several more weeks of production. In the future, if I resolve not to be so lazy about this, perhaps I, too, will be able to enjoy those late harvests.

Pole limas. As you surely know by now, these are the pride of The Gardening Partner's gardening year, and his patience plus a wonderful late summer enable us to keep picking until the third week of October. After some of those cold nights in late September, I begged him to allow me to start tearing down the vines so we could plant the winter rye. He was convinced that some of the small pods would eventually mature—and he was right. In the future, I'll try to be more patient, too.

Good fences make good gardens

The Gardening Partner's step was full of bounce one May, and I heard him cooing with pride to the neighbors about his thriving, eight-inch-high pea plants. "The crop looks good—not bad for an old farmer," he would say. (I ignored the odd nature of the "farmer" concept, since he had been in the toilet-paper business most of his life.) I went away for a couple of days and returned to find him dejected.

"Someone, something ate three rows of my pea vines last night." We investigated. There were no telltale footprints, and the vines had been neatly and precisely cut down to about three inches high.

That evening, while we were eating supper, we saw the culprit. A fat, sassy groundhog lumbered its way up and over the three-foot wire fence surrounding the plants and resumed its neat chomping.

We urged our dogs down the hill. The lazy Labrador barely moved off the porch. Suzy, the crazy poodle, cornered the thief in the garden, but then we got scared that she wouldn't be able to handle it, so we called her off and retreated while the groundhog hurdled the fence and headed for the woods. A friend lent us a trap, but the groundhog evaded it. The devastation continued nightly. The clever critter even removed the melon rinds we used for bait.

The Gardening Partner jury-rigged an additional section of chicken wire onto the existing fence. The peas struggled to produce a new crop of shoots. And eventually, we enjoyed a few small bowls of delicious peas.

All summer, as the limas grew where the peas had been planted earlier, we debated putting up a taller fence. Finally, we erected a

141

massive enclosure. It's as ugly as can be, but it seems to be keeping out the groundhogs, rabbits, and deer. If you want to grow vegetables, there seems to be no other way.

Raising houseplants

One of the keys to success in raising houseplants is to know the plant's name so you can quickly check out its basic requirements in a gardening book. Most garden centers provide an identification tag for each plant; if your selection is not marked, be sure to ask for its identification before you leave the store.

Light is the critical factor for most home gardeners in determining which plants will survive in their homes. Plant books tend to talk about direct sunlight (which enters an unobstructed south-facing window most of the day); bright light (found in areas close to those that get direct sunlight); medium light (found close to a north window or near an east window where an outside object such as a tree deflects the sun's rays); and poor light (usually found in corners at least eight feet away from a direct source of light).

In summer, direct sunlight shining through glass may burn even such sun-tolerant plants as geraniums, but during winter, many plants will benefit from the rays in a south-facing window. When you bring a new plant home, place it in the area you think most appropriate, then watch it carefully for the first few weeks.

Cooler temperatures benefit most houseplants (and their owners, for that matter). But some, such as certain members of the gesneriad family, prefer it warmer. If you have a cool house, try succulents, dwarf pomegranates, citrus plants (such as Calomondin orange and Meyer's or Ponderosa lemon), and scented-leafed geraniums in locations with direct sunlight. In bright light, try begonias, cyclamen, pittosporum, streptocarpus, and podocarpus. In medium light, you should succeed with pony-tail palm, Swedish ivy (*Plectranthus australis*), German ivy (*Delairea odorata*), Swiss cheese plant (*Monstera deliciosa*), Norfolk Island pine (*Araucaria heterophylla*), and peace lily (*Spathiphyllum* Clevelandii).

In summer, the gardener who overwaters can usually get by without too many sick plants because high temperatures and good light mean that plants will need lots of water. In winter, when in doubt, skip the watering and wait until the next day. Cooler temperatures and lower light greatly reduce water needs from October through mid-March.

Drooping leaves are the most obvious indication that a plant needs water, but the color of the soil can also be a useful indicator.

If the soil mixture is shrinking away from the edges of the pot, the upper layers are dry.

Durable houseplants

Some houseplants, such as poinsettias or Easter azaleas, put on a magnificent show once a year and then their owners must either relegate them to the compost pile or wait many months before the next display. Then there are the durable houseplants that change little with the seasons and provide a green backdrop for flowering plants.

For a plant to fit in the durable category in our house, it must be long-lived, relatively slow-growing, and able to survive periods of neglect. Jade, Norfolk Island pine, Natal plum, and rhipsalis are some of the successes among the durable houseplants in my indoor garden.

The jade (*Crassula ovata*) came from a neighbor as a small cutting. Ten years later, it was about three feet high and two feet wide with a thick trunk. The branches are graceful and pendulous, creating a form very different from that of its younger days.

Jades are adaptable. Although they will do best in full sun, ours has grown successfully for many years in an east-facing basement window. From time to time, I rotate the pot to discourage the plant from becoming lopsided. The temperature in the basement may go as low as 50° F. at night, but jade will also flourish in warmer climates. Water your jade infrequently and only when the soil is completely dry. Feed it once in March and again in midsummer.

Sickly Norfolk Island pines, frequently seen in restaurants and office buildings, are usually the victims of high temperatures, too much sun, and dry soil. Keep these plants in good light but out of direct sun, water them when the soil gets dry on top of the rootball, and feed them on the same schedule as the jade. Plants grown in a daytime temperature of 65° to 70° F. with a 10- to 15-degree drop at night should remain green and healthy. Each year, a healthy Norfolk Island pine will grow about three to six inches, so make sure you can accommodate this plant later in its career as a durable houseplant.

In Florida, Natal plum (*Carissa macrocarpa*) makes an attractive hedge. Up north, dwarf varieties such as Boxwood Beauty and *C. macrocarpa* Nana make wonderful pot plants. By nature, the dwarf varieties are pendulous, so I grow mine in hanging baskets. The Natal plum needs full sun in a west-facing window and, despite its thick evergreen leaves, requires plenty of water. Dry soil causes the leaves to yellow and drop. In spring, this plant will produce fragrant, white flowers that must be pollinated before they will develop into red fruit. For several winters, our Natal plum has survived in 50° to 55° F. nighttime temperatures, but they will also grow in warmer situations.

Because the genus *Rhipsalis* is in the cactus family, it seemed logical to place my tiny new *R. capilliformis* in full sun and water it very sparingly. Apparently this was not the right treatment, and before it expired I discovered that unlike most cacti, rhipsalis is native to the jungle. In its native habitat, it is a plant that grows on another and derives moisture from the air, and it will grow, like an orchid, in osmunda fiber and other soilless mixes. Ours has flourished in a regular soil mixture with additional perlite.

Many rhipsalis are pendulous and look nice in hanging baskets. As in the jungle, a damp atmosphere is preferable. Some varieties have thin stems, others thick and fleshy, somewhat like a Christmas cactus. When small, plants may look ugly. As the basket fills out, it can become an attractive specimen. In summer, hang the rhipsalis outside in the shade well away from direct sun.

The cyclamen: Winter's finest

If you keep your house reasonably cool, there's no better investment for a winter flowering houseplant than a cyclamen. Some years, I've managed to keep my purchases in bloom from mid-November until early April.

In the old days, the large cyclamen looked good for only a few weeks after purchase, but selections and breeding developments in Holland and Japan have produced a new generation of cyclamen that is much more tolerant of home conditions. For the most tolerant of all, select the dwarf varieties, which also have the advantage of sweet-smelling blooms and in some cases attractive, mottled leaves.

Cool temperatures are the key to long-lasting blooms on cyclamen. Place your plant in an area where it will receive bright light, but not direct sunlight. Be sure to keep it away from heat vents, and if you can't keep the house cool all the time, at least turn down the thermostat at night.

It's best to keep the cyclamen with other plants on a tray of damp pebbles, because together plants will maintain higher humidity than if they are scattered around the house. When plants are on a tray of pebbles, watering is easy because you just let the water run out the drainage holes. If your plant is in a saucer, take it to the sink and let the water run out the drainage holes before putting it back in the saucer. Most plants—cyclamen included—don't like sitting in a pool of water. Fertilize cyclamen monthly throughout the winter with a houseplant fertilizer.

As flowers fade and leaves turn yellow, pull them off. Don't cut them. Although it's possible to hold cyclamen over to bloom the following winter, I've always found it to be unsatisfactory and would prefer to invest in a new plant the next fall.

Resume cuttings

For the propagator who has been taking it easy over the last couple of months, the time has come to get back into the business of plant reproduction. From mid-November through early January, the time is ripe to take cuttings of both hardwood deciduous plants and narrow-leafed evergreens.

By month's end, the leaves on most deciduous plants will have fallen completely and the cool weather will have stopped growth. Shrubs such as callicarpa, calycanthus, deutzia, forsythia, forthergilla, spirea, privet, and weigela as well as trees such as dawn redwood, franklinia, halesia, and willow are ready to propagate from hardwood cuttings.

With hand pruners, cut the current year's growth of pencil thickness into six- to eight-inch lengths with at least two nodes. Bundle the cuttings into groups of 10 to 25, label them, and tie with string, keeping all tops pointing in one direction.

Cuttings can be stored outside, in a well-drained location covered by at least four inches of soil, or in the refrigerator. In either case, first treat the bottom ends with a rooting hormone. If you plan to store them in the refrigerator, surround the cuttings with moist peat moss and seal the bag. If you place them outside, omit the plastic bag but mulch heavily with leaves to retard the ground from freezing.

Throughout the winter, the cuttings will gradually undergo the initial processes necessary for root production. In late March or early April, dig up the cuttings or get them out of the refrigerator, separate them, and plant them individually in a shallow trench. Make sure you keep all the tops facing upward, and plant with only the uppermost bud showing above the soil line. Firm the soil and water well, watering again during dry spells. Rooting should occur within several weeks, but leave the cuttings in the same place at least until the following spring.

Narrow-leafed evergreens can be successfully propagated in December and January using a simple propagating box covered with clear polyethylene plastic, such as I mentioned on page 91.

Make your cuttings early in the day and, if you are away from home, be sure to carry a plastic bag and some moist paper towels in which to transport the cuttings. If plants are frozen, wait for a warmer day. Make terminal cuttings six to eight inches long with a sharp knife or pruners. If you are propagating dwarf conifers, your cuttings will be much smaller.

Strip away about half of the needles, starting from the cut, and dip the ends into a rooting hormone. Buy only a small quantity of hormone at one time because its effectiveness diminishes with age. Knock off excess hormone before inserting about one-third of the cutting into the rooting mix. Be sure to label all cuttings with name and date.

Throughout the winter, your propagating box should sit in a cool location (45° to 55° F.) in good light but out of the sun. Direct rays will build up excessive heat under the plastic cover and damage the cuttings. Check the rooting medium from time to time. It should remain moist but not soggy. Rooting will take four weeks to several months. Next April, plant the cuttings outside in semi-shade, and water well in dry spells.

The possibilities for propagating among the needled evergreens are endless. Try arborvitae, chamaecyparis, cryptomeria, juniper, and yew for a start. You might also try some broad-leafed evergreens such as holly, leucothoe, andromeda, and skimmia using this method.

Tree care

Two scarlet oaks, one elegant white oak, one sweet gum, one large hemlock, some white ash, pines and spruce, and an assortment of dogwood trees are among my best-loved "possessions." The oaks shield the front of the house from the western sun; the black gum provides shade for the terrace; the hemlock obscures the neighbor's house; and the dogwoods are beautiful 12 months a year.

The trees in your garden are irreplaceable assets. A good sodding job can repair a lawn within 24 hours. A trip to the local garden center can help produce a gorgeous flower garden within a few weeks. But mature trees cannot be bought at any price. Even if you plant a large and expensive tree, it may be 20 years before it will give you the shade you need.

Such an asset deserves care, attention, and long-range planning. It also may entail considerable expense, so it pays to learn as much as you can about your trees and their needs. If you are well informed, you have a better chance of getting a good return on the money you invest to keep this asset viable.

Whether you have a new lot or an old house, your first challenge is to find a reliable arborist or tree surgeon. To get the right person may take time. Look for a person with whom you can establish a long-term relationship—someone who will take a personal interest in your trees and make long-term recommendations so you can spread out the expense over the years.

For the most part, you may find the extension service and local arboretums reluctant to recommend specific arborists. Endorsement of a commercial operator or product is not in keeping with their goals. Your best source of information will be lists provided by some of these organizations, and your friends and neighbors; failing these sources, check the Yellow Pages under "Tree Service" to find arborists in your area. Some of them have completed examinations to become Certified Arborists. This would be another good check.

Ask two or three companies to give you an estimate. Request that each arborist suggest a long-term plan for your property and then have him or her break it down into manageable annual chunks. Insist on receiving a written proposal for work you plan to have done this year. Be sure to ask your arborist for proof of full insurance coverage and, if you plan to do any pest control, make sure that the person is fully licensed to use restricted pesticides.

Insurance coverage is important in all cases and especially if you are dealing with a tree person who is moonlighting on evenings or weekends. Although these people may be covered when working for their employer, they may not be covered when working as individuals.

As with any other estimates, you may find large price discrepancies. If one of the tree estimates is very low, check into it carefully before signing. Abnormally low estimates can mean that the operator plans to use low-grade chemicals or fertilizers; that he or she may ruin the trees by pruning carelessly in a hurry; or that he or she is an inexperienced estimator and therefore may be an inexperienced arborist.

As with any other important work on your property, it's best to be on hand while your tree work is being done. And remember, pruning your trees is like painting the Brooklyn Bridge. As soon as you get to one end, it's time to start all over again.

By the way, if some of the work requires getting access to drive chippers or getting other equipment across the lawn, make sure that work is done in the winter, when the ground is frozen and the damage will be minimal.

147

DECEMBER

A Month of Rest, But Not Too Much Rest

You've earned a rest, and this is the month to get it. And how's this for getting extra bang for the buck: Many of the month's gardening tasks—acquiring and disposing Christmas trees, choosing plant gifts, growing orchids—involve fun holiday activities, too.

Some tips for early December ...

꿈 If you plan to purchase a live, balled and burlapped Christmas tree, dig your planting hole now rather than face solid, frozen ground on New Year's Day. Put the fill dirt in an area where it will not freeze and keep the hole open by filling it with loose mulch. Surround the hole with stakes to avoid accidents.

꿈 If you haven't already taken this precaution, turn off the lines to your outside water faucets and drain the pipes. If you did some planting this fall, give the newly planted trees and shrubs one last dose with the hose before you close the pipes.

꿈 Cyclamen make wonderful holiday plants. If you buy them now and keep them in a cool room with high humidity, you should have blooms through early spring.

꿈 Take another turn around the garden, and remove leaves in flower beds and on the lawn.

🌿 **In the vegetable garden:** Before it gets too uncomfortable to hold onto the pruners, cut back your raspberries and blueberries. With the raspberries, you should have removed the old and weak canes last summer after they bore fruit. Cut back the remaining canes to shoulder height to lessen the chances of their breaking. For the first few years after you plant them, confine your pruning of blueberry bushes to removing dead branches. Once the plants start to mature, your goal is to rejuvenate each bush on a five- to six-year cycle by removing a few of the older branches each year. You should also remove branches that grow toward the center of the bush. ... If you still have root vegetables such as beets and carrots in the ground, plan to mulch them with four to six inches of chopped leaves after the soil starts to freeze.

🌿 **For the flowers, shrubs, and trees:** If you laid amaryllis bulbs on their sides in the late summer so they could go dormant for a few months, pull out the pots, place the bulbs in fresh soil, and water to encourage them to develop new growth. Water only when the soil dries out. ... If you bring home cut blooms, recut the stems on an angle so that only the points of the stems rest on the base of the container. Place the stems in a tall vase or bucket of warm water for several hours, preferably overnight, before arranging them. ... Gardeners who potted bulbs to bloom in the spring should check them from time to time to be sure the soil is moist. If you have them outside in a coldframe with the lid up, things are probably all right. If they are stored in the cellar, the attic, or a window well, they may need attention. When you water, be sure there's a place for the water to drain away so the pots are not sitting in a pool. If you stored the bulbs covered in a refrigerator, check not only for moisture, but also to make sure that there's no mold growing on the soil. If there is, scrape it away and cut a few holes in the covers to increase ventilation.

Some tips for late December ...

🌿 Before you start ordering from next summer's seed catalogs, go through your seed storage box or drawer to determine what will germinate next year and what should be tossed away. Before you order, make a plan for the vegetable garden that includes some new experiments along with all your old favorites.

🌿 When you take down the holiday tree, cut the limbs from the trunk and use them as mulch for perennials, strawberries, and small, delicate shrubs. The danger for these plants in winter is that they get

149

heaved out of the ground as it freezes and thaws. When the inevitable midwinter warm spell occurs, your pine or fir branches will help keep the ground frozen.

❧ Poinsettias will do best in good light, with night temperatures around 65° to 70° F. and moist but not soggy soil.

DECEMBER: THE DARKEST MONTH

A monthly overview

December should be a fairly restful month for most area gardeners. The lawn mower is tucked away, the leaves have been cleaned up, and after a hard frost you won't even have to feel guilty about the vegetable garden you never got around to digging over. But just in case you get restless, here are a couple of reminders to keep you busy until the first of the year.

First, the outdoor garden.

For starters, hose down hand tools, remove mud, allow them to dry, then spread a light coat of oil on their metal parts. If you haven't done so already, be sure to drain outside faucets and bring in all hoses and watering cans.

If weeds such as chickweed are growing rampant among the late crops, remove as many as you can before the freeze to prevent them from taking over your garden in the spring.

December through early March is the time to prune fruit trees. Start with the apples and pears in early winter, leaving the peaches and nectarines until early March.

In mid-December, check your evergreens to see if there are some you might prune to use as holiday decorations. Yew, holly, box, juniper, pine, and spruce are among those that will last well indoors. Use a sharp pair of shears and make all your cuts just above a node. By pruning to a node, you will avoid unsightly stubs.

Next, tend to your indoor garden.

For the friend who seems to have everything, why not pot up a few paperwhites as a holiday gift? Find an attractive five- to six-inch bowl, half fill it with pebbles, and set the paperwhites on the pebbles, touching each other. Depending on the size of the bulbs, you may get six to eight into each bowl. Pack more pebbles around the bulbs, fill the bowl with water, and set it in a shady, cool place (one with a nighttime temperature of 50° to 55° F.). When the foliage emerges, move the bowls into a well-lit, cool area. The bulbs will bloom in three to four weeks.

Try to provide as much humidity for the houseplants as possible by grouping them together, or at least setting each one in a saucer filled with damp pebbles. Water according to the needs of the plants, rather than on a schedule. With the low light of winter, most houseplants will need less water than they do in the other seasons. Water heavily and infrequently, rather than a little several times a week. And do it over the sink so the water can run through. Never leave a plant in a saucer full of water.

Careful monitoring will take you a long way toward preventing outbreaks of pests and diseases. Clear away yellow and rotting leaves promptly. Inspect plants frequently, searching for the pests most common on houseplants. Suspect sticky residue on leaves or the surface on which the plants sit—the floor or a table. Aphids will sometimes excrete this sticky material, but they're relatively easy to spot. Scale also creates a sticky mess, and this is harder to pick up early because you often don't notice the little brown bumps.

Red spider mites are minuscule, so you need to be wary of the symptoms rather than looking for the culprit. Yellowing leaves and webbing will clue you in. The best preventive measure is washing the plants frequently under the kitchen faucet or in the shower.

Good news: Orchids have gotten easier

Orchid growing was once shrouded in mystery and because plants were propagated mainly by division, the most desirable varieties were extremely expensive. Today, the scene has changed and both amateur and professional growers generously share their information. In addition, many new and easier-to-grow hybrids have been developed, and propagation by tissue culture has reduced the cost per plant of even the choicest varieties.

An orchid plant makes a wonderful gift for a gardener because the blooms will last for several weeks and because the person to whom you make the gift should, with a few tips, be able to bring it back into bloom in subsequent years.

Good light is essential to ensure bloom. On north- and west-facing windowsills, orchids probably will put out only vegetative growth. On south- and southeast-facing sills, they should bloom.

Here are some suggested orchid choices:

Phalaenopsis. These orchids, known as moth orchids, are the ones most commonly sold as houseplants. Their mothlike flowers form on a long spike that will stay in bloom in normal house tem-

151

peratures for several weeks. Ideally, the day temperature for this orchid should be 70° to 85° F., with a drop to 60° to 65° at night. I'm stingy with the heat and can regretfully assure you that a phalaenopsis won't work for you if you like your house really cool at night. Give this orchid bright light without direct sun.

Paphiopedilum. This plant requires light conditions similar to those for phalaenopsis, but the green-leaf varieties can tolerate cooler temperatures, as low as 50° to 60° F. at night. Those with mottled leaves prefer temperatures similar to those for phalaenopsis. The cooler the temperature, the more care you need to take in watering to avoid rotting.

Cattleya. This is another very popular orchid for home display and is often used as a cut flower for corsages and bouquets. Like most cultivated orchids, these plants are epiphytic, or air plants, and have developed water-storage organs and large, fleshy roots covered with a spongy, water-retentive layer. As with most orchids, pot them in a porous, free-draining medium such as fir bark. Give a cattleya bright light, with some sun and night temperatures between 55° and 60° F. Since home-growing of orchids has become so popular, breeders have developed a whole range of mini-cattleyas, which are well suited to growing on windowsills or under lights.

Cymbidium. These are best suited for people with a garden or an outdoor porch because the plants must have a cool period in the fall (to 40° F. at night for several weeks) to induce flower buds. For the rest of the year, they require bright light with nighttime temperatures between 45° and 60° F., although the miniature cymbidiums are more temperature-tolerant and can handle warmer temperatures throughout the year.

Oncidiums. These orchids do best in an intermediate to warm growing condition and have wonderful, delicate sprays of flowers. They, too, like bright light, but not full sun. During spring and summer months, water oncidiums frequently and do not let the plants dry out between waterings.

A few general thoughts:

Windowsill growers must watch for leaf burn. From early November through late January, there is no danger of leaf burn in our area, but in February, the stronger light can push the leaf temperature beyond 105° F., the point at which the leaf will burn and become disfigured. To eliminate the potential for burning, tack up a piece of gauze over the window frame. After the middle of May, orchids can be placed outside, until the nights turn cool at the end of September.

Orchids need a daily variation in temperature, such as a house temperature in winter of 65° to 70° F. during the day, with a

10-degree drop at night. On all fertilizer containers, you will find a series of three numbers, indicating the percentage of nitrogen, phosphorus, and potassium. For orchids, select a fertilizer such as 15-30-15, with a high percentage of phosphorus.

One key to success with many orchids is the potting mixture, and each grower has a favorite. Some use tree fern, some fir bark, and some combinations of both, mixed with charcoal and perlite.

High humidity is important to all plants and especially for successful orchid growing. Humid-grow trays, which can be placed under lights or on windowsills, are now available through orchid supply catalogs and dealers and have worked well for orchid growers. Each tray is equipped with a grate that sits on top of the tray. When you water, the excess flows into the tray, which acts as a basin and a source of humidity. Periodically remove the plants and wash the trays and grates in soapy water to hold down diseases.

In with the Christmas tree

Buying a Christmas tree is largely a matter of personal preference. I tend to favor orphan trees of strange shapes. The Gardening Partner places more emphasis on symmetry and abhors the ones I select that

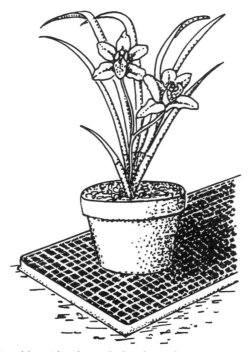

To provide additional humidity for orchids, place plants on Humid-grow trays.

have more than one bad side. Regardless, though, the early birds who buy their trees in mid-December and store them under the right conditions have the best chance of seeing those trees last once they're inside the house. Cut holiday trees are best kept out of sun and wind. When you get the tree home from the nursery or roadside stand, recut its base and place the butt in a bucket of water.

All cut evergreens inevitably dry out, but some dry out and lose their needles faster than others. Concolor fir is probably the best needle-holder, followed by Douglas fir, Fraser fir, white pine, Scotch pine, Colorado spruce, and Balsam spruce. Once you get the tree into the house, be sure that the base is in water, that the tree is kept away from a heating vent or from the dry heat of a wood stove, and that the room is as cool as possible.

Live trees are increasingly popular, and almost any live evergreen can be used as a holiday tree. Let your home-landscaping needs determine the variety you choose. Good spruces are Colorado, Norway, white, and Serbian. Douglas firs are also good for this area, although Fraser fir has problems handling our warm summers. White pines are also popular, and the irregular character of the black pine complements design elements in contemporary homes.

Buy a tree with a decent-sized ball, but not so big that you have to hire a crane to get it into the house. Avoid dramatic temperature changes moving the tree in and out. If it's very cold when you plan to bring the tree into the house, do it in stages. For instance, use an unheated garage as a way station—and reverse the process when you put the tree outside.

The rootball must be kept damp, so set the tree in a waterproof container or in several layers of heavy plastic, then cut slits in the top of the ball and gradually pour in enough water to dampen it. Add more water as needed, but never let the ball sit in a pool of water. That's a quick way to a dead tree.

Out with the Christmas tree

There's always a debate in our household as to when the Christmas tree should be taken down. If it's a live tree, I suggest not keeping it in the house for more than 10 days. There are two schools of thought about the best planting time for a live holiday tree. Some gardeners recommend holding the plant in a garage or unheated shed until spring. Others suggest planting as soon as possible after the holidays when the temperature outside is above 30° F. Whichever method you choose, when you plant it outside, set the ball at the same height as it was in the nursery, even an inch or so higher, water heavily, and add a three- to four-inch layer of wood-chips or pine bark mulch to retard freezing of the soil around the ball.

A cut tree can obviously stay in the house longer, but as it dries in the house its potential as a fire hazard increases. The branches of holiday trees make great protection for parts of your garden throughout the rest of the winter. You may even want to pick up discarded trees and piles of cut greens in the neighborhood to swell your mulch inventory. Evergreen boughs make good protection for perennials, newly planted bulbs, strawberry plants, and even plants such as camellias, whose thick evergreen leaves may burn in the late winter sunshine.

The theory behind winter protection for perennials, bulbs, and strawberries is that once the ground is frozen, you should try to keep it frozen. In most winters, a period of severe weather is followed by a couple of weeks of warmer weather during which the ground thaws, then quickly freezes again. Under these circumstances, the perennials and strawberries are heaved out of the ground, leaving their roots exposed. If you cover the ground with a layer of boughs, it is less likely to thaw and thus you reduce the possibility for heaving and root damage.

If you are a camellia fan, or have some special large-leafed evergreens such as rhododendrons, consider using your evergreen boughs to protect these plants. In the Northeast, February and March are key months in the battle for survival of the large-leafed evergreens. The strength of the late winter sunshine increases, but the ground still may be frozen. As the sun beats down on the leaves, the leaf temperature rises and transpiration begins. The plant cannot, however, supply the required moisture through its roots because the soil is frozen. So the leaves become disfigured by sun scald.

Shelter your plants from the damaging rays by placing boughs, or even whole trees, between the plants and the sun. For plants close to the house, remove one side of the branches of your Christmas tree and lean it against the building, creating a little sun tent for the large-leafed evergreen.

Plants make good gifts

As you might expect when it comes to holiday gifts, I'm biased toward greenery and flowers, mostly because I think of plants as a luxury that most people won't buy for themselves.

When you're shopping, be picky. Don't hastily take the first plant at the front of the bench. Pick a couple of likely candidates and turn them around, inspecting for yellowing leaves, pests, or diseases. Look for buds rather than flowers so the plant will last a decent length of time. And, most important as you shop, think of the recipients and consider their home growing conditions.

Poinsettias are the most popular plant for the holiday season, and for good reason. Breeders have worked hard to produce plants that bloom cheerfully for several weeks, often under impossible conditions. Just imagine spending your holiday season in a hot, dry, dusty lobby of an office building.

To get the most out of a poinsettia, set it in an area with good light, keep the soil moist, and give the plant some dilute fertilizer from time to time. If you can reduce the temperature at night, so much the better. Inadequate light and blasts of dry air will cause leaves to drop prematurely, so keep the plant away from air ducts.

People often ask if they can hold their poinsettia over for another year. The answer is yes, but you will never be able to produce the same effect it had the year you bought it. Growers start poinsettias fresh from cuttings each year, then grow them in conditions where the day length is adjusted to make sure the plant puts on a show at holiday time. If you put the poinsettia outside for the summer and treat it as you would any houseplant, it will thrive, but once you bring it back into the house in the fall, it's unlikely that you will be able to reproduce the conditions the plant enjoyed in a greenhouse the year before. So, once its leaves start to yellow, add the plant to the compost pile.

Amaryllis. This bulb will thrive almost anywhere, be it a cool house or an overheated apartment. For the gardeners on your holiday list, look for a precooled and preplanted bulb and suggest that they set the pot in a bright window and water it generously. Others like an immediate splash and would prefer to receive the plant in flower. In either case, the adventurous gardener should be able to get the amaryllis to bloom again the following year.

Ardisia. With leathery leaves and delightful red berries that may last several months, this plant will grow in a north or east window where the temperature is 65° to 70° F. in the daytime, 10 degrees cooler at night. Keep the soil moist and fertilize once a month with an acid-forming, soluble fertilizer. Lightly spray foliage weekly to remove dust, and set the pot in a shaded location during the summer.

Azaleas. These plants require treatment similar to ardisia and should bloom in future years if you can provide semi-shade in summer and cool temperatures next fall in preparation for blooming.

Cinerarias. With brightly colored flowers, these are the perfect plants for friends who might not enjoy the challenge of figuring out what to do with a plant a couple of weeks after receiving it. Once its blooms are over, there's little point in keeping the plant around. Keep cinerarias away from drafts and place them in full to filtered light in cool areas with their soil kept constantly moist.

Cyclamen. These are my favorite gift plants. There's nothing raucous about their red or pink flowers, and the white varieties are better yet. Grow them in a cool (60° to 65° F. by day, 10 degrees cooler at night), humid atmosphere, and water the soil before it dries out. Strong filtered light and a monthly dose of houseplant fertilizer may keep them blooming until March or April.

Gloxinia. Elegant, sensitive plants that resent environmental changes, gloxinias will be hard to rebloom unless you have a greenhouse or plant room. To make them last as long as possible, grow them in strong, filtered light in daytime temperatures of 65° to 70° F., and lower the thermostat at night. Provide as humid an atmosphere as possible by setting the plants on a tray of pebbles and keeping the pebbles and the soil in the pot constantly moist.

Fresh flowers: Springtime in the winter

There's nothing I like better than having fresh flowers around the house. Even a small bunch of freesias makes it seem like spring when the winter wind is howling outside.

If you go on a binge and buy flowers this winter, take special care to keep them fresh as long as possible. Save your flower purchases until you've done your other errands, so you can get the blooms home as quickly as possible. Once you take the flowers out of the wrapper, strip all the leaves that would be below the level of the water, then cut a small piece of stem using a sharp knife. If you make your cut with pruners you'll crush the stems, whereas a slanted cut with a sharp knife or razor blade allows the stem to take up the maximum amount of water. Plunge all stems into a deep container filled with water.

Let the flowers sit in the bucket for several hours or overnight before you arrange them. Use a floral preservative in the vase water. Commercial products are available from florists.

If you're using one of those green blocks (a common brand is Oasis) that go in a container to keep the flowers in place, be sure to soak the block for several hours before you put it into the vase and start arranging.

Look around the house for suitable containers to use as vases. Jugs or pots with edges that flare out at the top are the easiest to use. Keep them clean by washing with detergent and household bleach after use. Once your arrangement is in place, top off the vase with fresh water daily.

The carefree houseplant

Do you ever get the feeling that your houseplants tie you down? Or that you forget to water them more days than you remember? If your answer to either is yes, maybe you should give up your thirsty begonias, African violets, and spider plants and concentrate on succulents.

"Succulent" is the descriptive term for all plants that store water in fleshy leaves and stems. Within this group is found the cactus family as well as genera such as Echevaria, Rhipsalis, and Lithops. In winter, many succulents can go for weeks without water. In summer, they need more water but you can usually go away for a week's vacation and leave them untended.

My succulent collection is small, but with even a few plants I have a marvelous diversity of foliage colors and leaf shapes. If I had to pick one genus as a favorite, I would go for the echevarias. They grow in rosette form with leaf colors varying from blue-green to purple to shades of pink. The intensity of the foliage color will vary with the growing conditions; the more light, the more intense the foliage color. When echevarias become leggy and unattractive, cut off the top rosette and root it in perlite or sand. Within a few weeks you will have the beginning of a new compact plant.

Species in the genus Graptopetalum are also available in a dizzying array of foliage colors. These leaves also form rosettes. If you are just beginning with succulents, this is a good place to start because species such as *Graptopetalum paraguayense, G. pachyphyllum,* and *G. filiferum* are adaptable and easy to grow. Euphorbias such as *Euphorbia bupleurifolia, E. multiceps,* and *E. francoisii* are also good for home gardeners.

These are just a few succulents for starters. Now the question is how to take care of them. In winter, all succulents will benefit from full sun in a south-facing window. From March to November, succulents from the jungle, such as Thanksgiving and Christmas cacti, ephiphyllums, and rhipsalis should be placed in filtered light out of direct sun.

Happily, succulents will tolerate a wide range of temperatures. Most can be grown in 70° F. homes as well as 40° sun porches. In summer, I place all but the jungle cacti outside in full sun.

All succulents should be planted in a quick-draining soil mix. I prefer to use equal parts commercial potting soil and sand or perlite. For top-heavy succulents, I use the sand mix to give additional weight to the pot.

Your watering schedule will vary with type of plant, soil mixture, and pot size. As a general guideline, from October through April most succulents (other than those native to the jungle that need more water) will require water only once every three to four weeks. By midsummer, you will be watering every five to seven days, depending on the amount of sunshine. Fertilize succulents once a year in early summer. Jungle types should be fertilized once a month from April through October.

Houseplant resolutions

With the new year just ahead, now is the time to sow a few suggestions about New Year's resolutions regarding houseplants. Healthy houseplants, like healthy children and pets, don't just happen. They need lots of tender, loving care mixed in with a good dose of common sense. Even then, you may have some failures.

I tend to discard my failures quietly and without ceremony in a compost pile. Sometimes I know what went wrong—scale, red spiders, lack of water, cold temperatures. Often, though, I have no idea why the plant did not make it, so I make a point of asking my gardening friends their recommendations for my next attempt. In the end, their advice usually boils down to a few basic ideas. The key is to get the right combination.

The most basic of all necessities is the plant's need for light. If you have a poorly lit apartment or office, do not expect cyclamen or gloxinias to bloom well for you. There are several foliage plants such as aspidistra, philodendron, dieffenbachia, aglaonema, or the parlor palm that are well suited to such situations. To be sure, none of these has the glamour of a cyclamen in full bloom, but I would prefer a healthy aspidistra to a sick cyclamen. If you really cannot pass up some of those bloomers, buy yourself a fluorescent light unit and you can have the best houseplants on the block.

Watering problems, too, are always high on everybody's list of complaints. It's important to remember that the pot and soil structure are all part of the watering scene. If your plant is in a plastic, metal, or glazed container, be extra careful not to overwater. Because they are wonderfully porous, clay pots are more forgiving of gardeners who are heavy-handed with the watering can.

Making certain that the soil is well drained is another excellent way to avoid overwatering. Many of the plants you buy in garden centers and supermarkets are potted in a very porous mixture containing plenty of perlite or sand. If you make your own potting mixture, mix at least one-third perlite or sand with the compost or potting soil.

Try to water in the morning and, where possible, to avoid dropping water on the leaves. And then there's the most basic of all watering recommendations—be sure your container has a drainage hole. Maybe someone gave you an elegant dish garden and the container has no drainage hole. If you want the collection to survive, you should replant it in a clay pot with a drainage hole.

While on the subject of watering, we should also consider fertilizing. In general, I do not fertilize my houseplants from the end of September through early February. There are exceptions, such as plants growing under lights or orchids that I hope will bloom later in the winter. On the whole, though, it is safer to lay off that insidious blue stuff during the short days of winter when your plants need less water and nutrients. Excess fertilizer will build up at the base and on the sides of the pot and will burn the plant's vital feeder roots. In mid-February and early March, you can resume a modified feeding program, increasing the frequency as the light gets stronger.

Temperature is another of the plant lover's concerns. In our house, we creep around covered in sweaters, knee socks, and tweeds trying to pretend it is not Antarctica. The Gardening Partner doesn't much like it, but many plants love it if the temperature is between 50° and 60° F. at night. Be careful about locating plants near cold windowpanes. Tropical plants such as African violets, marantas, and fittonias may suffer from "freezer burn" and will greet you with floppy leaves if you forget to pull the curtains at night.

Successful houseplant growers are always on the alert for a problem. The smallest infestation of scale can develop into a major catastrophe unless you catch it early in the game. That innocent pair of whiteflies will produce thousands of progeny within a couple of weeks as you vacation in the sunny South. Get into the habit of dousing your plants in the sink or under a hose once a week. If this is impractical, I am sure they would settle for an early morning shower.

Yes, vegetables in December

Harvesting vegetables in midsummer is fun, but the bounty I brought in one early-December weekend gave me real pleasure. I don't want to sound smug, but we had broccoli one night, carrots the next, lettuce, mustard greens, and arugula in salads, and parsley, cilantro, and dill for seasonings.

A warm autumn should help you harvest fresh vegetables until at least mid-December. If you live in a city or another warm microclimate, you'll do even better. The key is to plan ahead, in the spring, when you get the garden going.

If you can, arrange the garden so you plant the fall-winter crops in areas from which you removed early-spring crops such as peas, lettuce, and spinach. Our garden isn't big enough for such an orderly transition, so I just squeeze things in wherever I can.

If your family likes them, the biggest bang for your buck (and energy) will come from planting root crops, because even if heavy frost is anticipated in mid-November, you can cover them with leaves and keep harvesting. We've had fun with parsnips, celery root, and beets, but the most consistent favorite is carrots. To get decent production in our garden, which doesn't get as much sun as it should, I try to sow no later than early July.

You'll get better carrots if you thin the seedlings once they're a couple of inches high. If I don't get around to thinning, the Chantenay types seem to be the most productive with such neglect. The broccoli has been good, but it would have been better if I'd searched for seedlings earlier to get them in the ground by mid-August instead of at the end of the month. Of the greens I mentioned before, arugula is a favorite for its tangy leaves in salads and sandwiches, and it seems more resistant to frost than lettuce or mustard greens.

Hollies: Landscaping gems

Hollies with prickly evergreen leaves may not be your favorite plants when you brush against them by mistake, but overall this group provides a wonderful selection of attractive plants for our landscapes.

Consider the diversity. Besides those with prickly leaves, there are evergreen varieties with smooth leaves, such as the Japanese and longstalk hollies. And if you're looking for a bright winter splash, try the winterberry.

For starters, many homeowners are familiar with the American holly (*Ilex opaca*). American hollies become large, open plants with age, so if you want them to continue to provide good screening, you must prune selectively to keep them tight.

English and Chinese hollies have wonderful, shiny leaves, but they're not reliably hardy in this area. That's why the development of the blue or Meserve hollies created a lot of excitement among landscapers and home gardeners. The stems are bluish purple and the evergreen foliage is finer in texture than that of American or Chinese types. Blue Princess, Blue Prince, Blue Maid, Blue Angel, and Blue Stallion are excellent choices.

Longstalk holly (*I. pedunculosa*) has cherry-red fruits on slender stalks, while this tree's smooth-edged foliage resembles that of a pear tree. Its shape is upright and elegant, and the plant is not susceptible to the diseases that prey on American hollies.

Japanese hollies are frequently used on landscape jobs because their fine-textured, smooth foliage creates an excellent hedge or edging. Rounded, spreading, and upright forms are available, and all take well to shearing. They thrive in sunny and partially shaded locations. In this area, they'll do best if sheltered from wind. Choose from cultivars with a wide variety of shapes and ultimate sizes depending on the planned use.

Deciduous winterberry holly (*I. verticillata*) is native from Nova Scotia to Florida, and ranges from four to 15 feet in height and width. Although they can be used as specimen plants, I prefer winterberries massed together in a site where the berries can be enjoyed from the house in winter. Full sun is their preference and they grow best in moist, clay soil that retains water. Opinions differ as to which varieties produce the best crop of fruit. One variety, the Sparkleberry, has received a good deal of recognition.

Hollies are usually either male or female; both sexes have flowers, but only females have berries. To ensure fruit production, you must place a male plant of the same type nearby.

Beautiful berries

When the lawn is brown and the perennials have lost their punch, some plants come into their own. Trees and shrubs with shiny berries, for example, light up the garden in late fall and winter. Crabapples, hawthorn, viburnums, and hollies are old favorites, but also consider callicarpa, with purple berries on long, arching stems, and heavenly bamboo, or nandina. Native to southern China, nandina may defoliate in hard winters, but its bright-red berries make it worth taking the chance. In spring, the foliage is tinged pink to bronze as the leaves emerge; in fall, the leaves turn scarlet. Nandina can take dry soil. Once the plants are established, prune out one quarter of the old canes in spring to encourage new growth. For smaller gardens, look for Harbors Dwarf, a compact form of heavenly bamboo that grows into a three-foot-high compact plant.

Among the crabapples, if you are interested in fall fruit, buy varieties with small fruits. *Malus floribunda*, for example, produces abundant quantities of yellow and red fruits. Dorothea has yellow fruits, and Donald Wyman and Indian Magic both have red berries.

Several viburnums produce excellent crops of bright berries if you plant them in full sun, including tea viburnum (*Viburnum setigerum*), linden viburnum (*V. dilatatum*), and the siebold viburnum (*V. sieboldii*).

JANUARY

Where the Possibilities Are

My idea of a perfect January gives me one weekend when I'm snowed in and, toward the end of the month, a couple of days with unusually warm temperatures. I'll spend the snowy weekend with catalogs, dreaming about the upcoming year's garden. I'll spend the warm days digging up the first set of bulbs from the coldframe for forcing inside the house.

Some tips for early January ...

❧ When the weather warms up, get out the pruning shears and remove dead wood from shrubs such as lilacs.

❧ Midwinter is a good time to call in the tree surgeon and ask for a multiyear plan for pruning and other related work. Tree care is expensive and is best considered as one of those perpetual maintenance jobs for which you make a budget allocation every year or two. If whole trees or large sections need to be removed, try to do it in the winter when the ground is frozen and the damage to your lawn is reduced.

❧ It's not too early to begin thinking about spring planting. Before the avalanche of new seed catalogs arrives in the mail, toss out the old copies. Before you start scanning the new catalogs, check your leftover seeds. Each packet should have a date stamped on it indicating the year in which the seed company tested the contents for viability. The length of time that seeds remain capable of germinating will depend on the type of plant and the conditions in which the seeds were stored. Seeds of peas, beans, beets, and tomatoes will remain viable for several years. Lettuce, parsley, and onions, however, may not germinate as well in subsequent years. Test germination by placing a few seeds on a piece of moist paper towel and keeping them in a warm location. If germination is poor, discard the seeds and buy a new packet.

❧ If it snows, lift the weight from your evergreens as soon as possible by beating the plants gently from below with a broom. If you work from above, you are liable to break the overladen branches.

❧ Allow cacti to go semi-dormant in the winter. Water only to keep them from shriveling.

❧ Apply an antitranspirant to recently planted evergreens or to those that might suffer from sunburn and windburn. These products reduce desiccation, a major cause of winter damage. Apply when the temperature is above freezing.

❧ Take cuttings of holly and root them in a mixture of equal parts sand and peat in a cool, well-lighted location. Set your propagating container on a heat cable to speed rooting.

❧ Check summer bulbs in winter storage for rotting or drying.

❧ If you have woods on your property, there's almost sure to be winter work awaiting you. One of the most important tasks is the removal of vines, such as bittersweet, honeysuckle, and wild grape, that will eventually strangle your trees.

❧ When watering houseplants such as African violets, which have fuzzy leaves, take care not to spill water on the foliage. You'll find that the moisture leaves spots.

Some tips for late January ...

❧ When the blooms die on your amaryllis, remove the stalk and continue to water the plant throughout the spring and summer, as you would any houseplant. If the straplike leaves get long and unwieldy, stake them and contain them with string. Your goal is to increase the size of the bulb, so fertilize the plant generously.

❧ Mealybugs favor ficus, jade, citrus, and cacti among houseplants. Check plants frequently for white, fluffy mealybug bodies, which tend to cluster in the crotches where leaves meet stems. Remove with a cotton swab dipped in rubbing alcohol.

❧ In light of the frequently asked question, "What should I do with my paperwhite bulbs once they've bloomed," I'll repeat my suggestion: Send them to the compost pile. Hardy bulbs, such as tulips, crocus, and various types of daffodils, can be planted outside in spring following forcing and will bloom again. But paperwhites are not hardy in this area and your planting efforts will be wasted.

❧ Another question that gardeners often ask in late winter is whether they can still plant the bulbs they mistakenly left in the garage over the winter. First, check to see how they feel. If they are mushy, toss them onto the compost pile. If they are firm, get them into the ground as soon as the soil thaws. You may get only foliage this year, but you will probably get both flowers and foliage in subsequent years.

❧ To clean crusty clay pots, add one cup each of white vinegar and household bleach to a gallon of warm water and soak the pots. For heavily crusted pots, scrub with a steel-wool pad after soaking for at least 12 hours.

❧ Tulips require special attention for maximum vase life. Remove the bottom leaves, cut the stems on an angle, and place all heads level before rolling the flowers in bunches of 10 or 12 in newspaper, just covering their heads. Once the flowers are covered, place the bunch in a vase of water for several hours before making the arrangement. Bunched in this way, the tulips will remain stiff and upright; once you let them go, the blooms will lean toward the closest light source.

JANUARY: READY, SET, GO

A monthly overview

January is the month to get ready, February the month to get set, and March the month to get going in the garden.

My idea of a perfect January gives me one weekend when I'm snowed in and, toward the end of the month, a couple of days with unusually warm temperatures. I'll spend the snowy weekend getting out the plan for last year's garden and a load of catalogs, and dreaming about the coming year's garden. And when the weather turns warm, I'll seize the opportunity to dig up the first set of bulbs from the coldframe for forcing inside the house.

Plan your garden by laying out both the vegetable and flower areas on paper so you can estimate the required seeds and equipment. I find one-half inch to the foot a good scale at which to work for our vegetable garden, and I refer to the plans for the previous couple of years to remind me to rotate the crops where possible. In a small garden, crop rotation is hard, but if you can rotate the solanaceous crops (tomatoes, potatoes, eggplants, and peppers) with legumes or other crops, you will lessen the chances of your plants becoming infected with soil-borne fungal diseases such as verticillium and fusarium wilts.

If you cannot rotate the tomatoes, be sure to buy disease-resistant varieties. In most garden catalogs, you will notice the letters "VFNT" following some of the variety names, indicating resistance to verticillium and fusarium wilt, nematodes, and tobacco mosaic virus. In my area, the first two are the most prevalent.

In catalogs, you will find a dizzying array of tomato selections. If you have space to grow several varieties, pick one for its early fruiting, such as Early Girl, others for their large, beefsteak fruits, such as Burpee Supersteak Hybrid, and yet another, such as Better Boy, Big Boy, or Celebrity, for a dependable mid-season crop.

The Gardening Partner is such a fan of large, juicy tomatoes that I can never get him interested in eating cherry tomatoes, but varieties such as Super Sweet 100 are most rewarding because they produce thousands of delicious, bite-size fruits. Ruby Pearl is also delicious and you can harvest by cutting a whole cluster with one snip of your shears. I like the aesthetic effect you can achieve by arranging a plate with slices of red tomatoes and slices of Lemon Boy, Husky Gold, Sun Gold, and other yellow-fruited varieties. If you want to can or make pints of soup or sauce to freeze, grow Italian plum tomatoes.

Some of the older varieties of open-pollinated tomatoes may not be as perfectly shaped as today's modern varieties, but they taste terrific. One of the most widely sold is Brandywine, an heirloom variety dating back to 1885.

With their mailboxes overflowing with catalogs in January and February, gardeners can feel like the most popular people in late winter. Some companies now even send theirs in December. There's a lot to learn from these catalogs, and I have included a short list of my favorites in the Appendix. If you get intrigued by seeds and want to join a group of 7,000 backyard gardeners around the world who collect, grow, and save seeds of heirloom vegetables, fruits, and grains, join the Seed Savers Exchange, whose address is in the Appendix on page 194.

If your garden plans include slow-growing annuals such as begonias, petunias, and geraniums, late January through early February is the time to start these from seed. Begonias and petunias have tiny, dustlike seeds; geraniums are bigger but equally slow in getting from seed stage to flowering plant. Plant seeds in a well-drained, sterilized mixture (available at garden centers and hardware stores) and search for a warm location to ensure speedy germination. Propagation mats will accelerate the process. Cover pots with plastic bags or plastic wrap to prevent soil from drying out too rapidly.

Assess and design

Even though St. Patrick's Day, the traditional date to begin spring planting, is still a couple of months away, it's time to rough out a plan for your vegetable garden. I urge you to come up with a plan that tries at least one new vegetable variety.

The best starting point, even before you actually draw a design, is to think back to last year's garden and assess its successes and failures. Did the tomato crop, for example, come in when you were on vacation? If so, check out the dates you expect to be away this year; perhaps you can plant a variety that will mature before you leave or after you return.

Making the most out of a piece of land means starting early, then planting in succession so you have crops to harvest throughout the growing season, which can extend until late fall. Seasoned vegetable gardeners will debate endlessly about the merits of rushing to get the peas in by St. Patrick's Day. My theory is that if you can work the soil, get the peas in whenever you can.

Lettuce, spinach, and onions can be planted at the same time as the peas. As you plant the peas outside, sow seeds of broccoli, cabbage, and cauliflower in containers inside and then plant the seedlings in the garden in mid-April. Some years, I've tried planting seedlings of broccoli and cauliflower outside in late March, but the results have been disappointing. However, if you protect these seedlings with floating row covers (see page 169) or hoops of plastic, you'd probably have better luck. The seedlings need several weeks of cool weather to reach maturity before the heat sets in, but they just don't seem to like soil as cool as peas and lettuce can tolerate.

Mid-March is also the time to sow tomato and pepper seeds in containers indoors; these can be planted outside after the last frost. If you plan to sow eggplant from seed, start these about two weeks ahead of the tomatoes.

All garden planning revolves around the last expected frost date in your neighborhood. Some vegetables, such as cabbages and lettuce, can stand an occasional nip, but tender tomatoes won't survive a frost, and peppers and eggplants may be stunted for the rest of the summer if you plant them too early.

Generally, May 15 is considered that magic date in my area, but there are exceptions wherever you may be. In the middle of a city, you probably won't have a frost much beyond the first week of May. In a frost pocket, on the other hand, you'd be wise to leave your tomato seedlings inside the house almost until Memorial Day. Once you have decided what to plant and the date of your last frost, make a chart, listing all the crops, with columns for planting indoors and outdoors.

Most seed packets and some catalogs will tell you when to plant each crop outdoors. The packet won't list a specific date, but on a packet of tomato seeds, for example, it will say, "Sow in late winter, six to eight weeks before transplanting outdoors in spring." For hardy vegetables, such as lettuce, the instructions may read, "Plant in average soil in early to late spring."

Some years, my vegetable garden has looked like a fabric store, with white covers over the rows of early or late vegetables. Made of synthetic fabric, these lightweight strips are called floating row covers. They don't really float, but they are so light that they seem almost to be floating when they're draped over a row of vegetables.

Gardeners can use them either for sheltering plants from the cool winds of spring or fall or as a mechanical barrier against pests, such as Mexican bean beetles. More than 80 percent of the available sunlight can penetrate the covers, and they also allow for passage of rain. These covers do break down in sunlight, but they will last for a couple of seasons if you take care not to rip them. Drape the covers over the plants, then fasten them down on all sides with soil. When you remove them, wash the dirt off, dry in the sun, and store until the next season.

New Year's resolutions in the garden

I try to accompany my dreaming with some New Year's gardening resolutions. Mine, for instance, would include a promise to save the labels from all new plants so I can avoid the embarrassment of

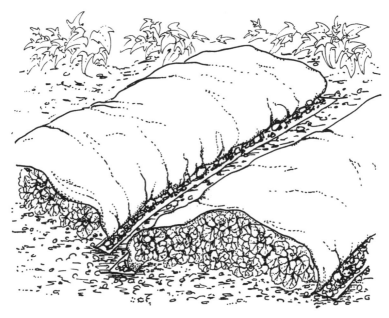

Floating row covers can be used to protect plants from low temperatures in spring and fall and also as a barrier against pests.

having to tell friends I can't remember the names any more than I can figure out how to look up their cultural requirements in the encyclopedia.

Furthermore, I would vow to keep a garden diary and to record planting dates as well as first and last harvest dates for all of The Gardening Partner's favorite vegetables. On tasting the first peas or the last good tomato, we always have lengthy discussions on how they compared with those of past years. A well-kept garden diary would counter the outrageous claims he tends to make.

Forced bulbs, continued

If you planted some hardy bulbs in a coldframe in October, intending to bring them indoors for early forcing, now is the time to check on them. Choose as warm a day as you can to lift out the bulbs, not only to make the business more pleasant for you, but so that there will be the minimum possible change in temperature from outside to inside for the bulbs.

If you sank your bulbs in leaves in the garage, just lift them out. If they're in a trench in the coldframe, or in a sheltered spot, dig very carefully into the top layer of soil to prevent damaging any shoots.

Dig up a couple of pots and check to make sure the roots are well-developed. If you can't see roots emerging through the drainage hole in the bottom of a pot, turn it upside down and knock the bulbs out so that you can inspect the root system. Bulbs will differ in the speed with which they mature. Should you dig them up before the roots are developed, it's likely they will not bloom well.

Dig only a few pots of bulbs at a time so that you can spread out their forced blooming over several weeks in the house. Once you have the pots out of the ground and in the house, find a cool, dim spot to place them for a few days. If the soil is frozen, let it defrost gradually; if it's dry, water until the moisture runs out through the drainage hole.

Within a few days, the shoots will start to turn green, at which time you can put the pots in bright light, but try to keep them cool (below 65° F. at night) because with lower temperatures, you'll get better flowers and they'll last longer.

If you're growing smaller bulbs, you probably don't have to worry about staking. With taller varieties of daffodils and tulips, however, it's best to stake when the shoots are small, rather than waiting until they're flopping all over the place. Use small, green bamboo stakes and green twine, or black or dark green, heavy-duty sewing thread.

As the foliage develops, keep the soil moist and use a houseplant fertilizer once a month. As the blooms fade, remove them and continue watering and fertilizing until the leaves start to turn yellow. In early April, I remove the bulbs from their pots and plant them outside. Some experts say to wait until all danger of frost has passed, but I get very bored seeing all that yellowing foliage around and my forced bulbs never seem to have suffered from this treatment.

What a genus!

They bloom from early spring until late summer, come in a host of colors, are deciduous and evergreen, and boast more than 900 species. I'm describing the genus Rhododendron, which includes all azaleas, and I'm blessed to be gardening in a region with excellent growing conditions for many plants in this group. One reason is that our soil is, by and large, acidic. Here are a few that have given me and The Gardening Partner special pleasure in our garden:

Rhododendron carolinianum gets my vote because the ones we planted many years ago outside our front door, in a difficult situation with less than perfect soil, rewarded us year after year with lots of small, pink flowers in early May. Another bonus was that the plants remained low, perhaps three feet tall, with minimal pruning.

171

The Exbury hybrids stand alone because of their gloriously colorful yellow, orange, and bright pink fragrant flowers. The plants can be tall and the foliage is deciduous. Plant them in full sun and be prepared to prune from time to time to keep the flowers at a height where you can enjoy them. In summer, their leaves may turn white from mildew. But don't worry about it; the leaves will drop in fall. My plants of Gibraltar, an Exbury azalea, with flame-orange ruffled petals, came from cuttings taken when I was working for Sally the Propagator, whom you met in the July chapter.

Our plumleaf azalea (*Rhododendron prunifolium*) was given to us by a friend, and I love to see its long, pink flowers in July. When I take Candy the poodle out at night, I walk by just to catch a whiff of the fragrant blooms, which open a few at a time and last for several weeks.

And finally, that princess of rhododendrons, the yak or *R. yakusimanum*, a dense, rounded plant that has dark green leaves with wonderful, woolly, pale tan undersides. We have two plants, given to us as a house gift by an English garden writer, and every spring I take enormous pleasure in seeing their beautiful, fat blooms emerge. At opening, the flowers are a deep pink, later fading to white. After a decade, the plants are still only about 30 inches tall. I could wish I had planted them in a little more sun, where I think they would have bloomed even better.

Scented geraniums

As a child, one of the favorite spots at my grandmother's house was the Paved Garden, a walled area sheltered from the brisk Scottish winds and filled with scented geraniums. Midwinter makes me long for those scented, velvety leaves. In full sun and well-drained soil, they are easy to grow and will bring many months of enjoyment. Even better, the deer don't seem to have them at the top of their grazing list.

Start with the easiest, the rose-scented geranium, which not only looks nice in the garden, but can also be used in baking or to make a rose-scented jelly. Lemon-scented geraniums are excellent for making potpourri. And how about *Pelargonium grossularioides*, whose magenta leaves have a coconut aroma? There are also varieties with peppermint scents, such as Chocolate Mint, with huge, velvety leaves. Grow this in full sun to get the best color in the leaves.

Several mail-order houses offer sumptuously wide selections of scented geraniums. Once you have your own plants, make cuttings each year in August or September. Take multiple cuttings because they are somewhat unpredictable in rooting. Avoid using either very new growth or old brown stems. Perlite and vermiculite work well as rooting mediums; then, when you pot up the rooted cuttings, be sure to add plenty of perlite or vermiculite to the soil mixture. Scented geraniums do not fare well in heavy soil.

The unsung heroes

Once those holiday plants start to fade, it's time to turn your thoughts to the background greenery—to the plants that give a solid performance in all seasons, providing a backdrop for the Christmas poinsettia, the Easter lily, and the Thanksgiving mum. Ferns make terrific year-round plants for gardeners with cool houses.

Successful fern culture requires a cool temperature (65° F. during the day and 50° to 60° at night), a bright but not too sunny location, and as much humidity as you can provide.

Greenhouses or sun porches facing north or east are fern havens. North- and east-facing windowsills can also be successful if you keep the thermostat low and raise the humidity by setting pots on saucers or trays filled with damp pebbles. If your room faces south or west, place the ferns away from the direct sun near the window.

For those who find their apartments or offices hopelessly dry, humidifiers or terrariums may be the answer. Consider converting that old fish tank into a terrarium when the goldfish lovers decide they have bigger fish to fry.

In addition to cool temperatures, most ferns need a loose soil mixture consisting of equal parts garden or packaged soil, peat moss, and perlite or sand. Some will grow best in moss baskets or, as in the case of the staghorn ferns, on boards. Many will thrive in the relatively shallow containers called azalea pots. Grow them in either clay or plastic.

Wait until the plants are truly potbound before you repot, and then transfer only into the next pot size, avoiding the temptation to swamp a tiny plant in a giant-sized pot. Not only will it look ridiculous, it will develop slowly and poorly. It's best to repot in April or May as the plants develop new growth.

In general, keep house ferns moist from late February through October, adding a regular houseplant fertilizer to the water every three to four weeks. During the balance of the year, when light levels are low, omit the fertilizer and water only when the soil feels dry on top.

Here are a few ferns you might want to try in your house:

Bird's-nest fern (*Asplenium nidus*). Shiny, thick fronds make this a handsome plant, but watch it carefully for scale.

Boston fern (*Nephrolepis exaltata* Bostoniensis). This is more rugged than most house ferns because it can stand more sun in winter and generally lower humidity. Many attractive cultivars such as Whitmanii, Fluffy Ruffles, Teddy Junior, and Wanamaker are available. Do not mist fluffy varieties because fronds do not dry out fast enough and you may run into disease problems.

Button fern (*Pellaea rotundifolia*). This plant is harder to grow because it requires high humidity, but it's easily overwatered. It's native to limestone cliffs, so add a teaspoon of ground limestone per quart of soil mixture. Excellent for hanging baskets and, when small, for terrariums.

Delta maidenhair fern (*Adiantum raddianum*). This delicate-looking fern likes low temperatures and high humidity. I find that it grows best untended in the ground under the bench in our very cool greenhouse. If your plant looks ratty next spring, cut all fronds back to one inch from the soil and allow new growth to develop from old roots.

Holly fern (*Cyrtomium falcatum*). This fern has long, thick, shiny fronds. It's easy to grow and it will do well at very low temperatures.

Mother fern (*Asplenium bulbiferum*). This is one of the easiest to grow because it survives in lower humidity. Small bulbils, which sprout on fronds, make this an easy one to propagate.

Rabbit's-foot fern (*Davallia fejeensis*). Be sure to start this one out in a wire basket so that its hairy, brown rhizomes (hence the name rabbit's-foot fern) can spread around the basket and down the sides. Surround the interior of the basket with long-fiber sphagnum moss and fill it with soil before you place the fern on top, anchoring the rhizomes with wire or hairpins until the plant is established.

What every garden needs

Every garden needs at least one viburnum, and in my case, I couldn't get by without at least two. My first came from Aunt Marion, that dear, wonderful aunt of The Gardening Partner who nurtured my horticultural interests when I first came to live in America. Though she is long since gone, our memories of her live on in the fragrant viburnum I grew from a cutting taken from her shrub. We planted it on the well-lit south side of our house, but not in full sun, and in late April or early May the scent from its white blooms wafts in through our bedroom window. *Viburnum carlesii*, sometimes called the Korean spice viburnum, is one of the smaller species, growing six to seven feet high with as wide a spread, but you can easily keep it smaller if you prune annually after bloom.

The Gardening Partner loves our doublefile viburnums, grown from a few cuttings from Sally the Propagator. They grow on the edge of the woods and we can see their layers of white flowers from the window of the family room. I took the cuttings about 20 years ago and now the plants are more than 10 feet high and as broad. There are many cultivars of *V. plicatum* var. *tomentosum* on the market, some with white flowers, some with pink, and with a good deal of confusion in the nursery trade about the subtle differences between each. Whichever you get, I know you will enjoy the spectacular show of flowers, and their timing is perfect – appearing right after the dogwood blooms have faded. The doublefile viburnum will grow vigorously and will expand its territory by layering itself. Anytime you want to reduce it in size, just take it back to the ground and remove suckers as they encroach on other plants. Several viburnums, including the doublefile, have excellent fall color and there are also several species, such as *V. setigerum*, the tea viburnum, that have very colorful berries.

Ornamental grasses

In my early gardening days, I thought grass was lawn grass, and when I studied perennials at the University of Delaware, I don't even remember hearing the term "ornamental grass." These grasses are deservedly popular now, not only because they are attractive but because they bring a new element into the garden with their upright and mounding forms and, with many, their seedheads provide a focal point in a perennial bed in winter, when most plants have been cut to the ground. Furthermore, they are tough and adaptable and most of them seem to resist deer-browsing. When you grow ornamental grasses, be especially careful to understand their growth habits and ultimate sizes because some of them can grow very quickly into enormous plants. Also, be warned that they take a while to get going in the spring.

First, a few cultural directions. Most grasses will benefit from spring planting. Many nurseries carry wide selections and you will also find them in mail-order catalogs. In general, most of them will take a variety of soil conditions and many grow best in full sun. How closely you space your new plants will depend on how quickly you want to cover the soil and how deep your pockets are. For starters, figure on spacing them as far apart as their ultimate height. If you are planting on a bank, and soil erosion is a problem, plant closer to get a quicker cover. Avoid planting too deeply.

As a substitute for the burning or grazing that would take place in their native habitats, you should plan to cut back your ornamental grasses once a year. Some may choose to do it as part of the fall cleanup, but most gardeners prefer to enjoy the seedheads and foliage over the winter, then cut back in early spring. Just get it done before the new foliage starts to appear. Cut back to within a few inches of the soil line, using either a pair of pruners or a weed trimmer.

Grasses definitely need to be divided and thinned every three to four years to maintain their shape and character. Those left undivided for too long will develop large dead centers. Once you have tried to divide one of the large grasses, you will realize why I caution you not to plant grasses larger than your garden—or your muscles—can accommodate. When you are deciding which grasses would be good for your garden, first check them out in an arboretum in September and October, when they are at full height.

Arm yourself with forks and shovels, and perhaps an ax or saw for the large varieties, and divide grasses in early spring, after you cut them back and just as new growth starts. If you divide grasses during the growing season, cut back the foliage by one-third to reduce transpiration. If you have severe deer problems, plant grasses with the sharper-edged leaves.

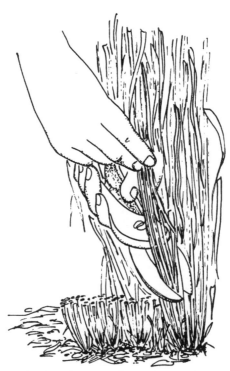

Cut ornamental grasses back to the ground in early spring.

Here is a small selection of grasses to get you started:

Fountain grasses (*Pennisetum alopecuroides*). The Gardening Partner brought home one of these fountain grasses for me at a time when the only place we had to plant it was too close to the roots of a spreading hemlock. The plant is still there—and thriving, which is a testimony to its durability in the face of the competition with the hemlock roots. Clumps of fountain grass look attractive in borders or in larger plantings and will tolerate shore conditions. The stiff foxtail flowers look good through most of the latter part of the summer.

Hakone grass (*Hakonechloa macra*). Unlike the other grasses mentioned below, hakone grass will grow in partial shade. In our garden, it seems to survive in dry shade under an ash tree. The cultivar Aureola has variegated foliage, which is always an asset to brighten up a shady location.

Japanese blood grass (*Imperata cylindrica* Red Baron). Sometimes known as cranberry grass, the foliage of this low-growing grass starts out bright green with red tips and gradually turns brighter and brighter as the season progresses until it's vivid red in fall. Plant in full sun and moist soil. If Red Baron reverts to the nonred form, remove it at once because this grass can be very invasive.

Japanese silver grass (*Miscanthus sinensis*). No discussion of ornamental grasses for this area would be complete without mention of miscanthus, or eulalia. This is a tall grass, which can take shore conditions, grow with its roots in shallow water, or grow in good garden soil in full sun. There are some wonderful cultivars on the market, including Morning Light, which has a white band on the leaf margins; Purpurascens, with medium green foliage and a red tint that turns bright orange-red in fall; and my very favorite, *M. sinensis* var. strictus, or porcupine grass, that has bright yellow horizontal bands across each leaf.

Switch grass (*Panicum virgatum* Heavy Metal). Heavy Metal switch grass is really handsome, with powder-blue foliage that turns yellow in fall. It's tall and upright and makes quite a statement toward the back of a border. Other excellent cultivars of switch grass include Hameln and Moudry, the black-flowered pennisetum, and Little Bunny, which makes a nice little mound in our flower garden.

So what's in that bag?

Soilless potting mixtures have become increasingly popular in recent years as both commercial growers and home gardeners have reaped benefits from their use. Garden loam, once the main ingredient in potting soils, serves the purpose admirably when in the open ground. But when packed into the confines of a pot, the soil compacts, leaving few air spaces and resulting in poor drainage and waterlogged roots. If you can wean yourself from the notion that all good potting soils need a dose of garden loam, you could become a convert to soilless mixtures.

So what's in that bag? Peat moss is one key ingredient. On account of its structure, sphagnum peat is slow to decompose and will hold 15 to 30 times its dry weight in water. Although the peat itself contains no nutrients, it binds mineral nutrients and water to its particles, releasing them in a manner the plants can use.

Inert materials such as vermiculite and perlite are also included in potting mixtures to increase the number of air spaces in the mix, providing both improved drainage and oxygen, an essential element for root development. Vermiculite is an ore and once heated, its mica flakes expand like an accordion, providing endless air pockets. Like peat, vermiculite is active in binding and releasing nutrients. The mica flakes, however, tend to collapse with age, destroying the air pockets and good drainage. Perlite is a volcanic silicon dioxide sand. Once heated, it increases 20-fold in volume, creating tiny, water-holding surface cavities. Unlike vermiculite, it is not active in binding nutrients, but its particles do not break down, so it makes a better long-term drainage material than vermiculite.

A soilless mixture is not easy to work with when you first open the bag because it is so dry. Before you start potting, mix it thoroughly with water and let it stand for several hours. Also, you may decide to adapt the mix for special needs. Some cacti, for example, will require more drainage material, so you should add more perlite for these plants. If you use bagged potting soils for plantings that will dry out quickly, add more peat.

FEBRUARY

Winter is Broken, But Spring is Still a Promise

> *The best garden plans are often made in midwinter when, yearning for the delights of spring and summer, you stare out the window and find a landscape devoid of color—and fragrance.*

Some tips for early February ...

෨ If the weather encourages you to do some midwinter pruning of small trees and lower branches of larger trees, remember to make two cuts for heavy branches. Your final cut should be just beyond the "collar" of the branch; make the first cut about three inches farther away from the trunk and on the underside of the branch to prevent the bark from peeling down the trunk.

෨ Insecticidal soaps can help control pests on houseplants. Buy the combined spray with soap and pyrethrins. Follow the directions on the container and, for maximum effectiveness, spray on a regular schedule.

෨ **In the vegetable garden:** When buying seeds of crops that do well in spring and fall—such as lettuce, spinach, and herbs (dill and coriander, for example)— order enough to carry you through fall planting. If you try to buy them in late summer in a garden center, you'll probably find them out of stock. ... Leeks make a tasty vegetable. Grow them from seed, starting in the next couple of weeks. Sow the seeds thinly in a small flat indoors. When the plants are a couple of inches high, thin and space them on one-inch centers. Plant in the garden in late April. Onions can be grown in the same manner, or you can purchase sets or small plants for planting in late March. ... If you used your coldframe for forcing bulbs, it should be almost empty by now, so why not get a jump on spring and start some cold-tolerant crops? Lettuce, mustard greens, and spinach will give you wonderful early salads.

🌱 **For the flowers, shrubs, and trees:** There's still time to start slow-growing annuals such as geraniums, petunias, and verbenas from seed. The soil temperature in the planting medium should be 75° F., both day and night. ... Cut a few forsythia branches and bring them into the house to force them into bloom. Place them in water in a cool, dimly lit location so that the buds open slowly. Forsythia is the easiest to force. Experiment with branches of early-blooming trees, such as cherry and crabapple. While you're outside, remove sticks from the lawn, leftover leaves from the flower beds, and any dead-wood you find in evergreens. ... Don't forget those bulbs placed in cold storage last fall for forcing. Bring them into a cool place, and let them adjust gradually to brighter light. ... Curled leaves, malformed buds, and a "honeydew," or sticky substance, on plant leaves indicate aphids. Spray plants weekly with an insecticidal soap.

Some tips for late February ...

🌱 Now that the days are longer and the light is brighter, resume fertilizing the houseplants. If you want to fertilize every time you water, use one-quarter the recommended strength of fertilizer. If you plan to use full strength, use it once every couple of weeks until April, when you may want to give some plants more nutrients by fertilizing weekly.

🌱 With only a few weeks to go before St. Patrick's Day, the day by which you should traditionally (and, weather permitting) have planted your first row of peas, it's time to sketch out your vegetable and flower gardens on paper. Once these plans are done, you'll find you can be more economical in your seed ordering, or when purchasing transplants.

🌱 If your evergreens have suffered damage on odd branches—or sections, as in the case of the sarcococca—prune them out whenever you can. If the whole shrub or tree appears dead, don't remove it until late April, just in case new growth starts to sprout.

𝄢 Got a few ratty-looking Boston ferns around the house? First, check them for scale. If scale is evident, you're probably better off tossing them, but if they're not infested, rejuvenate them by pulling each one apart and repotting the more vigorous-looking sections in fresh soil.

𝄢 **In the vegetable garden:** Prune blueberries in late winter by removing canes more than six years old at ground level. If your bushes are becoming thick and lack air circulation, also remove shorter, twiggier branches at ground level to make way for stronger ones.

𝄢 **For the flowers, shrubs, and trees:** It hurts, but when paperwhite bulbs have finished blooming, put them on the compost heap instead of trying to save them for another year. Paperwhites are not hardy in this area and so will not bloom for a second year. Hardy daffodils, tulips, and hyacinths will bloom again, so keep them growing in good light, water as you would houseplants, and plant them in your garden when it warms up. ... If you received a gardenia for Valentine's Day, give it 60° F. at night and 70° to 75° during the day. If your house is warmer at night, it may cease to produce new flower buds. ... Check perennials. If frost has heaved them out of the ground, wait for a thaw and then firm them gently to make sure roots are in contact with soil. ... If you have a cover crop, such as winter rye, on your garden, till or dig this in as soon as the soil has thawed so it has a chance to start decomposing before you plant.

FEBRUARY: A HALFWAY MARK

A monthly overview

For the gardener, February is something of a halfway point. On the one hand, there's winter to clean up after, and on the other it's the time to make serious preparations for spring. The best garden plans are often made in midwinter when, yearning for the delights of spring and summer, you stare out the window and find a landscape devoid of color—and fragrance.

First, let's tend to the winter chores. If it still looks decent, keep on watering your Christmas poinsettia and providing it with the occasional dose of fertilizer. But if it's turning ugly, do us both a favor and put it on your compost heap, which is where it has to go before winter is over. (Yes, you can keep poinsettias around, watering and fussing over them all summer, but only the really dedicated gardener with special lighting can get a poinsettia to look even halfway decent for a second year.)

Cyclamen are another story, and if yours is still blooming, you can probably count on having it around for another couple of months. Keep it in the coolest possible room, in good light, and fertilize it with your other houseplants. By April, I've usually had enough of my cyclamen, and I tend to hustle them to the compost pile. My friend Cynthia puts hers outside in the shade and keeps them growing throughout the summer. Then in the fall, she brings them back in for another season in the house. The plants are not exactly the bouncing beauties they were the first year, but they do have green leaves and they do flower.

You can bring a little early spring cheer into the house by cutting branches of shrubs and trees to force into bloom. Forsythia is the best-known plant for this, but try other early spring-blooming plants such as fruit trees and pussy willows. More on those in a moment.

Seedlings should be your next area of consideration at this time of year. Leeks and onions, which should be sown shortly, are two that germinate easily, even in cool soil. If you have never tried growing leeks, join me as one of their greatest fans. They're delicious in soups and stews or braised for a winter supper. And though they belong to the same family, the leek's flavor is wonderfully different from that of the onion.

Sow seeds this month in a flat in the house, using any sterilized sowing medium. Sow thinly, and when the seedlings are an inch or so tall, thin them to stand an inch apart. After the first month, fertilize the seedlings monthly until mid-April, when you can transplant them into the garden. In the house, I trim the tops to force more growth into the roots, and when I transplant, I trim both roots and shoots.

To produce long, white, tasty leeks, you must dig a trench for planting, then hill the leeks throughout the summer. At planting time, I dig down to about 18 inches and put a layer of compost in the bottom of the trench before adding the leeks. Plant leeks in rows two feet apart with 18 inches between plants. About a month later, when the roots are established, I sprinkle dry fertilizer around each plant and then gradually fill in the trench, adding small doses of fertilizer each time I add more soil. Leeks require lots of nutrients, and if you don't have manure handy, slow-release fertilizer seems to be a good substitute.

Sooner or later you will run out of the soil you excavated in April, and you will need additional materials to cover up the plants. We have successfully used leaf mold, which keeps the soil moist with little watering throughout the summer. Furthermore, in some ways it's better than soil because it's less likely to get into the folds between the leaves, which makes leeks hard to clean for the kitchen.

If your dreams include fresh berries in future years, get out the catalogs and order them this winter. If planted this spring, strawberry and raspberry plants will bear a small crop the summer after this. Blueberries will take longer, but you can expect a healthy picking within five years. Mail-order catalogs and fruit specialists offer a range of varieties.

With strawberries and raspberries, be sure to get disease-free plants. Heritage remains my favorite raspberry, from which you can expect good crops in both spring and fall. If you would rather have the whole crop in June, try Taylor or New Hilton. When choosing blueberries, be sure to purchase early-, mid-, and late-season varieties to ensure adequate pollination.

Tender geraniums (pelargoniums) are a mainstay in many summer gardens and, with the introduction over the years of varieties that are easier to grow from seed, you can have a large number of plants on a relatively small budget. For late May blooms, sow seeds no later than mid-February, placing the container in a location where the mixture will remain at 75° F. until germination.

Germination of geraniums can be sporadic, with some seed leaves appearing within a week, other seeds taking as long as three weeks to germinate. In view of this, it's best to use peat pots, sowing one seed per pot rather than sowing several seeds in a small flat.

The scent of a garden

Early in the season, many of the best scents in your garden will come from daffodils and other bulbs. Because of their wonderful fragrance, grape hyacinths are some of my favorites, both for growing outdoors and for forcing. The standard hyacinth, which has very fragrant flowers, strikes me as rather ungainly when planted in the garden.

Among the summer-blooming bulbs, some of the lilies provide wonderful scents in the garden, and the flowers will last well when picked and brought in the house. Sweet alyssum (*Lobularia maritima*) makes a wonderful, sweet-smelling border for the flower garden. Start seeds indoors or buy flats of seedlings to

183

transplant toward the end of April. As a half-hardy annual, sweet alyssum will stand light frost. It does best in April, May, and June, and probably will stop blooming in midsummer, then start again when the nights turn cooler in September. Plant where it will receive shade in the afternoon. I like the white cultivars (Carpet of Snow, Tiny Tim), but if you enjoy purple or lavender-pink edging plants, you will find both seeds and seedlings available in these colors.

Heliotrope is another purple-flowered annual with a wonderful fragrance. Its color makes it rather difficult to incorporate into a garden plan, but it goes well in summer borders, combined with pinks and lavenders. Buy plants each spring, or sow seeds 10 to 12 weeks before transplanting after the last frost. Germination may take up to three weeks.

Flowering tobacco (*Nicotiana alata*) has a more delicate fragrance than heliotrope. The white, pink, and chartreuse blossoms are most fragrant in the evening, and the plants can be started easily from seed six to eight weeks before the last frost. Seeds need light to germinate and plants will do best in light shade.

Come summer, the most vicious enemies of this flowering tobacco are aphids and the Colorado potato beetle. Anyone who grows potatoes and eggplant will be familiar with this beetle, which can ruin a planting within a few days by chewing leaves and flowers. Keep watching for the yellow- and black-striped beetle and gray-black larvae. Control it by handpicking or spraying with rotenone at weekly intervals after you first notice the insects.

The shrub group has a wide range of possibilities for fragrant flowers, including such old favorites as lilacs, roses, and many azaleas and rhododendrons. In early spring—often in February and March—the Chinese witch-hazel (*Hamamelis mollis*) has small, highly fragrant, spidery flowers with ribbonlike petals. This small tree may eventually grow 30 feet tall, and although it's not what I would recommend if you have room for only a couple of small trees in your garden, it has an attractive, rounded shape and those early fragrant flowers are an asset in a larger garden.

Several species of daphne are hardy in my area, some of which grow for several years, then suddenly die. *Daphne caucasica,* the Caucasian daphne, has the reputation of lasting longer than some others. Its white flowers appear on and off from April until frost. The winter or fragrant daphne (*D. odora*) has special significance in the garden because its blooms start when the weather warms in late winter—perhaps as early as February. Plant in a sheltered location.

Valentine's Day flower shopping

No essay on February would be complete without a few words about Valentine's Day. If my valentine were to take me shopping at a gardening center, here's what I'd be looking for.

First on my list would be an orchid. Hey, you might as well start at the top and see how it goes. Orchids have the reputation of being delicate and hard to grow, but if you have a well-lighted windowsill, or a light unit, they can be one of the most satisfactory plants, blooming for weeks on end. For more details, see page 153.

Perhaps there's a peach-colored amaryllis waiting for you. These develop rapidly in warm rooms and usually produce a couple of blooms per pot. Once the blooms are spent, remove dead flowers and stalks and keep the plant growing with the same light, water, and fertilizer you give your other houseplants.

Azaleas are always popular as spring plants, giving welcome dashes of pink, red, and white around the home or office. Try to get one in bud; otherwise the flowers will be over before you know it.

And just in case you *do* receive those red roses, what about caring for them? Take them out of the box with appropriate "oohs" and "aahs" and lots of kisses, then recut the stems on an angle with a sharp knife, remove any leaves that will be under water, and plunge the roses into warm water.

Shorten the road to spring

The days are longer, the sun is stronger, and we gradually seem to be getting closer to spring. To hurry it along by a few weeks, bring flowering branches indoors and force them into bloom.

Forsythia and pussy willow are two of the easiest, but you'll also have good luck with such fruits as apple and peach, early-blooming rhododendrons (*Rhododendron mucronulatum*), quince, and daphnes. Generally, the earlier the plants come into bloom, the easier it will be to force them indoors this month because their buds are already swollen and ready to pop.

Look around the garden for the most likely branches to cut, bearing in mind that you should cut only those that you won't miss for the rest of the season. In other words, do a good pruning job as you cut. With forsythia, it's rarely a problem because there are so many branches anyway, but with slower-growing plants, you must be careful not to ruin the shape.

If the fall was warm, some forsythia buds may have come into bloom. Avoid cutting these by searching for branches with an abundance of fat buds. On most plants, the fat buds are flower buds, and the slender buds produce foliage.

Cut your branches with pruning shears on a warm day, one with a temperature above freezing, and bring them indoors. Cut each to a size you can use in a vase, and then smash the stems, using a hammer on a hard surface, to encourage water to enter the stems easily. Place branches in a bucket of warm water, in a spot that is cool and well-lit but not sunny. Cover the branches overnight with a plastic cleaner's bag to reduce the shock of coming from the damp outdoors into your dry house. Or you can completely immerse the branches overnight in a tub of warm water and then place them in a bucket. Once they come into bloom, put them into a vase.

These longer, brighter days mean better days ahead for your houseplants, and you should help them take advantage of that situation by giving them good grooming and maintenance. Remove dead leaves and flowers promptly to lessen the spread of disease. If a heavy pruning job is in order, now is a good time to do it so you can take full advantage of the spring and summer growing seasons. Also, mid-February is a good time to resume spring and summer fertilizing schedules.

Seed sowing

I love those weekends in February and March when it is finally time to get out the seed pans, the soil, the labels, and the seed packets to start up another year's garden under lights and on the windowsill.

Producing your own annual and perennial flower and vegetable transplants can be very satisfying. Of course, when it all goes wrong and diseases destroy the crop, it can be utterly frustrating, so try to avoid these frustrations by providing the optimum environment for the seedlings.

Assuming that you already have bought your seeds or have a list of the ones you intend to buy, make a calendar outlining the appropriate sowing date for each variety of seed. By sticking to the calendar, you'll avoid the temptation to plant everything so early that you end up with a mass of straggly seedlings on every windowsill.

Guidelines for the time required from seed sowing to transplanting into the garden are usually listed on seed packets. If you plan to sow seeds of geraniums, begonias, petunias, or impatiens, start them at the beginning of February. In mid-March, sow collards, cabbage, broccoli, and cauliflower for transplanting into the garden in mid-April. Save the tomatoes, eggplants, peppers, and ageratum seed for sowing by mid-April, six weeks before you plan to transplant them into the garden.

Armed with your calendar, you are ready to search for shallow containers with drainage holes to serve as seedpans. The deeper the pan you select, the more germination mixture you'll need to use and the greater the chance that the soil will become waterlogged, so stick with containers that are less than three inches deep. One friend sows all her seeds in egg cartons because she finds the shallow nests just the right depth.

The scourge of seed-starters is a group of diseases called "damping off." Everything looks wonderful, then suddenly your seedlings drop. Before you know what's happening, your crop is lost. These are fungal diseases and you must take precautions from several fronts to avoid problems:

Make sure your containers are free of disease. Soak them overnight in a mixture of one part bleach to 10 parts water, then rinse well and let containers dry before using them.

Use only sterile seed-starting mixes, which are available in garden centers. Before you sow, thoroughly wet the mixture and let it drain.

As an added precaution, I cover seeds after sowing, not with the seed-starting mixture, but with a shallow layer of well-moistened, milled sphagnum moss. This moss, also available in garden centers, has a property in it that inhibits disease, and it's worth using if you've had problems with damping off.

And most important is to figure out a place where you can keep the soil temperature for the seeds of tender plants consistently above 70° F., preferably around 75°. If you don't have the perfect place in the house, buy a propagating mat or cable.

To maintain the desired humidity, slip each pot into a polyethylene bag, and place the container in good light but out of direct sunlight. As soon as you see seed leaves on the soil surface, remove the plastic cover and place the containers in a sunny window or under lights, where the seedlings should get as much daylight as possible. Once they have germinated, they do best at 55° to 65° F.

The seedlings soon will become crowded in their germinating containers, so when the bulk of them have two true leaves (the initial leaves above soil level are seed leaves), transplant the seedlings into larger seed pans, allowing sufficient room for growth until you finally transplant them into the garden.

Your spacing will vary, depending on the variety of plant and the length of time you plan to keep it in the container. I usually put nine transplants per seven- by five-inch seed pan. Use either a topsoil-perlite mixture or prepackaged potting soil.

When you transplant the seedlings, dig carefully into the germinating mixture with a plant label or a pencil and extract a handful of seedlings. Pull them apart gently, always holding the leaves rather than the delicate stems, which are easily damaged. Replant them in the new container at the same depth that they were in the original seed pan, water lightly, and place out of direct sun for a couple of days until the seedlings become acclimated and start to develop new roots. Once they have reached this stage, give them full sun.

An ode to the onion

The onion, in its various forms, is truly a plant for all seasons.

In early spring, chives flavor the first salad; later, it's the spring onions. By midsummer, large onions are ready for salads or stews, and shallots can be used in stir-fries. Late summer brings the main crop of onions, and from October through March, heavily mulched leeks can be pulled from the garden.

Buy a pot of chives in March, place it on a sunny windowsill, and cut leaves now and again to flavor food. In April, divide the clump and plant the divisions outside in a sunny location, where they should last through future winters.

Onions are easy to grow if they get full sun and rich, well-drained soil. They can be grown from sets (small bulbs), seeds, or small plants. Sets should be planted in mid- to late April and only bulbs that are smaller than half an inch across should be used. Larger sets often produce a one-sided bulb and an unwanted flower stalk.

The simplest planting method is to scatter the bulbs on the ground and top them with a light cover of shredded leaves. The more precise gardener may want to grow onions in rows. Dig a three-inch-deep furrow with the back of the rake, scatter a fertilizer into the bottom of the furrow, and cover it with one inch of soil. Sets should be planted four inches apart, with soil barely covering them.

Some years, I have started onions from seed, finding that crops produced from this method are less likely to go to seed and that they tend to keep better through the winter. Check the catalogs for long-keepers such as Southport Yellow Globe or Fiesta Hybrid, and sow seeds in late February or early March. The seeds should be scattered onto a sterilized mix, covered lightly, and the container placed in a warm location.

Within a few days, a green fuzz will appear. When the seedlings are two to three inches tall, cut the tops back by half an inch with a pair of sharp scissors to encourage root development. In early

May, transplant the seedlings into the garden, using a furrow and fertilizer as described for the sets.

No matter how they are started, onions require plenty of fertilizer. Keep the bed free of weeds, and fertilize two or three times during the growing season. Scatter the fertilizer alongside the bulbs, then water heavily. If many of your onions have gone to seed in past years, insufficient nitrogen may be the reason.

Shallots, which have a milder flavor than many onions, are also easy to grow. They keep well in cold storage throughout the winter. Bulbs grow in a cluster attached at the base. Before planting, separate the bulblets and plant in similar conditions to onions, but on three-inch centers. As they develop, the bulblets will multiply in number but not in size.

Many cooks believe that leeks make the best soups, the best stews, and the best quiches. They are delicious stir-fried, braised, or combined with a cheese sauce. Sow seeds the same as for onions, in late March or April, then transplant the seedlings into the garden in May.

Growing broccoli, eggplant, and okra

I also love broccoli and would happily eat it several times a week. The Gardening Partner isn't as wild about it, but his level of interest rises considerably if it has been grown in our garden. Broccoli grows easily from seed and should be started in the house three to four weeks ahead of transplanting into the garden in late April or early May.

As with all seedlings, these broccoli transplants should be hardened off (March, p. 6), so don't move the plants directly from the warm, cozy atmosphere in your house into the potentially hostile environment of your garden in spring. If you have a coldframe, set the flats in there for several days; if not, put the plants overnight in a protected spot, such as a porch or garage, and put them in full sun during the day.

Plant broccoli in rows three feet apart with two feet between plants in a row, and surround each with a collar of plastic or heavy paper to deter cutworms from severing the stems at ground level.

If there are folks who can produce successful eggplant crops on a dozen or more acres, it seems illogical that The Gardening Partner and I can't manage to keep even six plants in good shape through the summer. At first, it was a breeze. We had eggplant coming out of our ears. We fried it and froze it until we never wanted to see it again. But in later years, the plants would look wonderful only until about the beginning of July, when the leaves would start to pale, and finally turn brown and fall off. The fruit that had started to grow would mature, but there wasn't much of it.

Experienced eggplant growers will have no trouble diagnosing our problem as verticillium wilt. If you have never seen it in your garden, cross your fingers and hope it never arrives. It's a soil-borne disease, and what makes it so difficult to avoid is that members of the solanaceous family (tomatoes, potatoes, peppers, strawberries) can all play host to it.

The secret is to rotate crops, which requires a fairly large planting area. With plenty of land and crops such as zucchini and butternut squash to use in the rotation, it's not too hard to do. But The Gardening Partner lays claim to more than half of our growing space for planting his limas, which leaves little space for all the other things I love to grow, not to mention rotating crops. For us, and for anyone with a small garden, the only way to beat verticillium wilt is to grow the eggplant in pots filled with sterile soil.

Another warm-weather crop that is susceptible to disease is okra. Again, this is a favorite of The Gardening Partner, not just for the bright green edible pods, but also for the beautiful, pale yellow flowers that precede them. If you've noticed that your okra does fine for a couple of months, then starts to drop its lower leaves, it's probably wilt, and again, there's no way but rotation to solve this problem.

Oh, deer; a big problem

When The Gardening Partner and I decided to start a vegetable garden, we chose the sunniest spot (in the middle of the lawn), turned over the soil, stuck in the vegetable seeds and plants, watched them grow, and enjoyed our harvests. It seemed so easy, so we expanded and developed additional plots for more vegetables and, later, for fruits such as raspberries, blueberries, and strawberries.

Meanwhile, I started to plant flower gardens. A few years later, we had to erect a small chickenwire fence to keep the rabbits out of the places where we grew lettuce and beans. Later still, The Gardening Partner spent hours pounding in stakes to put up higher fences around the vegetables to protect them from animals. I'm sure our tale is no different from that of other gardeners in my area who now have to share their gardens with animals. The most voracious of those animals is the deer.

Our vegetables are now behind larger fences, but since it's not possible to fence the ornamental plantings, we produce the best garden we can by limiting plantings to varieties the deer seem not to favor. Every herd of deer is different, so some of the plants that have survived in our garden may be tasty to deer in other areas, but I hope the varieties listed below will help other gardeners faced with the same problem.

First, a few words of guidance. Where possible, locate the specimens deer love as close as possible to the house and, if you are so inclined, spray these plants with a deer repellent to deter browsing. I am notoriously lazy about spraying because the sprayer never seems to cooperate and I just get frustrated. But because it's so easy to apply, I am prepared to sprinkle Milorganite around some of the plantings close to the house to try and deter deer. Milorganite is a sewage-sludge product sold as a fertilizer. In wet summers, you have to apply it more frequently because the odor (which *I* don't find offensive in the garden) washes away with the rain, but I have found that it gives some protection and that the damage increases if I forget to sprinkle it around.

If you're planting in popular deer territory, look at each plant for a feature that may deter browsing. Those with spines (such as barberries), rough leaves, or gray leaves seem less popular. Among the shrubs, I have never seen deer damage in our garden on junipers, barberries, buddleia, viburnum, cotoneaster, deutzia, *Spirea japonica alpina*, leucothoe, caryopteris, or andromeda. They have consumed azaleas such as Delaware Valley White, but don't seem to bother *Rhododendron carolinianum*, the Carolina rhododendron, our plumleaf azalea (*R. prunifolium*), or a couple of yakusimanum rhododendrons. All of the above are quite close to the house and the leaves of the yak rhododendrons have fuzzy undersides to their leaves, which could be a deterrent.

Among the ground covers, the evergreen sarcococca has come through unscathed, as have *Vancouveria hexandra* and its relatives the epimediums, many ferns, and European wild ginger (*Asarum europaeum*). And not even deer bother the rampaging yellow archangel (*Lamium galeobdolon* Variegatum).

In the flower garden, plants with odors, such as allium, grow untouched, along with those with fuzzy leaves, such as lamb's ears, and the gray-leafed *Veronica incana*. Some herbs have the double protection of odor and fuzz, and rather naturally, some of the plants I now like best are herbs such as salvias, which are untouched by deer.

That charming little plant that produces yellow flowers in the front of the border in April, *Euphorbia myrsinites*, has never been browsed, perhaps because all euphorbias have a caustic, milky sap in their stems. The Siberian bugloss (*Brunnera macrophylla*) has

191

rough leaves and has survived several years for us, as has the low-growing plumbago (*Ceratostigma plumbaginoides*) that produces such glorious blue flowers in late summer.

Chrysanthemum pacificum, which also seems deer-resistant, has recently become popular more for its white and green variegated foliage that looks good most of the summer than for the small yellow flowers that appear in late September. Just be careful where you plant this because it can spread very quickly. The sharp leaves of ornamental grasses also seem resistant to chewing by deer, as do the fragrant leaves of scented geraniums.

My defensive strategy going forward is to keep trying plants with gray leaves, fuzzy leaves, sharp thorns, and other kinds of deterrents. It might not make for the prettiest garden, but Katie the lab is too old to chase the deer, Candy the poodle finds squirrels much more interesting, and The Gardening Partner and I have no influence over them whatsoever.

Appendix

Listed in this section are resources that I have found useful over the years and that I think would prove useful as well to many gardeners using this book. I begin with a listing of catalogs, books, and periodicals. This is followed by a listing of horticultural organizations from around the country. This section concludes with information about the Pennsylvania Horticultural Society's Gold Medal Program, which, since its inception, has tried to recognize little-known plants of exceptional merit.

Catalogs

Trees and shrubs
Brittingham Plant Farms, P.O. Box 2538, Salisbury, MD 21802
The Cummins Garden, 22 Robertsville Road, Marlboro, NJ 07746
Fairweather Gardens, P.O. Box 330, Greenwich, NJ 09323
Forestfarm, 990 Tetherow Road, Williams, OR 97544
Foxborough Nursery, 3611 Miller Road, Street, MD 21154
Hartmann's Plantation, P.O. Box E, Grand Junction, MI 49056
Siskiyou Rare Plant Nursery, 2825 Cummings Road, Medford, OR 97501
Stark Brothers Nurseries, Louisiana, MO 63353
Woodlanders, 1128 Colleton Avenue, Aiken, SC 29801
Yucca Do Nursery, P.O. Box 655, Waller, TX 77484

Flowers
American Daylily & Perennials, P.O. Box 210, Grain Valley, MO 64029
Andre Viette Farm & Nursery, Route 1, P.O. Box 16, Fishersville, VA 22939
Antique Rose Emporium, Route 5, P.O. Box 143, Brenham, TX 77833
Bluestone Perennials, 7211 Middle Ridge, Madison, OH 44057
Carroll Gardens, P.O. Box 310, Westminster, MD 21157
Charles H. Mueller Co., 7091 North River Road, New Hope, PA 18938
The Daffodil Mart, Route 3, P.O. Box 794, Gloucester, VA 23061
Dutch Bulbs, P.O. Box 200, Adelphia, NJ 07710
French's Bulb Importer, P.O. Box 565, Pittsfield, VT 05762
Gardens of the Blue Ridge, P.O. Box 10, Pineola, NC 28662
Geo. W. Park Seed Co., Greenwood, SC 29647
Harris Seeds, P.O. Box 22960, Rochester, NY 14692
Heirloom Seeds, P.O. Box 245, West Elizabeth, PA 15088
Heronswood Nursery, 7530 288th Street N.E., Kingston, WA 98346
Johnny's Selected Seeds, Albion, ME 04910
Klehm Nursery, 4210 North Duncan Road, Champaign, IL 61821
McClure & Zimmerman, P.O. Box 368, Friesland, WI 53935
Kurt Bluemel, 2740 Greene Lane, Baldwin, MD 21013
Merry Gardens, Camden, ME 04843
Orol Ledden & Son, P.O. Box 7, Sewell, NJ 08080
Otis Twilley Seed Co., P.O. Box 65, Trevose, PA 19047

P. de Jager & Sons, P.O. Box 2010, South Hamilton, MA 01982
Pinetree Garden Seeds, P.O. Box 300, New Gloucester, ME 04260
Plant Delights Nursery, 9241 Sauls Road, Raleigh, NC 27603
Prairie Moon Nursery, Route 3, P.O. Box 163, Winona, MN 55987
The Rosemary House, 120 South Market Street, Mechanicsburg, PA 17055
Roses of Yesterday & Today, Brown's Valley Road, Watsonville, CA 94076
Sandy Mush Herbs, 316 Surrett Cove Road, Leicester, NC 28748
Stokes Seeds, P.O. Box 548, Buffalo, NY 14240
Swan Island Dahlias, P.O. Box 700, Canby, OR 97013
Thompson & Morgan, P.O. Box 1308, Jackson, NJ 08527
Van Bourgondien Bros., P.O. Box 1000, Babylon, NY 11702
Vintage Gardens, 2227 Gravenstein Highway South, Sebastopol, CA 95472
W. Atlee Burpee Co., Warminster, PA 18974
We-Du Nurseries, Route 5, P.O. Box 724, Marion, NC 28752
Well-Sweep Herb Farm, 317 Mt. Bethel Road, Port Murray, NJ 07865
White Flower Farm, Litchfield, CT 06759
Woodside Nursery, 327 Beebe Run Road, Bridgeton, NJ 08302

Vegetables and Herbs

The Cook's Garden, P.O. Box 535, Londonderry, VT 05148
Kitazawa Seed Co., 1111 Chapman Street, San Jose, CA 95126
Le Jardin du Gourmet, P.O. Box 7, St. Johnsbury Center, VT 05863
The Pepper Gal, P.O. Box 23006, Fort Lauderdale, FL 33307
Ronniger's Seed Potatoes, Star Route, Moyie Springs, ID 83845
Seed Savers Exchange, 3076 North Winn Road, Decorah, IA 52101
Seeds Blum, Idaho City Stage, Boise, ID 83706
Shepherd's Garden Seeds, 6116 Highway 9, Felton, CA 95018
Southern Exposure Seed Exchange, P.O. Box 170, Earlysville, VA 22936
Tomato Growers Supply Co., P.O. Box 2237, Fort Myers, FL 33902
Vermont Bean Seed Co., Garden Lane, Fairhaven, VT 05473

Inside the House

Glasshouse Works, P.O. Box 97, Church Street, Stewart, OH 45778
Logee's Greenhouse, 141 North Street, Danielson, CT 06239
The Plumeria People, P.O. Box 820014, Houston, TX 77282
Tinari Greenhouse, 2325 Valley Road, P.O. Box 190, Huntingdon Valley, PA 19006

Miscellaneous

Bamboo & Rattan Works, 470 Oberlin Avenue South, Lakewood, NJ 08701
Gardener's Supply Co., 128 Intervale Road, Burlington, VT 05401
Gardens Alive! 5100 Schenley Place, Lawrenceburg, IN 47025
Green Spot, Department of Bio-Ingenuity, 93 Priest Road, Barrington, NH 03825
Kinsman Company, River Road, Point Pleasant, PA 18950
Mellinger's, 2310 West South Range Road, North Lima, OH 44452
Smith & Hawken, 117 East Strawberry Drive, Mill Valley, CA 94941

Books

Bailey, L.H. *Hortus Third*. Macmillan, New York, 1976.
Bales, Suzanne Frutig. *Ready, Set, Grow: A Guide to Gardening with Children.*

Macmillan, New York, 1996.

Ball, Jeff. *Rodale's Garden Problem Solver*. Rodale Press, Emmaus, PA, 1996.

Ball, Jeff. *Smart Yard: The Guide to 60-Minute Lawn Care*. Fulcrum Publishing, Golden, CO, 1995.

Brooklyn Botanic Garden Handbooks (published quarterly on various gardening topics). Brooklyn Botanic Garden, 1000 Washington Avenue, Brooklyn, NY 11225.

Burpee American Gardening Series (various gardening topics). Prentice Hall, New York, 1995.

Collins, John F. *Livable Landscape Design*. Cornell University Press, Ithaca, NY, 1988.

Darke, Rick. *For Your Garden: Ornamental Grasses*. Little, Brown, Boston, 1994.

Dirr, Michael. *Manual of Woody Landscape Plants*. Stipes Publishing, Champaign, IL, 1990.

Fell, Derek. *Perennial Gardening*. Michael Friedman Publishing, New York, 1996.

Fell, Derek. *The Pennsylvania Gardener: All About Gardening in the Keystone State*. Camino Books, Philadelphia, 1995.

Heath, Brent. *Daffodils for American Gardens*. Elliott & Clark, Washington, DC, 1995.

Index of Garden Plants (derived from *The New Royal Horticultural Society Dictionary of Gardening*). Timber Press, Portland, OR, 1994.

Klein, William M. *Gardens of Philadelphia and the Delaware Valley*. Temple University Press, Philadelphia, 1995.

McClure, Susan. *The Herb Gardener: A Guide for All Seasons*. Storey Communications, Pownal, VT, 1996.

McDonald, Elvin. *The New Houseplant: Bringing the Garden Indoors*. Macmillan, New York, 1993.

McGrath, Mike. *Best of* Organic Gardening. Rodale Press, Emmaus, PA, 1995.

McKeon, Judith C. *The Encyclopedia of Roses: An Organic Guide to Growing and Enjoying America's Favorite Flower*. Rodale Press, Emmaus, PA, 1995.

Mackey, Betty. *The Plant Collector's Notebook, Rev. Ed.* B.B. Mackey Books, Wayne, PA, 1996.

Mackey, Betty. *Cutting Gardens: The Complete Guide to Growing Flowers and Creating Spectacular Arrangements from Your Garden*. Simon & Schuster, New York, 1993.

Martin, Tovah. *Well-Clad Windowsills*. Macmillan, New York, 1994.

Northen, Rebecca Tyson. *Home Orchid Growing*. Prentice Hall, New York, 1990.

Ottesen, Carole. *Ornamental Grasses: The Amber Wave*. McGraw-Hill, New York, 1989.

Ottesen, Carole. *The Native Plant Primer*. Harmony Books, New York, 1995.

Platt, Ellen Spector. *The Ultimate Wreath Book: Hundreds of Beautiful Wreaths to Make from Natural Materials*. Rand McNally, Skokie, IL, 1995.

Platt, Ellen Spector. *Flower Crafts: A Step-by-Step Guide to Growing, Drying and Decorating with Flowers*. Rodale Press, Emmaus, PA, 1993.

Prittie, Joni. *The Crafter's Garden*. Meredith Press, New York, 1993.

Pryke, Paula. *Flair with Flowers*. Rizzoli, New York, 1995.

Rodale's Successful Organic Gardening (series on various gardening topics). Rodale Press, Emmaus, PA, 1995.

Schmidt, R. Marilyn. *Gardening on the Eastern Seashore*. Barnegat Light Press, Barnegat Light, NJ, 1993.

Taylor, Patricia A. *Easy Care Native Plants: A Guide to Selecting and Using Beautiful American Flowers, Shrubs and Trees in Gardens and Landscapes*. Henry Holt, New York, 1996.

195

Taylor's Guides. Series titles: *Annuals; Bulbs; Container Gardening; Fruits and Berries; Garden Design; Gardening Techniques; Ground Covers, Vines and Grasses; Heirloom Vegetables; Herbs; Houseplants; Natural Gardening; Orchids; Perennials; Roses; Seashore Gardening; Shade Gardening; Specialty Nurseries; Shrubs; Trees; Vegetables; Water-Saving Gardening.* Houghton Mifflin Company, New York.

Van Sweden, James. *Gardening with Water.* Random House, New York, 1995.

Woods, Christopher. *Perennials: A Gardener's Guide.* Brooklyn Botanic Garden, Brooklyn, NY, 1991.

Wyman, Donald. *Wyman's Gardening Encyclopedia.* Macmillan, New York, 1986.

Yang, Linda. *The City and Town Gardener: A Handbook for Planting Small Spaces and Containers.* Random House, New York, 1995.

Magazines and newsletters

Alan Lacy's Homeground
P.O. Box 271
Linwood, NJ 08221
Quarterly newsletter

The Avant Gardener
P.O. Box 489
New York, NY 10028
Monthly newsletter

Fine Gardening
Subscription Department
The Taunton Press
63 South Main Street
Newtown, CT 06470-5506
Bimonthly

Garden Design
P.O. Box 5429
Harlan, IA 51593-2929
Monthly

Gardens Illustrated
U.S. subscriptions from:
Fenner, Reed & Jackson
P.O. Box 754
Manhasset, NY 11030
Bimonthly

Green Scene
The Pennsylvania Horticultural
    Society
100 North 20th Street, 5th floor
Philadelphia, PA 19103-1495
Bimonthly

The Herb Companion
Interweave Press
201 East 4th Street
Loveland, CO 80538
Bimonthly

Horticulture
P.O. Box 51455
Boulder, CO 80323-1455
Monthly (10 issues)

HortIdeas
Greg and Pat Williams
460 Black Lick Road
Gravel Switch, KY 40328
Monthly newsletter

Journal of Garden History
U.S. subscriptions from:
Taylor & Francis
1900 Frost Road, Suite 101
Bristol, PA 19007
Quarterly

Kitchen Garden
Subscription Department
The Taunton Press
63 South Main Street
Newtown, CT 06470-5506
Bimonthly

Landscape Architecture
American Society of Landscape
    Architects
4401 Connecticut Avenue, N.W.
Washington, DC 20008-2369
Monthly

National Gardening
National Gardening Association
180 Flynn Avenue
Burlington, VT 05401
Bimonthly

Organic Flower Gardening
Rodale Press
33 East Minor Street
Emmaus, PA 18098
Twice a year, available at bookstores

Organic Gardening
Rodale Press
33 East Minor Street
Emmaus, PA 18098
Monthly (9 issues)

Professional Floral Designer
American Floral Services
P.O. Box 12309
Oklahoma City, OK 73157-2309
Bimonthly

Plant and horticultural societies

African Violet Society of America, Inc.
P.O. Box 3609
Beaumont, TX 77704-3609
409-839-4725

American **Bonsai** Society, Inc.
P.O. Box 358
Keene, NH 03431
603-352-9034

American Association of **Botanical
    Gardens and Arboreta**
787 Church Road
Wayne, PA 19087
215-688-1120

Cactus and Succulent Society of
    America
1535 Reeves Street
Los Angeles, CA 90035
213-556-1923

National **Chrysanthemum** Society
10107 Homar Pond Drive
Fairfax Station, VA 22039
703-978-7981

American **Community Gardening**
    Association
100 North 20th Street, 5th Floor
Philadelphia, PA 19103
215-988-8800; fax 215-988-8810

American **Conifer** Society
P.O. Box 314
Perry Hall, MD 21128
301-256-5595

American **Daffodil** Society
1686 Grey Fox Trails
Milford, OH 45150
513-248-9137

American **Fern** Society
Department of Botany
University of Vermont
Burlington, VT 05401
423-974-6219

Garden Club of America
598 Madison Avenue
New York, NY 10022
212-753-8287; fax 212-753-0134

National Council of State **Garden
    Clubs**
4401 Magnolia Avenue
St. Louis, MO 63110
314-776-7574

The **Gardens** Collaborative
9414 Meadowbrook Avenue
Philadelphia, PA 19118
215-247-5777 ext. 104

Hobby **Greenhouse** Association
8 Glen Terrace
Bedford, MA 01730
617-275-0377

Hardy Plant Society
Mid-Atlantic Group
49 Green Valley Road
Wallingford, PA 19086

American **Hemerocallis** Society
1454 Rebel Drive
Jackson, MS 39211
601-366-4362

Herb Society of America
9019 Kirtland Chardon Road
Mentor, OH 44060
216-256-0514

Pennsylvania **Horticultural** Society
100 North 20th Street, 5th floor
Philadelphia, PA 19103
215-988-8890

American **Horticultural
Therapy** Association
9220 Wightman Road, Suite 300
Gaithersburg, MD 20879
301-948-3010

Holly Society of America
304 North Wind Road
Baltimore, MD 21204
301-825-8133

American **Hosta** Society
5206 Hawksbury Lane
Raleigh, NC 27606
919-851-4784

American **Iris** Society
7414 East 60th Street
Tulsa, OK 74145
918-627-0706

Native Plant Society of
New Jersey
P.O. Box 1295
Morristown, NJ 07962-1295

Natural Resources Defense Council
1350 New York Avenue, N.W.
Washington, DC 20005
202-783-7800; fax 202-783-5917

Nature Conservancy
1815 North Lynn Street
Arlington, VA 22209
703-841-5300; fax 703-841-1283

American **Orchid** Society
6000 South Olive Avenue
West Palm Beach, FL 33405
407-585-8666

Perennial Plant Association
3383 Schirtzinger Road
Columbus, OH 43026
614-771-8731

National **Pond** Society
P.O. Box 449
Acworth, GA 30101
800-742-4701

American **Rhododendron** Society
P.O. Box 1380
Gloucester, VA 23061
804-693-4433

American **Rock Garden** Society
P.O. Box 67
Millwood, NY 10546
914-762-2948

American **Rose** Society
P.O. Box 30000
Shreveport, LA 71130
318-938-5402

Delaware Valley **Water Gardening**
Society
c/o Fred Weiss
339 Valley Road
Merion Station, PA 19066
610-667-7545

National **Wildflower** Research Center
2600 FM 973 North
Austin, TX 78725-4201
512-929-3600

National **Xeriscape** Council
P.O. Box 163172
Austin, TX 78716-3172
512-392-6225

New England **Wildflower** Society
Garden in the Woods
Hemenway Road
Framingham, MA 01701
508-877-6574

The Pennsylvania Horticultural Society's Gold Medal Plant Award Plant Portraits, 1988-1997

The Pennsylvania Horticultural Society's Gold Medal Plant Award program honors little-known and underused woody plants of exceptional merit and promotes their use. Awards have been given to 56 plants since 1988. This section describes the award winners; all are superb garden plants.

For additional information, contact the Pennsylvania Horticultural Society at 215-988-8800.

Abies nordmanniana, a disease- and insect-resistant fir, is better adapted to the warm climate of the Delaware Valley and the broader region the Gold Medal program serves than other members of the genera. Rich, dark-green and pyramidal in shape, this evergreen reaches to 50'. Hardy from zone 5 to zone 7. (1994)

Acer griseum is a native of China that has made itself at home in the American garden. This aristocrat is a standout in the winter landscape at 20'–30' high with exfoliating, cinnamon-red bark. Planted in rich, moist soil in full sun, the paperbark maple is a great small shade tree with no pest or disease problems. Hardy to zone 4. (1993)

Japanese cutleaf maples have long been garden favorites. *Acer palmatum* var. *dissectum* 'Tamukeyama', selected in the early 18th century, remains a best choice. Growing to 6' with a 12' spread in 20 years, this maple is a hardy, long-lived specimen tree. Unlike many cutleaf maples, this cultivar retains its red

color through the heat of summer. Its dome shape and twiggy habit provide winter interest. Hardy to zone 6. (1997)

Acer triflorum is a small specimen tree unrivaled for fall color. Growing to 25' in height with a 20' spread, this maple will consistently put on a dazzling fall display in yellow-orange to flame orange. Prefers an acidic, moist, well-drained soil in partial shade but tolerates sun, shade and neutral soils. No pest or disease problems. Hardy to zone 5. (1996)

Aesculus pavia is a native buckeye that blooms in May with red to coral panicles, 3"–6" long. With no pest or disease problems, this species is far more resistant to leaf scorch than other aesculus. Growing to 20' with a 30' spread, this is a great tree for residential gardens. Plant in full sun and moist, well-drained soil. Hardy from zone 6 to zone 9. (1995)

Betula nigra 'Heritage' sports a creamy white bark that mottles as older pieces exfoliate. The river birch can be trained as a single stem or grown with multiple stems. Mature height can reach 40'–60' and 'Heritage' can handle moist or dry soils, though it needs a fairly acid site. Hardy from zone 3 to zone 8. (1990)

Boxwood evokes images of stately gardens of yesterday. *Buxus* 'Green Velvet' is the best choice for today's gardens. Growing to 3' with a 3'–4' spread, 'Green Velvet' is easily maintained as a short border plant. Tolerant of a broad range of soil types, grown in sun or light shade, this boxwood retains its color through the winter—a real advantage in northern gardens. Deer-resistant. Disease-free. Hardy to zone 5. (1997)

Callicarpa dichotoma is noted for its cluster of striking lavender-colored berries in September, unusual for fall fruits. A deciduous shrub, this beautyberry grows 3'–5' tall with graceful arching branches. It grows rapidly, preferring full sun to part shade, and its size is manageable with pruning. Hardy from zone 5 to zone 8. (1989)

Cephalotaxus harringtonia 'Prostrata', an evergreen shrub widely tolerant of soil types, reaches to 30' in height with a spread of 12'. No pest or disease problems. A great alternative to Japanese yew, it's deer-resistant. Hardy to zone 6. (1994)

Cladrastis kentukea (*C. lutea*) is an American native. When planted in full sun the yellowwood is broadly adaptable and long-lived. In late May to early June, pendulous white flowers, 8"–14" long, adorn this pest-free tree. Prune in summer to avoid excessive "bleeding." Hardy from zone 4 to zone 8. (1994)

Clematis 'Betty Corning' is a vigorous woody vine with finely textured foliage and nodding lavender flowers from July through August. Plant in full sun. Grows to 6' in height by 10' in width and has no pest or disease problems. Maintenance is limited to a spring pruning to 4'. Quite drought-resistant. Hardy from zone 4 to zone 8. (1992)

Clethra alnifolia 'Hummingbird' is a dwarf summersweet that displays full-size flowers on a compact 3' plant. A fragrant, summer-blooming shrub, this American native is a vigorous spreading plant but is not drought-tolerant. Hardy from zone 3 to zone 9. (1994)

Cornus kousa x *C. florida* 'Rutban' Aurora™ is a vigorous hybrid that offers hope for dogwood lovers. A white-flowering selection from Rutgers University's breeding program, this cross is more resistant to leaf spot, canker, and borer than *Cornus florida*. Aurora is highly adaptable to many garden situations. Its upright habit supports a multitude of large white blooms in mid-May. Grows to 19' in 20 years. Hardy to zone 6. (1993)

Cornus kousa x *C. Florida* 'Rutlan' Ruth Ellen™ is another product of the Rutgers University's breeding program. The flowering bracts are more distinct than Aurora's and rest on a low-spreading *C. florida*-type tree. Early in May a profusion of bloom begins that will last up to two weeks. Like all the Rutgers hybrids, Ruth Ellen has to date shown resistance to dogwood anthracnose. Grows to 19' in height by 22' spread in 20 years. Hardy to zone 6. (1993)

Cornus sericea 'Silver and Gold' is named for its yellow twigs in winter and white-variegated leaves in summer. This shrubby dogwood will grow enthusiastically to around 7'. It will withstand summer heat and humidity in this region better than other variegated forms of cornus. Hardy to zone 4. (1990)

Crataegus viridis 'Winter King' is resistant to cedar-apple rust and air pollution, and tolerates heavy pruning. Masses of white flowers cover the tree each spring, followed in fall by orange-red berries, larger than those of the species. A great asset to any winter landscape. Attains a rounded habit with age, growing to 30'. Plant in full sun; prune during the late winter. 'Winter King' will withstand a broad range of soil types and is hardy from zone 4 to zone 7. (1992)

Cryptomeria japonica 'Yoshino' is by far the best of the Cryptomeria species. Planted in light shade with adequate moisture, 'Yoshino' overcomes the winter browning and loss of lower branches from which other cryptomeria suffer. A conical-shaped evergreen, it grows to 30' in height by 18' wide in 30 years. It is resistant to fungal problems and no pest problems have been reported. This cryptomeria makes a great evergreen screen with a wonderful texture. Hardy in zone 6 to zone 9. (1993)

Daphne caucasica is adorned with delicately scented white flowers from April until frost, with leathery leaves and almost billowy habit. It is longer-lived than most daphnes and valued for its compact size; prefers good drainage and will grow in full sun or partial shade. Hardy to zone 6. (1990)

Deutzia gracilis 'Nikko' is a compact, fine-textured shrub suited to the small garden at 2' tall with a 5' spread—an excellent groundcover. A rapid grower with abundant small white flowers starting in late May and burgundy color in the fall, the deutzia prefers a light afternoon shade in areas with high summer temperatures. Hardy to zone 6. (1989)

Fothergilla gardenii 'Blue Mist' matures at 3' to 3.5' with white, bottlebrush-shaped flowers and the added attraction of blue-green foliage. The dwarf fothergilla is easily propagated; will grow in full sun or light shade and moist, well-drained soil. Hardy from zone 5 to zone 8. (1990)

Halesia diptera var. *magniflora* grows to 25'-30' in open, wooded, or full-sun conditions. A heavy and prolonged flowering variety, this halesia will dazzle you with large white flowers. Plant in the spring in any moist, well-drained soil. A real show stopper! Hardy to zone 6. (1995)

Hamamelis mollis 'Pallida' is a witch-hazel with fragrant lemon yellow flowers that offer a pleasant burst of color in February and March. This hamamelis grows to 15' and also does well as an espalier. Hardy from zone 5 to zone 8. (1989)

Hamamelis x *intermedia* 'Diane' adds a sparkle to your winter landscape with its strong red flowers. This witch hazel blooms in January with a few warm days, and reaches its peak in February and March. A fall color that rivals the maple makes this large (to 15') vase-shaped shrub a real winner. Plant in full sun to partial shade. Hardy to zone 5. (1991)

Hedera helix 'Buttercup' is a versatile ivy with colorful foliage, excellent as a groundcover or trained to climb. New leaves are bright yellow-green, later turning butter yellow. Mature leaves are dark green with distinct light veins. It grows to 8" as a groundcover, up to 90' trained as a vine. 'Buttercup' tolerates a variety of soil conditions and will grow in full sun to heavy shade; it may require heavy pruning to keep it within bounds. Hardy to zone 5. (1988)

Heptacodium miconioides is a large shrub, growing to 20', which will delight from an early age. In autumn red buds open to a fragrant profusion of white flowers. Once the petals drop, red flower-stems continue interest until red fruit appears. Broad soil type and pH tolerance makes this a great plant. Exfoliating bark. No pest or disease problems. Can be trained into tree form. Hardy to zone 4. Hardy to zone 5. (1995)

Hibiscus syriacus 'Diana' brightens any garden with its pure white single flowers from July until frost. Flowers remain open into the evening so they may be admired by moonlight. Will tolerate a variety of soil types, prefers full sun. 'Diana' can be cut back yearly to 2' to maintain a blooming height of 4'. It sets no visible seed so it will not become a garden weed. Hardy to zone 5. (1991)

Hydrangea macrophylla 'Blue Billow' was discovered here on a Korean island and introduced here for its masses of small, fertile summer flowers. 'Blue Billow' is reliably hardy in this region and is best grown under the shade of trees in slightly acid soil. Hardy to zone 5. (1990)

Hydrangea quercifolia 'Snow Queen' is sleek and elegant with its deep green foliage and panicles of white flowers that bloom through June and July. The old flower heads turn a handsome russet before the final burst of spectacular wine-colored fall foliage. This oakleaf hydrangea will grow to 6' with an equal spread and does well in sun or shade. Hardy to zone 5. (1989)

Ilex glabra 'Densa', an upright and compact holly, tolerates heat, drought, sun, shade, and transplanting without missing a beat. Suited to problem and urban sites, 'Densa' grows to 4' with a 4' spread in 9 years. Pest- and disease-resistant, this broadleaf evergreen is a great alternative to boxwood. Hardy to zone 4. (1994)

Ilex x *meserveae* 'Mesid' Blue Maid™, the best of the blue hollies, keeps lustrous green foliage year-round. Bright red berries attract birds from October through December. Reliably hardy and far more heat tolerant than her sisters, Blue Maid™ is a great evergreen shrub. Reaching to 15', slightly broader than tall at maturity, Blue Maid™ takes well to pruning. No disease problems. Male pollinator needed. Hardy to zone 5. (1996)

Ilex verticillata 'Scarlett O'Hara', growing to 10' with a 12' spread in 11 years, extends garden interest into the winter. An abundance of small, clear-red fruit persist through the cold months. Clay-soil tolerance, with no

pest or disease problems, makes this an ideal plant for the home garden. 'Rhett Butler' is her preferred pollinator. Hardy in zones 3 to 9. (1996)

Ilex verticillata 'Winter Red' is a deciduous holly, laden with red fruit through the winter. Growing to 10' with an 8' spread, 'Winter Red' performs best in moist, well-drained, acidic soils. Male pollinator necessary. Hardy to zone 4. (1995)

Ilex x 'Harvest Red' sports abundant small Christmas-red fruits on a finely textured, well-shaped deciduous holly. The leaves in fall turn to wine and then drop; the fruit persists long into the winter and is admirable after a snowfall. Hardy from zone 3 to zone 9. (1991)

Ilex x 'Sparkleberry' is valued for its superior fruit production. A large, multi-stemmed deciduous holly with brilliant red berries often lasting through the winter, 'Sparkleberry' will grow to about 12' with a similar spread. This holly is best planted in full sun and is tolerant of most soils. A pollinator of either parent species must be planted nearby to ensure good fruiting. Hardy from zone 3 to zone 9. (1988)

Itea virginica 'Henry's Garnet' is a tough, adaptable native shrub with great contrast from summer to fall. Fragrant, long white flowers bloom in late June against green foliage; fall foliage is a striking red-purple that lasts well into winter. This itea grows to 6' with an 8' spread and is best planted in slightly cool, moist sites— though it will tolerate drier sites. Hardy to zone 5. (1988)

The native juniper is available in every size and shape. *Juniperus virginiana* 'Corcorcor' Green Sentinel™, well-suited for a tall screen, is upright and grows to 25' with a spread of 6'. Junipers tolerate a broad range of climatic and site conditions. Host to cedar-apple rust. Pest-resistant. Hardy to zone 4. (1997)

The bright yellow flowers of *Koelreuteria paniculata* 'September' provide this tree its common name—Golden rain tree. The glory of 'September' is its late August through September bloom period, when few other trees are in flower. In October the leaves turn yellow and blooms are replaced by rose-pink fruits that persist for 5 to 6 weeks. Koelreuteria is sparingly branched and forms a rounded tree at 30'–40' by 30'–40'. No pest or disease. Hardy to zone 5. (1997)

Magnolia 'Galaxy' is adorned late each April with a profusion of dark pink flowers, escaping the frost damage of early spring. As a young tree, 'Galaxy' suckers, but if properly pruned it becomes an upright pyramidal shade tree well-suited to the home landscape. No pest or disease problems. Hardy in zones 5 through 9. (1992)

Magnolia grandiflora 'Edith Bogue' is hardy from zone 6 to zone 9 and does not suffer winter damage in northern regions of its range. Blooming in June and July, the creamy 9"–12" blossoms fill the air with a sweet, lemony fragrance. Lustrous dark-green foliage grows upright along the branches. Plant in full sun to partial shade. 'Edith Bogue' tolerates some moisture but prefers rich, well-drained soil. It can grow to 60' high with a 30' spread. (1992)

Magnolia kobus var. *stellata* 'Centennial' blooms late in April, giving it a better chance of escaping frost damage to its flowers than other magnolias. Starting with a pink tinge, 5" flowers fade to white. Growing to 15'–20' with a spread of 10'–15', this floriferous cultivar prefers full sun. Disease- and pest-resistant. Hardy to zone 4. (1997)

Magnolia x 'Elizabeth' has creamy, pale yellow, lily-like flowers and grows to 25'–35' with a 10'–15' spread. Works well as a shade or specimen tree and is best grown in an open space with full sun and slightly acid soil. Hardy to zone 5. (1988)

Malus 'Donald Wyman' is an outstanding crabapple, fast growing to 20' with equal spread and highly disease-resistant. 'Donald Wyman' is useful as a street tree or garden specimen, with pink buds opening to white flowers in mid- to late April. Glossy, bright red fruits last well into winter, often into March. Hardy to zone 5. (1989)

Malus 'Jewelberry' is a dwarf crabapple growing to only about 6' high. Shows dark pink buds in spring that open to pink and white flowers. In cooler springs, the flowers will be deeper in color. Glossy red fruits follow the bloom. 'Jewelberry' is another highly disease-resistant crabapple. Hardy to zone 5. (1989)

Picea orientalis' graceful appearance makes this evergreen a standout in the landscape. Branches of fine dark-green needles descend and smoothly rise upward again. This spruce holds its lower branches as it ages, unlike others of the genus. Wind-tolerant, the Oriental spruce grows into an effective screen. It is slow-growing and should be planted in full sun and well-drained soil. No pest or disease problems. Hardy in zones 5 through 8. (1992)

Prunus 'Hally Jolivette' has pink buds that open to white blooms over a succession of 10–20 days in early spring. A small bushy tree, growing to 15' with an equal spread, 'Hally Jolivette' starts blooming in its second year. Ideal for small properties, the fine twiggy habit even adds winter interest. Plant in full sun. Hardy to zone 5. (1994)

Prunus x 'Okame' does well in many sites and produces an abundance of blooms. This cherry grows to 25' with a similar spread. Pink flowers appear early in the season—late March to mid-April. Fall foliage is bright orange

203

and yellow and, except for early shaping, pruning is minimal unless grown in smaller gardens. Plant in full sun. Hardy to zone 5. (1988)

Sciadopitys verticillata, the Japanese umbrella pine, offers the richest dark-green foliage of any evergreen. Long, thick needles are borne in whorls on a handsome dense tree. Plant in rich well-drained soil in a sunny location. Although the largest trees normally seen are between 20'–30' spreading to 15', in time this tree will mature to 60'. Hardy to zone 5. (1991)

Stewartia pseudocamellia var. *koreana* grows to about 30' in this country, with interest throughout the seasons: saucer-shaped white flowers from mid-June through July, orange-red fall color, and a smooth exfoliating bark that is most striking in winter. Native to Japan and Korea, stewartias should be grown with some shade and will do best in acid soils. Hardy to zone 5. (1990)

Syringa reticulata 'Ivory Silk' blooms reliably in midsummer with large creamy-white panicles. Flowering begins at a young age on this sturdy, compact tree. Grows to 20' with 12' spread in 15 years. Drought-resistant; no pest or disease problems reported in the Gold Medal region. A great street tree. Hardy in zones 1 through 9. (1996)

Viburnum 'Eskimo', a selection of the U.S. National Arboretum's plant breeding program, is a handsome, compact shrub. Grows to 4'–5' in height with an equivalent spread. Pest and disease problems are absent, and 'Eskimo' is resistant to bacterial leaf spot. Early May finds 'Eskimo' covered with creamy white 4" flowers set on horizontal branches. Fruit ripens in August from dull red to black. Tolerates partial shade conditions; semi-evergreen; plant in full sun. Hardy in zones 6 through 8. (1992)

Viburnum dilatatum 'Erie' is a large, deciduous shrub worth the space in your garden as it grows to 10'–12'. With frost, the abundant and well-displayed fruit turns from red to coral and lasts long into winter. Mid-May brings creamy white flowers, and fall color ranges from yellow to orange-red. 'Erie' flowers best in full sun but grows well in many exposures and soil types; it is pest- and disease-resistant. Hardy to zone 5. (1993)

Viburnum nudum 'Winterthur' is in its full glory in autumn. The mix of pink and blue berries set against a rich purple foliage make this shrub a knockout. 'Winterthur' will grow in rich, wet, shaded sites as well as in sunny, well-drained locations. Creamy white flowers in the spring round out a year of show for this wonderful little plant. Grows to 6' in 20 years. Hardy from zone 7 to zone 9. (1991)

Viburnum x *burkwoodii* 'Mohawk' is another deciduous viburnum, slightly smaller at 8' with a spread of 10'. In late April red buds open to fragrant white blossoms for a splendid addition to any garden. Plant in full sun for most flowers or in partial shade for more persistent flowers. 'Mohawk' is notably resistant to powdery mildew and bacterial leaf spot and is hardy to zone 5. (1993)

Viburnum plicatum f. *tomentosum* 'Shasta' is a doublefile viburnum without equal when it comes to flowering. In the spring there is hardly a spot on the shrub that is not covered by a large white blossom. Growing best in rich soil, in sun to part shade, its compact habit makes 'Shasta' a great addition to any garden. Grows to 6' with a 12' spread. Hardy to zone 6. (1991)

Viburnum x *burkwoodii* 'Conoy' displays a branching habit ideal for foundation plantings and the small garden. This evergreen shrub, the last selection of Dr. Egolf's breeding program at the U.S. National Arboretum, withstands pruning and shearing. Growing to 5', with a spread of 7', 'Conoy' prefers sun but will tolerate part shade. In May red buds open to white flowers. Red fruit ripens to black each autumn. Pest- and disease-resistant. Hardy to zone 6. (1997)

Zelkova serrata 'Green Vase' is a fast-growing hardy shade tree, well suited for home gardens or urban sites. 'Green Vase' is especially useful as a street tree as it tolerates airborne pollutants, drought and heavy clay soils, though it will not tolerate sandy soils. It grows to 60'–70' with a 30'–40' spread in a neat, upright habit. Hardy to zone 5. (1988)

Index